Disney Declassified
Tales of Real-Life Disney Scandals, Sex, Accidents, and Deaths

Aaron H. Goldberg

Copyright © 2016 Aaron H. Goldberg
All rights reserved.
Quaker Scribe Publishing
ISBN-13: 978-0692256176
ISBN-10: 0692256172

No part of this book may be used or reproduced in any matter whatsoever without written permission except in the case of brief quotations embodied in critical articles and journals.

This book makes reference to various copyrights and trademarks of the Walt Disney Company, commonly known as Disney; this book is in no way authorized by, endorsed by, or affiliated with Disney or their subsidiaries.
The mention of names and places associated with Disney and their businesses are not intended in any way to infringe on any existing or registered trademarks but are used in context for educational purposes.

The author and publisher are neither affiliated with nor a representative of the specific companies, organizations, or authorities in this book. The opinions and statements expressed in this book are solely those of the author and/or people quoted by the author and do not reflect the opinions and policies of the specific companies mentioned.

While every precaution has been taken in the preparation of this book, neither the author nor publisher assumes responsibility for errors or omissions.

First Print: 2014

Media inquiries and comments: quakerscribe@gmail.com

Dedicated to my late mother, Susan

Thank you to Walt Disney for his creations and to you, the reader, for buying this book!

Table of Contents

Introduction ix
1 Mickey Mania 1
2 Lights, Camera, Accident! 39
3 Peter Pan's Fight 77
4 Disney Debauchery 95
5 Making a Mint Off the Mouse 113
6 Pirates of the Court Room 135
7 It's an Accessible World After All 145
8 Morality in the Movies 157
Bibliography 171

Introduction

The word "Disney" means different things to different people. For most, the Walt Disney Company stands for all things wholesome, family centric, moral, and entertaining. For others, the cynics and the haters, they feel the company sustains and promotes unrealistic images and story lines to children. Their view is the company isn't "healthy" for children but is rather a self-perpetuating global consumerism machine interested only in profits—your uncle Walt Disney doesn't love you; he loves only your money.

As for Walt Disney, the man, he too still garners much attention nearly fifty years after his passing. There are millions of people who still love him. Not only did he change our childhoods with movies, television, and how we vacation with our family but also his fingerprints are all over American culture.

For the millions who still embrace Walt, his voice is like music to their ears. The grainy black-and-white and early color-television footage of him is almost magical. He still looms larger than life as he stands watch over his vast entertainment empire. This is due to the prolific Disney-marketing machine. This machine keeps Walt both relevant and in the hearts of millions of children—so much so, that in one survey, many children didn't know Walt Disney was a real person and thought he was a character created along the lines of the Pillsbury Doughboy.

Since Walt's death, there is another public persona of his that has grown and evolved into mythical proportions as well. Walt has been called everything from a bigot, racist, chauvinist, anti-Semite—even his own grandniece lobbed this matzo ball out into the public eye in 2014—and a micromanaging ass of a boss.

Clearly the Walt Disney Company and Walt Disney, the man, can be very polarizing topics. Disney and their theme parks, television shows, movies, and the man, have been analyzed six ways to Sunday; even yours truly is guilty from time to time. This book really isn't about the analysis or judgment (although there is a smattering of social commentary here and there) of the Walt Disney Company at a deeper or philosophical level—it's actually quite the contrary.

Disney Declassified at its core is an interesting collection of real-life stories with Disney being the setting or catalyst in a situation that is usually very un-Disney like. Some of the situations are heartbreaking, others are head scratching, and probably all of them are tales the company would rather you not hear.

Wherever your point of views may lie, whether you are a Disney lover or hater, this book will be interesting to you. It isn't an attempt to sully the company's name but to give you the glimpses of reality that does seep into one of the most prolific, entertaining, and omnipresent companies in American culture and history.

CHAPTER 1

Mickey Mania

In 1998, the United Kingdom's maximum-security prison, Whitemoor, home to murderers, sex offenders, and IRA terrorists, paid their inmates five pounds a week to assemble and package Disney's *The Lion King* lamps that went on sale in the country.

In late 2013, Disney launched a new marketing campaign and slogan: "Show Your Disney Side." According to Disney, "It's the side you simply can't wait to share. It's the side of you that laughs more, screams more, and just plain lives life to the fullest. It's the side of you that comes out to play the moment you and your family step through the gates of a Disney theme park."

Sounds like fun, right? Surely everyone has captured the excitement of Disney at some point on his or her trip to visit Mickey Mouse. The stories in this chapter are of people showing a different side of Disney, a side that is, well, a bit crazy. I'm pretty sure when Disney rolled out their campaign, this wasn't the Disney side they were talking about and imploring people to embrace. These are the stories that may make you want to scream—not in joy and excitement but in horror and disbelief.

Oftentimes Disney is the catalyst or setting for people to do crazy, irrational things. This is what "Mickey Mania" is all about—going crazy with, for, and about Mickey. Fortunately or unfortunately, depending on your views and sense of humor, there are an enormous number of stories that are noteworthy enough to be included in this chapter. While all of them can't be covered, a considerable number of them can be and are classified for our purposes into several sections.

This chapter is composed of the following sections: (1) "Plain Crazy"— here the heading speaks for itself—is about generalized batty behavior and antics, (2) "Theft and Fraud" that is pretty self-explanatory, (3) "Dying for Disney" that narrates the stories about faking cancer to get a trip to Disney, (4) "Dubious Disney" that speaks of the moves that the Walt Disney Company has made over the years, and lastly, a couple of good, heartwarming stories show that Walt Disney does bring out the good in people, after all.

Plain Crazy

Plane Crazy was Walt Disney's first animated short featuring Mickey Mouse in 1928. The six-minute cartoon helped countless people around the world fall in love with Mickey Mouse. However, no one loved him more than Walt himself; he loved him like a family member. Over eighty years later, the words "Plane Crazy" still resonate with some Disney family members. In their case, you'll have to add an "i" and drop the "e" in the word "Plane," to fully describe their situation.

It's only fair that stories featuring erratic behavior with an element of Disney start with a story involving some Disney drama in its purest form: real Disney drama with real Disney family members—no, not Donald or Goofy but Walt's former son-in-law and Walt's grandchildren.

Economic Research Associates (ERA) was the firm that Walt utilized to research the best location for Disneyland. In the early 1960s, Walt utilized the firm once again for selecting a site for his Florida project. In 1963, William "Bill" Lund worked for ERA and traveled to Florida to research the best locale for Disney's East Coast enterprise. We all know the story. Bill was obviously successful, as the land was selected, deals were made, and Walt Disney World came to fruition in October of 1971.

Helping to select a site for Walt Disney World wasn't the end of Bill's relationship with Disney. His relationship actually got more intimate. In 1968, Bill married Walt's daughter, Sharon. In 1970, Sharon gave birth to their twins, Bradley and Michelle. By 1977, their marriage soured, and Sharon and Bill divorced. Despite their marital strife, before her passing in 1993, Sharon appointed Bill as one of four trustees to their children's trusts, which today are worth roughly $400 million.

The trusts would pay both Brad and Michelle yearly installments of roughly $1 million a year. At certain age milestones, lump sums ranging from $20 million to $35 million would also be disbursed. One of Bill's duties as a cotrustee was to determine if his children were competent enough to receive the money. This is when the family's financial feud started, when an accident happened to Michelle.

On Labor Day of 2009, Michelle was out with some friends when she suffered a brain aneurysm and was rushed to the hospital for emergency surgery. During her recovery and a lengthy hospital stay, physicians told the family her prognosis was grave. This is where things started to unravel not only for Michelle, physically, but also for all parties, financially and emotionally.

When Michelle was seriously ill and hospitalized, Bill wanted to have her transferred out of Southern California and to a rehab closer to him in Arizona. Certain family members and those closest to Michelle disagreed with Bill's intentions. They implored him not to do this, as leaving California for Arizona would be the last thing Michelle would want. A line was drawn in the sand, so to speak, and the two sides squared off over her care.

To make it easier here, as there are a lot of first names to throw around in the story, let's break this into teams. Team Michelle was composed of close friends, some family, and a cotrustee. Team Bill included himself; his wife, Sherry; some of her children; and Michelle's twin brother, Brad.

Team Michelle felt Team Bill was trying to keep them away from Michelle, restricting access to her, and causing stress and drama in an effort to keep her isolated from everyone else. Team Bill complained of the same thing. It basically became a "he said, she said" of each team blaming the other in an effort to control Michelle. Each side complained that the control over Michelle was an effort to isolate her and have access to her money and have absolute control over her.

One of the members on Team Michelle, a longtime friend and cotrustee, moved to have Bill's medical power of attorney for Michelle removed. This was granted, and a childhood friend from her team was granted the temporary medical power of attorney and temporary guardianship.

Soon after, Michelle started to make a recovery and regained consciousness, albeit with some short-term memory issues. She was, however, lucid enough to understand not only her health situation but also the pressing situation with her father.

Michelle gave statements and agreed with everything Team Michelle was doing. She also agreed that perhaps some of Team Bill's actions were malicious and too controlling. Additionally, her biggest fear was to end up in Arizona with Bill controlling her and calling all the shots in regards to her health care and finances. Michelle even noted that, before her aneurysm, she decided she wanted to rescind her father's power of attorney. The actions of Team Michelle were appropriate and appreciated.

Well, the plot continued to thicken while Michelle was incapacitated. When her attorneys were working to attain the temporary power of attorney, they uncovered improprieties in some of her trust finances, and Bill's name was allegedly all over them.

Apparently, Bill was receiving money from secret land deals he put together for several years, utilizing the funds of the trust—something obviously immoral and, more importantly, against California law. As per the law, trustees can't benefit personally from transactions involving a trust. Court records showed that Bill made in excess of $3.5 million on the land deals he orchestrated with the trust's funds.

With Bill's shady business deals revealed, which the other cotrustees were unaware of, Team Michelle decided to sue to have Bill removed from Michelle's trust. Interestingly, Bill didn't deny the dealings. He said he had permission and submitted a document to the court that showed Michelle's and Brad's signatures giving him permission to make the deals. The deals were actually quite lucrative for the trust—$163 million to be exact—a fact Bill says everyone fails to mention in their legal case.

As the legal case proceeded, it was determined that the signatures Bill offered as proof of consent for the deals from Brad and Michelle were forged. A handwriting expert was brought in, and it was determined that Michelle's signature had been taken from another document, something for which Bill didn't have an answer.

Bill's legal fight to stay on as a trustee on his children's trusts didn't last much longer. Blaming concerns for his health, he stepped down from being a trustee, but not without a parting gift. As a settlement, he will be paid $500,000 a year for the rest of his life, exclusively out of Brad's trust. In light of everything that happened when Michelle was critically ill, the attention turned to her twin brother, Brad, and Bill's influence over him.

Michelle and her aunt, Walt's other daughter, Diane Disney Miller, were concerned about Brad's welfare. They wondered if he was under too much control from his father and stepmother. Michelle and Diane filed legal documents in the Maricopa, Arizona, probate court, claiming they feared Brad was being isolated and was not allowed to go out or receive phone calls. They questioned if he (and his $1 million yearly trust allowance) was being held captive by Bill and his wife.

Brad apparently suffered from developmental disabilities and lived in a house next door to his father. Michelle and Diane wanted to make sure Brad was there willingly and could do as he pleased. The duo urged the court to assess his state and the situation to determine his well-being and determine if he was being manipulated financially or mentally.

They suggested to the court that if Brad did need care or a guardian, perhaps it should be independent from his father. Their petition showed that in 2006 Brad had filed court papers wanting his father and stepmother to become his guardians, as he had developmental disabilities, which affected his competency for receiving the funds from his trust. Michelle and Diane thought this adoption might be monetarily motivated.

On Brad's thirty-fifth birthday in 2005, his trust indicated that he could receive a payment of $20 million. The trustees, Bill included, voted four to zero not to disperse this money to him. Yet five years later in 2010, another large distribution was due, and the trustees voted three to one against the payment; the one vote "for" came from Bill, who indicated his son was doing better than five years before and was now capable of managing his money—although the papers filed in 2006 declared otherwise. Brad refuted all of the above claims by his sister and aunt. He claimed he loved his father and stepmother and was happy where he was living.

Brad was so irritated by the situation and the intrusion into his life that he initiated adoption proceedings, again, to have his stepmother adopt him. Although Michelle still contends this was money motivated and just another situation created to gain control over Brad and his money, at one point, there were even claims of sexual shenanigans going on between Brad and his stepsister, Sherry's daughter, in an attempt to gain control over him and his trust.

In the end, it appears as though everyone got what they wanted. Michelle got her financial freedom, Bill received some more money, Brad wasn't bothered anymore by the courts, and probably a few attorneys bought new cars with the legal fees accrued from some infighting over real Disney dollars.

So what to make of all of this on a deeper, voyeuristic level? Who knows? There was a lot of money at stake from a grandfather long gone. There's a very old saying: "Money is the root of all evil." There's another prophetic saying: "Whoever said money is the root of all evil does not have any." If nothing else, it makes all of us regarding our own family dysfunctions feel a bit better!

This next story may seem all too familiar for frequent visitors to any of the Disney theme parks, especially when the parks are very crowded, but accident reports submitted in both Florida and California have shown incidents with guests driving scooters/power chairs into other guests. Usually the incidents are harmless, but back in 1995, the outcome was different. This time, the person behind the wheel had some consequences to deal with.

Back in August of 1995, thirty-five-year-old Katrina, who suffers from cerebral palsy, was visiting Disneyland in her motorized scooter, just as she did countless times over the previous four years. However, this day would end differently for her, for she lost the use of her beloved Disneyland annual pass for one month as a repeat offender of speeding and hitting walking guests.

This case of reckless driving Disneyland-style happened on Main Street when she was driving at an estimated speed of 4.5 miles per hour and bumped into someone who complained about it after being hit. Katrina denied ever hitting the person, but she admitted she might have been driving faster than usual, as she wanted to get across Main Street to the Pocahontas show before the *Lion King* Parade blocked her way. Disney spokesman John McClintock said this was the third time Katrina was cited for speeding, and something had to be done. The yearly pass she saved up for out of her monthly social-security payments was put on suspension.

This next story takes us over to the Walt Disney World police blotter. In July 2012, Dario, a forty-one-year-old physician vacationing with his family from Italy, was arrested for allegedly kicking his three-year-old son in the face. The little guy was crying and buckled into his stroller in front of the Mexico

Pavilion at EPCOT's World Showcase, when the incident happened.

According to the witness's statements in the arrest report, the doctor was arguing with his wife and children in front of the pavilion. The next thing people witnessed was Dario kicking his son in the face as the child's mother was screaming no repeatedly. The little tyke's left eye was swollen with a cut and bruising around it. An EPCOT employee went up to the child and noticed the child bleeding and crying hysterically. The cast member contacted police.

Dario and his family did not speak English, but, through a translator, both parents told a different story than what nearby people witnessed. In turn, they blamed their oldest son. The family wouldn't allow the child to be taken to the hospital, as the father deemed him okay after checking his son's injuries. The father was then promptly taken to jail.

Another heart-wrenching story involving a child took place one Saturday night in November of 1997 at Walt Disney World's Magic Kingdom. Kathleen walked into the ladies' restroom in Fantasyland around 9:00 p.m. She noticed blood on the floor and heard a whimpering sound. Kathleen opened the stall door and discovered a newborn baby in the toilet bowl. The baby was feet first in the toilet with her head barely above the waterline and with the umbilical cord around her neck. The good citizen sprang into action, grabbed the baby, and started to scream for help. Another woman quickly gave up her sweatshirt to wrap around the baby and get the cold toilet water off the newborn.

Sometimes fate works in mysterious ways, even in horrific situations like this one. Just a few feet away, Kenneth and his family just got off Space Mountain when he heard screams. One of his instincts kicked in, the instinct of a family physician. Dr. Kenneth saw a woman holding a baby, not an uncommon site at Walt Disney World. This baby was blue in color and still had a placenta and umbilical cord attached.

Yep, a woman had given birth in the bathroom and fled the scene. The good doctor sprang into action, putting the baby in a head-down position to hear if she was breathing; she was, but barely, and with a very faint pulse. Improvising with whatever pseudomedical instruments he could get his hands on, he used a pen to clear the mucus in her throat, opening her airway so she could breathe. Next he took a shoelace to tie off the umbilical cord.

Moments later, rescue workers arrived, covered her in a blanket, and off she went to the hospital. The newborn's body temperature was only ninety-one degrees when she was admitted to the hospital. The hospital kept her in a warmer, stabilized her, and named her Jasmine after the princess in the Disney movie *Aladdin*. After five days in the hospital, Jasmine was doing well and had hundreds of families inquiring about adopting her. She was released into the custody of the Florida Department of Children and Families for the time being.

With Jasmine thriving, there was still a bigger mystery: Who in their right mind would do such a thing? Who could leave a newborn in the toilet to die and go on about their business, let alone in one of the most family-centric places on earth? Speculation from authorities thought it was most likely a teenage girl concealing her pregnancy. The teen probably couldn't reveal her situation to family and just happened to give birth while she was at the park and panicked. Interestingly, as busy as the parks can be, there were no witnesses that came forward claiming to have seen anything.

Three months would pass before the mother to baby Jasmine was found. Jasmine's mother wasn't a teen at all, nor was she panicked at the notion of giving birth. Jasmine's mom was a forty-three-year-old mother of eight (nine including Jasmine) and was on vacation from the Philippines. Madona was vacationing at Walt Disney World with family members for nine days.

Even her own family members initially had no idea she was pregnant, as she was overweight. Eventually, Madona's sister-in-law from New Jersey contacted the Orange County Sheriff's Office. She revealed the information about the missing and negligent mother in February of 1998. Officials then ran DNA tests to verify the relation to Jasmine. Madona's sister-in-law stated that in the days after she gave birth, Madona continued her trip as if nothing ever happened, even commenting about what kind of a terrible mother and person could abandon a baby like that.

After the sister-in-law's call, authorities in Florida prepared an arrest warrant for Madona, seeking to charge her with attempted murder and aggravated child abuse and sought to extradite her back to Orlando, but the extradition never happened. As for Jasmine, the sister-in-law was already the adoptive mother to one of Madona's children, and baby Jasmine joined the family with her older biological sibling.

The next tale involving a baby doesn't take place at Walt Disney World. However, the theme park was the catalyst for the horrendous act. In September of 2011, thirty-three-year-old Bridget of Delaware gave birth to a baby boy. Instead of being overwhelmed with joy for her new bundle of joy, she sold her month-old son for $15,000 so that she could take her other two sons to Walt Disney World. Bridget's grandmother overheard her granddaughter's twisted Disney plan and tipped off authorities. She told them Bridget was going to "sell her newborn son to a homosexual couple for $15,000."

A short time later, police arrested both mother and baby buyer. Bridget eventually pled guilty but mentally ill and was sentenced to five years in prison. The judge suspended her sentence for eighteen months of intensive mental-health probation.

Another unsettling story with Walt Disney World as the backdrop happened in late June 2000 at Disney's BoardWalk Inn resort. What was shaping up to be just another day at work for Rafael, ended up turning into a nightmare he could have never imagined. Rafael was toward the end of his shift as a waiter at the BoardWalk Inn. He had one more room-service delivery to make—four beers for room 2326. The guest in the room had ordered room service four times before one o'clock in the afternoon; actually the person in the room had ordered room service nine times over the previous two days. When Rafael stepped in to make his delivery to the room, he was pistol-whipped on the head from a .357 Magnum pistol. He spent the next eleven hours as a hostage, with a gun pointed to his head as he prayed for his life.

Unfortunately, Rafael's delivery put him right in middle of a very dangerous situation and serious marital strife. The situation involved thirty-nine-year-old Bismark, who believed his wife, a former employee at the BoardWalk Inn resort, was having an affair with a room-service waiter named Alex.

Bismark apparently paid another BoardWalk Inn employee for information about Alex and his phone number. In late June, Bismark called Alex and left threatening messages on his voice mail. He told him he would beat him up or even kill him if he didn't provide information about his wife and children. He knew they were having an affair, and he wanted to speak with his family. After receiving no response from Alex, Bismark devised a plan to abduct and murder his wife's love interest. He bartered his services as a landscaper to a woman who agreed to register the hotel room in her name, so he wouldn't be identified. Bismark checked into the hotel with his four-year-old son on June 27.

By June 29, after repeated orders to room service and no delivery from Alex, who panicked after the threats and took the days off, Bismark became desperate and took hostage the next waiter that came to his room. Bismark was frustrated and needed to communicate with his wife, and Rafael was the one who was going to make it happen, unluckily for Rafael, who was in the wrong place at the wrong time.

As it turned out, there was no "other man" or love affair involving Alex. Bismark was grasping at anything to communicate with his estranged wife and the children. The whole story was a fantasy, as Alex and Bismark's wife had never met each other. What wasn't a fantasy was the gun directed at Rafael when he was held hostage in Bismark's room.

Bismark now had a hostage and wanted some action. He called down to the hotel's front desk and informed the hotel manager he had a gun and a hostage and that he wanted to kill himself. The police, SWAT team, and hostage negotiators were brought on site. As the hours went by, tensions grew. Frustrated by the negotiations with authorities, at one point Bismark fired a shot into the hotel room. One bullet down and ninety-nine left, the situation became more serious with this display of rage and a peek into Bismark's past. Over the years, he had been charged with beating his wife three times in the past decade and even threatened her family numerous times over the years with a gun.

By the eleventh hour, with a change in hostage negotiators and upon hearing a recorded message featuring his children saying, "I love you, Daddy" and "Please come out," Bismark walked out peacefully. He was charged with kidnapping, false imprisonment, aggravated battery, assault, shooting within a building, and attempted first-degree murder in a plot to kill Alex; if convicted on all charges, he could have faced life in prison.

Shortly after the situation, Rafael quit his position and sued Disney over being held hostage at work. He settled his lawsuit for an undisclosed amount almost immediately after it was filed. As for Bismark, an Orange County jury found him guilty of false imprisonment and two other counts for taking his son and Rafael hostage. They found him not guilty of the more serious charges of kidnapping and aggravated battery.

During the trial, Bismark took the stand and told the courtroom he never intended to hurt anyone and only wanted to see his children. He said he suffers from severe anxiety and a fear of crowds. "To this day, I can't figure out where my mind went."

The next story features someone who may as well have been on the Disney payroll. He's a man who lived much of his adult life as a walking billboard for Disney. George, who many call a character in his own right, is also known as the "Disney tattoo guy."

George had over twenty-two hundred Disney tattoos covering his body from head to toe. As he explained during many interviews, his childhood was very unhappy. The one thing that did make him happy was Disney. Over the next five decades, George became obsessed with all things Disney, from the fifteen thousand items in his Disney-themed home to the hundreds of trips to the parks. In all, his Disney indulgence cost him about $50,000 a year.

But all was not happy in the world of George. By 2010, he was undergoing Disney fatigue. He was tired of signing autographs and of the attention he received everywhere he went. He auctioned off the collection and started to slowly have his tattoos removed. Perhaps all of this happened because George found a new love, the love of a woman. In July of 2011, George too was charged with false imprisonment, criminal mischief, and misdemeanor battery. Where did the alleged crime take place? You guessed it, in his hotel room at Walt Disney World, with his fiancée.

If you think George spending $50,000 a year on all things Disney is a bit much, how about spending $400,000 on a trip to Disneyland Paris and Walt Disney World? This is the amount of money spent by Selangor Mentri Besar Datuk Seri Dr. Mohd Khir Toyo (the first few words are parts of a title: Menteri Besar is the head of the executive branch of government in Malaysia, in the state of Selangor).

Let's just call him Toyo to make the story a bit easier. In December of 2004, Toyo took his family over to Disneyland Paris. Feeling the need to see the mouse once again, this time on his home turf, Toyo and family, complete with his maid and staff, went down to Walt Disney World. The two trips cost in excess of $400,000 and were complete with a rented Mercedes, presidential suites, and travel accommodations for a group of traditional dancers from his country to greet him when he arrived at each location.

The reason for the trip? Toyo called it a "technical" visit for the government. Unless you call a face-to-face meeting with Mickey and Minnie Mouse in the parks a meeting of the minds, Toyo failed to meet with anyone from Disney in regards to the technicality of their parks.

Toyo and the man involved in this next story have a lot in common. They both blew through hundreds of thousands of dollars with reckless abandon and ended up in Walt Disney World. Both men also used other people's money to get there. However, their visits were vastly different. From 2006 to 2011, forty-five-year-old Jeffrey of Dublin, Ohio, ran a Ponzi scheme through his companies Superior Financial Resources and J. G. Kelly Equities. Jeffrey said his two companies dealt in stocks, annuities, and real-estate trusts. He boasted that he could offer clients a 7–10 percent return on their investment, even in the down economy.

Nearly twenty people invested to the tune of $1.5 million. After time, the schemes started to collapse under on their own, as the world saw with Bernie Madoff. These enterprises need to continually bring in new money to cover what money goes out to investors or is illegally pilfered by the mastermind behind it. Eventually it all starts to catch up. By 2011, this was what happened with Jeffrey's scam.

Little money was coming in, and his personal indulgences with other people's money were draining the coffers. Feeling the pressure, he left Ohio and decided to head down to the Happiest Place on Earth, where he started work as a boat captain. As we know, the Feds always get their man. FBI agents tracked Jeffrey down at work and arrested him while he was working at Walt Disney World. In December of 2012, he was indicted in US District Court on seventeen counts, including mail fraud, wire fraud, and interstate transport of fraudulently acquired securities. In March of 2014, Jeffrey was sentenced to five years in prison.

The next crazy story takes us aboard a Disney cruise ship. The actions of a few cast members aboard the *Disney Magic* brought new meaning to the phrase "life on the high seas." In August of 2012, *People* magazine and the *Daily Mirror* of the United Kingdom both ran stories about the crew members aboard the *Disney Magic* and their affinity for cocaine.

A whistle-blower aboard took pictures of several cast members allegedly doing cocaine and leaked them to the media. The crew was often seen in the photos cutting up and assembling their lines of nose candy with their Disney identification cards. But what would be some casual drug use without some casual random sex (note, the author does not condone either practice!)? From the stories narrated by some of the participants, the activities were quite rampant:

"It's all very family friendly. On deck, you have people in Mickey Mouse and Donald Duck outfits performing tricks. But downstairs, staff are sniffing coke. So many people are doing it; it's an open secret. People even do it during their shift. Staff work very long hours, and it's their only release. We'd go to whorehouses when we were docked. Or if we were at sea, we would have wild parties in the cabins. You'd just lock the door, and a few people would be sniffing almost straight away. Crew would all be sleeping with each other too. Girls never said no when they were high—it was wild. These parties happened almost every night. There were loads of girls around; people went crazy. People did coke during their shift; then at 11:00 p.m., as soon as you finished, you would have a party straight away and stay up all night, taking cocaine and drinking. Some people would go straight back to work. It's dangerous. The attitude seemed to be, as long as you smiled at the guests and did your job properly, it did not really matter what you did."

It can't get much crazier than snorting coke and going back to work and to interact with families and spread the magic of Disney aboard the *Magic*. Perhaps the ship's crew needed to take a trip over to Disney, Oklahoma, a town of two hundred inhabitants—with no relation to Walt, of course—which advertises a heck of a drug rehab facility for those addicted; seriously, I'm not making this stuff up.

In an effort to close out "Plain Crazy" on a high note—sorry, couldn't help myself with that one—how about a little creative craziness from a young couple. Why drop tens of thousands of dollars on a Disney wedding when a little ingenuity can deliver the same wow factor for just the price of admission?

On September 19, 2013, Tory and his soon-to-be bride, Nikki, boarded boats at Disneyland's Pirates of the Caribbean with their family and friends. Their mission was to tie the knot on the ride. Over the years Disney cast members have traded stories about couples feeling amorous and engaging in some lewd acts as they traverse the dark rides. There have even been cases where family members have scattered loved ones' ashes through the Haunted Mansion or Pirates of the Caribbean. But Tory and Nikki were bringing things full circle with Captain Jack Sparrow as their witness.

Just after the attraction's second drop, Tory's friend got the nuptials started with a two-minute ceremony, complete with the exchange of rings. By the time the newlyweds were at the battle scene with the large ship, they were already married. Some savvy planning and a secret seating chart allowed the couple to ask cast members to keep their friends and family together in each boat to witness the ceremony.

There you have it—a unique Disney wedding, orchestrated by a guy who named his children from a previous marriage Ariel, Belle, and Orlando. Now that is some Disney dedication and craziness—take *that*, Disney tattoo guy!

Theft and Fraud

Over the decades, Disney has accumulated countless accolades. It has been *Fortune* magazine's most admired company and *Forbes* magazine's most reputable company, to recount a few. One of the things that helped Disney earn these titles and set it apart from other companies is its customer service. Disney's customer service starts with employees that buy into "The Disney Way."

Walt Disney started "The Disney Way" back in 1955 with the opening of Disneyland. His rules were rigid, and his expectations were high for his cast members. Being clean cut, having a big smile, and always looking to lend a hand were the cornerstones. At times, Disney cast members and a few other folks have lost their way. They went astray of not only "The Disney Way" but also the law, especially when money was involved.

In August of 2013, Disney suspected a housekeeper from their All-Star Movies Resort hotel at Walt Disney World of stealing after several guests reported cash missing from their rooms, and twenty-nine-year-old Bruna cleaned each one. Disney security and the Orange County Tourism Police unit set up a sting operation. They planted a wallet in a dresser with $100 inside and another $400 in the locked room safe. With hidden cameras in the room, authorities witnessed Bruna take twenty dollars from the money planted in the safe. Upon approaching her about the theft, she denied doing anything. After recording the serial numbers on the bills and then comparing them to ones in her possession, the authorities proved otherwise. She was arrested and charged with petty theft.

Another noteworthy theft took place at Walt Disney World in April of 2006. An undercover sting operation would not be needed to catch someone stealing twenty dollars. This theft was much more brazen and bold. Jamie, forty years old, was stealing the cash registers from various stores on Disney property; yes, you read that correctly, stealing the entire cash register. Jamie would go into the stores during the day when they weren't as crowded. He waited until the clerk was distracted and then cut the wires. This allowed for the registers to be dropped into a garbage bag, and he then took off on foot. He hit eight cash registers in all from the Magic Kingdom, Polynesian Village Resort, and few others. He was eventually spotted at the Pop Century Resort where he was apprehended and arrested. Jamie was doing this to support his crazy cocaine habit. Guess the Disney Magic wasn't hiring at the time!

Someone once asked Willie Sutton, one of the most notorious bank robbers of the twentieth century, why he robbed banks. His response was brilliant, yet simple: "because that's where the money is." A few folks on Disney property tweaked Willie's retort and replaced the notion of a bank with Walt Disney World. Ever since the Magic Kingdom at Walt Disney World was built in 1971, people have been enamored with the underground tunnels that exist as a thoroughfare for employees to navigate the park below ground.

The "utilidors" have become a thing of urban legend and Disney lore. People often try and sneak in to see what is really going on down there. Is this where some of the illustrious top-secret Disney magic originates before it finds its way above ground and entertains the masses? Perhaps, perhaps not—it depends on your imagination.

What does traverse the "utilidor" system is often very magical in its own right: cold hard cash. In January of 1986, three cast members were shuttling cash through the tunnels at 2:15 a.m. when they were robbed at gunpoint.

Two men got away with cash bags through a stairwell that led to an employee parking lot. A hauntingly similar thing happened ten years later in July of 1996. This time, three men held up two workers at gunpoint underground. The men grabbed ten cash bags and went above ground to exit the Magic Kingdom just before midnight, as the park was still filled with guests. Both crimes were immediately considered "inside jobs," as the tunnel system is secure. In both cases, the criminals appeared to know specifics by either working there or being informed by someone who worked at Disney. The robbers were eventually apprehended in both situations.

Another theft happened in March of 1993, when a Wells Fargo courier was charged with stealing $20,500 that he was supposed to transport from "Disney's Hollywood Studios." Over four separate trips, Ramirez stole money from the back of his transport truck by stuffing the cash into his shoes and jacket pockets. Investigators noticed Ramirez had made a $13,000 down payment on a 1993 Pontiac Grand Prix and paid off his credit card and phone bill. He was arrested on one count of grand theft.

Moving along to some white-collar crimes, in October of 2012, a former Walt Disney World employee was accused of falsifying $120,000 in liability claims. Gregory was a forty-six-year-old Disney claims representative. He was responsible for investigating claims made against the resort by guests who allegedly had bodily injury or property damage while on Disney property. After investigating a claim, if he deemed it legitimate, Gregory would then offer compensation and negotiate settlements on behalf of Disney to settle the matter. He did so without needing approval from a supervisor.

Gregory's position led him to whip up some creative claims. Between January and June 2009, Gregory authorized eighteen fraudulent insurance settlement payments totaling $122,858. Through an elaborate scheme, he would either add payments to existing claims and get paid on it or increase the seriousness of the claims and add or change the recipient's name to divert the money to a fraudulent billing service in Georgia. After doing this, Gregory would then distribute the funds to his coconspirators in both New York and Georgia. The six-figure payout in such a short period of time was an anomaly for Disney accounting. The department noticed the large payouts and investigated. After Disney figured out the scheme, Gregory was arrested on seventeen felony charges of insurance fraud and racketeering.

Bonnie was a thirty-three-year-old executive assistant for Disney's head of communications. She was living her own fairy tale working for Disney in California. She had a good job and was head over heels for her own Prince Charming. Unlike most stories involving Prince Charming, this real-life tale didn't have a storybook ending. Bonnie and her boyfriend, Yonni, were arrested in 2010 on charges that they offered to sell secrets about the company's financial picture to investment companies. The minor snafu in their plan was that their insider information was going straight to an undercover FBI agent posing as a hedge-fund operator.

Here's how their intrepid scheme worked. Bonnie obtained information, such as Disney's quarterly earnings, before they were released to the public. She would tell her boyfriend, Yonni, who in turn tried to sell this insider information to over thirty investment companies via anonymous letters he sent to investment firms. Most of the firms went ahead and contacted the FBI, who then stepped in and posed as a financial big shot and offered to take the two entrepreneurs up on their offer for the insider information.

Bonnie and Yonni provided the FBI with Disney's May earnings report before it went public. In return for the information, Yonni met with their financial friend to receive a payment of $15,000 as compensation. He also promised more information in the future for a 30 percent cut of any profits made from the confidential info. Then the hammer dropped or shall we say the gavel. Both Bonnie and Yonni were arrested and charged with intent to commit securities fraud and wire fraud. In 2011, Bonnie received three years' probation with the first four months under home confinement plus one hundred hours of community service for each year of her probation. Yonni received two years and three months in prison.

In one of the more head-scratching entrepreneurial stories you'll hear in a long time, would you believe a drug dealer in Orlando actually stopped selling drugs and started selling fraudulent Walt Disney World tickets because it was more lucrative and carried less legal ramifications if he were caught? According to the Orange County Sheriff's Office, this is a true story.

Complete a quick Internet search, and you'll find countless advertisements for cheap or discounted Disneyland and Walt Disney World tickets. If you look within these same search queries, right alongside many of these ads and postings, you'll read about the countless people arrested for selling fake or already-used tickets. The problem of counterfeit tickets plaguing Disney goes back to day one, literally. In 1955, on the opening day of Disneyland, someone counterfeited a slew of tickets and inundated the park with guests. Today, it's not much different, except technology has gotten better both for the counterfeiter and Disney.

As of March of 2014, Disney was trying to toughen the laws in Florida for ticket scammers. Executives from Walt Disney World were aligning themselves with state politicians to bolster the laws. The Disney-backed bill would impose much longer prison terms for tickets scammers. Their new law would also work to include their MagicBands, which function as park tickets, hotel-room keys, and credit cards.

A Disney spokesperson said changes are needed because "fraudulent ticket sales can ruin family vacations." True, Disney can spin it in the media however they want. It is annoying for families that make the fake-ticket purchase—but more importantly for Disney, they are losing money. This is the second time Disney proposed this law but not the first time they had the state come in and write some laws to cover their ticket sales. In June of 1988, they had Florida write a law banning the sale of unused multiday tickets. If you buy a five-day ticket and only go two days, they don't want you to be able to sell the remaining days. At the time, Disney claimed it was losing $3 million in ticket revenue, and the state was being cheated out of $200,000 annually in sales taxes.

The first time this most recent ticket law came up, in 2013, it was killed off. Part of the reason it didn't make it was because of a provision Disney had in the legislation. The provision was the person selling the ticket would be arrested, as would the person (or family) buying it. So if a family or a group visiting from abroad doesn't know any better and makes the purchase, its members are now criminals. It certainly doesn't sound like Disney is too concerned with ruining the family vacation or giving the unsuspecting person or family a parting gift of a criminal record.

The changes to the laws are still pending and have not been determined by the state government. The new proposed law still has the provision in it for those buying the fake tickets. The changes to jail time for selling would increase from sixty days to up to one year for the first offense. The second violation would become a felony instead of a misdemeanor and carries a maximum sentence of five years.

With the legal stuff out of the way, here are a few of the more notable escapades in the world of Disney ticket fraud. Apparently, Grandpa Walt forgot to set up a trust fund for one of his "other" grandchildren, Stephen Disney. Stephen was so hard up for Disneyland tickets that he had to steal a few. Stephen Disney, not his birth name, was a fifty-one-year-old man who claimed to be a Disney heir; he even had a fake driver's license with his alter ego on it and a false tax return showing the Walt Disney Company as his employer.

In January of 2013, Stephen struck up a conversation with a classmate and told her of his family legacy. During their conversation, she mentioned she volunteered with a nonprofit organization. Stephen took an interest and replied that he could give her a pair of Disneyland tickets to use in a charity raffle to raise money for the nonprofit.

All seemed well, the raffle happened, the tickets and their new owners went over to Disneyland, and they were denied entry. The tickets hadn't been activated, as they were stolen. Stephen allegedly stole them from a retail store and then pawned them off to the unsuspecting nonprofit. Stephen Disney was arrested and charged with felony burglary and felony forgery of a state seal.

Another crafty ticket scam took place in September of 1996, when thirty-three-year-old Jacques worked as a desk clerk at Disney's Wilderness Lodge. Jacques would use the resort's computer system to process phony orders for tickets to guest's rooms. The tickets would arrive; he would cancel the room charges and pocket the tickets for resale. His scheme swindled $30,000 worth of park tickets until he was caught by Disney security.

With Disney ticket scams covered, let's up the ante a bit and go for flat-out credit-card theft. Credit-card fraud is more rampant than ever. At one time or another, you are likely to be a victim. In Mexico and the United States, 44 percent and 42 percent of people, respectively, with a credit or debit card are hit each year; Germany has the lowest with 6 percent. It appears as though one of the favorite hot spots to go on someone else's credit card is down to Walt Disney World.

The land of Lincoln is the birthplace of Walt Disney. Today, it's home to a guy with a wicked Disney obsession. Twenty-six-year-old Alexander was a former manager of a steak house in Lincolnshire, Illinois. Alexander loved Disney so much he visited Walt Disney World fifteen times and went on two Disney cruises, all within a five-month period. As everyone who visits knows, these trips don't come cheap. Alexander spent nearly $50,000 on his vacations with money he secured by stealing the identities of fifty customers and former employees of his restaurant.

Alexander used the stolen numbers from guest credit cards to buy gift cards and prepaid credit cards to fund his escapades. Alexander kept his theft and deception going by using phony names, addresses, phone numbers, and e-mail addresses to conceal his real identity. In July of 2013, authorities in Illinois caught up with him and charged him with identity theft and money laundering. In March of 2014, Alexander pleaded guilty to felony aggravated identity theft and was sentenced to six months in jail, along with paying restitution to American Express, Citibank, and Walt Disney World.

The next credit-card scam racked up tens of thousands of dollars in free Disney merchandise by working the system, the Disney reservation system. Three men from Florida—Robert, Steven, and Joseph—ran up $15,000 in charges at several Walt Disney World resorts and shops and then left without paying. Their scam exploited a loophole in Disney's reservation system. Here's how it worked. Each man would check into his hotel with a legitimate credit card. They would then change the card Disney kept on file for charging purposes. The change was made to a prepaid debit card with only a few dollars on it—just enough to clear the small dollar authorization Disney makes when you list the card on your account. The trio then went out to the parks and made purchases, billing everything to their hotel room. They would then flee the scene before Disney ever realized what transpired.

Walt Disney World allowed each guest to link their credit card to their room account charging privileges of up to $1,500 per room before Disney would reconcile and charge the credit card on file. These crafty guys would make their purchases, stay below the $1,500 threshold, and then leave with their goods. From February to April 2012 alone, they visited the resort seven times and ran the scam through thirteen hotel-room accounts.

The crew got pinched when Robert bought several hundred dollars' worth of pricey cigars, repeatedly. Robert reportedly bought large quantities and didn't care what the brands were. He would take anything and everything, which the shopworker thought was odd, as smokers usually favor certain brands. The shop contacted Disney Security who worked with law enforcement to apprehend the trio.

Fifty-year-old Jeffrey, who was homeless and jobless since the 1990s, devised another unique hotel scam. Jeffrey spent much of the previous two decades traveling across the country, moving from hotel room to hotel room on other folks' credit cards. Despite his grim situation, he possessed one attribute that made his life a bit easier: he had an incredible memory.

Law-enforcement officials were investigating a trespassing call at Walt Disney World's Coronado Springs in October of 2012. Jeffrey was at the resort at the time and didn't know the police weren't there to speak with him about his life on the lam utilizing other people's credit cards. Tired of living the crooked life, he spilled his guts about his decades of fraud. He explained to the police that he had a great memory and could remember credit-card numbers he would either briefly see or hear.

Walt Disney World was clearly one of his favorite places to squat, as he stayed there more than twenty-six times over the years. Jeffrey said it was very easy to bunk with the mouse. He would call over to the hotel of his choice, give them the credit-card number to reserve his room, receive a confirmation number, and head to the front desk to pick up his keys. After his powwow with police, Jeffrey was charged with trafficking stolen credit-card numbers, credit-card fraud, false statement as to financial condition or identity, and defrauding an innkeeper.

This next story of theft and fraud may be the most brazen yet. Most people around the world love Facebook. They love communicating with distant friends and family. People can stay abreast of all the latest gossip in their friend's lives. Oftentimes, folks even share their special moments and milestones in their lives for the entire world to see. How many times have you posted about your vacation or that significant moment in your life on social media? Most people partake in this guilty pleasure.

Social media is usually harmless, unless you're up to no good, then you're actually just helping authorities build their case against you. This is exactly what happened to a couple from New York. They shared their travels, indulgences, and exploits around the world with the world. The big problem here was their luxuries were afforded to them by credit-card and bank fraud.

As we all know, sooner or later, people's shenanigans tend to catch up with them. To quote the Staten Island District Attorney working this fraud case, "Make no mistake, Amanda is no Cinderella and Clyde is far from Prince Charming." It appears Bonnie and Clyde—er, scratch that, Amanda and Clyde—had a taste for the high life. Courtside seats to NBA finals' games, field-level seats to NFL games, an excursion to the Dominican Republic, and of course a lavish trip to Walt Disney World for the defrauding duo. The two left their trail of treachery on Facebook.

Like so many folks that get engaged, this couple posted their pictures online. The engagement happened at Walt Disney World. The photos from their trip featured the happy couple in an embrace in front of Cinderella's Castle. Another showed a Cinderella cake sitting next to a glass slipper with the words "Will You Marry Me?" As we all know, when the clock struck midnight for Cinderella, her magical ride ended. Well, the clock struck midnight for Amanda and Clyde in July of 2013, and it struck in a big way.

Amanda, twenty-six years old, and Clyde, twenty-nine years old, were charged with enterprise corruption, identity theft, falsifying business records, criminal possession of stolen property, grand larceny, and grand larceny as a hate crime, among some others. Here's how it all went down. Amanda worked as a nurse at a physician's office in Staten Island from 2004 to 2012. During this time, she had access to elderly patients' medical records that usually contained sensitive information such as social-security numbers and home addresses. Using this information, the two pilfered nearly $700,000 from fifty elderly patients. Amanda would relay the personal and financial information to Clyde, who would contact the financial institutions and do a change of address. He would then also order new debit and credit cards, having them sent to various addresses around New York City.

The couple's exploits on Facebook, along with authorities tracing the stolen bank accounts to the addresses Clyde established, built the case against them.

Over sixty charges were filed against the couple, but the case was still pending in July of 2014.

The disastrous Disney drama that was sketched out here is just a sliver of the mania and madness involving the masses, money, and the mouse. Disney has seen it all, from the abovementioned to numerous others. Unfortunately, these tales aren't the worst of the worst. Things actually take a more appalling leap, a leap down the slope of faking cancer to raise money—money people donated thinking it was going to help a dire situation, but instead it got spent at Disney.

Dying for Disney

What could be more sick, twisted, and appalling than lying to your friends and loved ones about having cancer? How about pulling the same hellacious ruse with your child? For most people it is unfathomable to fake cancer; it would be even more diabolical to tell people your child has cancer and the little one is going to die, even going as far as having your child believe this as well, forcing them to shave their head and alter their appearance to go along with this terrible act of deceit.

Most people, when they hear a friend or loved one has a terminal illness, react accordingly with devastation, heart-wrenching compassion, and a willingness to do anything to make their remaining days as tolerable and filled with love and joy as possible.

They organize fund raisers to help with medical bills and encourage them to go on a trip to the Happiest Place on Earth, urging them to have one of those magical days despite the looming cancer diagnosis. These actions and reactions are exactly what happen when people fake illnesses for donations—donations that often lead to trips to Disney that are just part of an evil stratagem for greed, attention, and a vacation.

Unfortunately, you hear about these stories from all over the country. People get diagnosed with cancer or a fatal illness, and the community springs into action, as they should with fund raisers, beef-and-beer parties, you name it. Friends and family come together to help this person in need.

More and more, stories are popping up that some twisted folks aren't really sick at all and sought out this attention and money for illnesses they never had. The scam always works, at least for a short time. The conscienceless people ultimately end up being revealed as the frauds they are. In the end they do get the attention they were seeking. They receive notoriety in the news when their antics put them through the legal system and often into prison.

So why do thousands of people fall for this over and over again? I think this is the easier question to answer than the one of "why do people perpetrate this heinous act?" These illnesses strike at the core of us. Everyone at some point in their life has had someone close to them get diagnosed with cancer or some other terrible illness. We see the destruction and devastation illnesses do, not only mentally but also physically. If pitching in a little bit may help this person, society in general is all for it. With that being said, where do many people go to escape reality and leave the "real world" behind with all its stresses and pressures, let alone a terminal illness? Disneyland or Walt Disney World.

If you can't afford your next Disney vacation, just follow the lead of these despicable folks and fake an illness to receive a free trip. In turn, you actually may end up getting two free trips, one to "the house of the mouse" and the other to the "big house," a.k.a. prison.

Men seem to be the anomalies in these stunts, so let's get started there. Jeffrey, forty-six years old and from South Jordan, Utah, told friends and family he was suffering from terminal cancer. The local Mormon congregation heard of Jeffrey's plight and organized a fund raiser on his behalf. The money raised went to Jeffrey, so he and his family could go on one "final" vacation together to Disney. The family set out on Jeffrey's farewell tour in September of 2011. After people became suspicious of his story, detectives checked his medical records and determined he didn't have cancer and wasn't terminally ill. He was arrested and charged with felony communications fraud.

Our first deceptive young lady was the then twenty-three-year-old Ashley from Toronto, Canada. She shaved her head and eyebrows, plucked her eyelashes, and starved herself to have her physical appearance coincide with her "chemotherapy sessions." If that wasn't enough to pull on your heartstrings, Ashley would update her illness status on Facebook and post photos with a big smile and fake tattoos emblazoned on her fingers that said "won't" on one hand and "quit" on the other.

Life was tough for young Ashley, as she was not only staring down the big *C*, she was also doing it alone. She frequently told people that she was disowned by her drug-addicted parents or that they were dead. The reality was that she didn't have cancer, and her parents were alive and supportive. They were divorced and both remarried, with three young children between them.

Why did she do it? Ashley said, "I was trying to be noticed. I was trying to get my family back together. I didn't want to feel like I'm nothing anymore. It went wrong, it spread like crazy, and then it seemed like the whole world knew."

The whole world knew indeed, because she told them. In late 2008, Ashley did have a medical issue. She had a benign lump in one of her breasts and had undergone a procedure for it, and all was well, except that she began telling anyone that would listen that things weren't well. Ashley said she had breast, brain, liver, stomach and ovarian cancer at various stages. Poor Ashley—she was really brave for dealing with such adversity with such a positive outlook. This is what her peers thought about her. Teenagers and young adults from all over embraced her. They organized benefits and concerts for her, printed T-shirts, and made online videos, all in an effort to keep her optimism up and help provide for her during this dire time.

Ashley also formed her own charity. A Facebook page was created to get the word out about Change for a Cure (meaning your pocket change can help fund a cure for cancer or at least line her pockets) with the tagline, "Together we can 'Change' the world one penny at a time." Cash donations started rolling in, and within two days the Facebook group had one thousand members—and months later, over four thousand.

At the concerts held in her benefit, Ashley set up "Change for a Cure" booths to collect donations, in addition to the ten- or twenty-dollar cover fee to enter. All of the money Ashley raised was going to be donated to the University of Alberta's research into dichloroacetate (DCA) a cancer treatment. Once she had collected all the money, she said she would walk from Burlington to Edmonton, Canada, starting on her twenty-third birthday, to deliver the money in person to the university. Keep in mind that Canada's health-care system is different than the United States'; most of the cost of the cancer treatments in the country is covered under the Canada Health Act of 1984. So her fundraising wasn't going to cover her exorbitant medical bills, as is often the case in the United States.

Even local companies contributed, as did the local skateboard community and charities. One such charity was Skate4Cancer, led by skateboarder Rob Dyer. Rob lost his mother and two grandparents to cancer. He launched this group as a cancer-awareness organization. Ashley wanted to go to Walt Disney World; it could be her last opportunity to visit Florida. She persuaded Skate4Cancer to foot the bill for her trip. When she returned back from her trip, she informed everyone that she had contracted an infection and was going to die soon.

Ashley was good. She may have missed her calling in theatre; everyone believed her story. Young people get diagnosed with cancer every day in this world, but there was one person who wasn't sure if the story was accurate, yet he too vacillated, and that was Ashley's father. Speaking only to her father once in the previous four years, she told him she had breast cancer and a brain tumor. She also told him that if she didn't get a bone-marrow transplant, she would be gone within six months. Her father thought it was another one of her "stories" and went along for the ride. The next day, he followed up with Ashley to find out the name of her oncologist to be informed of her condition and care.

After trying for ten days to reach her, Ashley finally responded and told him, "Stay the f—— out of my life." He stayed away from Ashley but called the hospitals where Ashley said she was being treated for cancer; there was no record of her. Skeptical but still not certain, he followed her on Facebook, along with thousands of other people.

Finally, he was able to get the truth out of her. He reached out to her on the phone repeatedly. They connected one evening, and he recounts, "I said flat out: 'You don't have cancer, do you?' There was silence on the phone, and she very quietly responded: 'No.'" He then gave her thirty days to go public with her admission, clear the air, and make things right.

Ashley did one interview with the *Toronto Star* to come clean, only after her father's ultimatum. In her interview she claimed she received only $5,000 worth of contributions. Volunteers say otherwise; they put it in the neighborhood of $30,000.

Ashely did offer up this quote in the interview: "I dug myself a big hole that I couldn't get out of. And there's nobody to blame but me."

Ashley was arrested on charges of theft and received ten months under house arrest, followed by five months with a curfew requiring her to stay home between 10:00 p.m. and 6:00 a.m. She also received two years of probation and community service, along with psychiatric treatment for a personality disorder, depression, and anxiety. All of this most likely led to a lenient sentence for her, as she could have faced up to fourteen years in prison for her crimes.

Two similar stories to Ashley's took place south of the border in the good old United States. Heather, thirty-five years old, from Racine, Wisconsin, bilked thousands of good folks out of their hard-earned money through donations and fund raisers over the period 2001–2004. Even the local newspaper ran a story on her. The *Racine Journal Times* ran the headline: "Facing her battle with a smile." It recounted Heather's bravery in her battle against a rare form of ovarian cancer. She told reporters she had surgery to remove her right ovary and uterus, only having to go under the knife a few weeks later to remove her kidney and shoulder muscle, as more tumors were discovered.

Donning a scarf over her bald head, Heather spoke of not only her physical and emotional battle but also her financial battle. She detailed the enormous medical bills she faced, as her health insurance only partially covered her care—a cue to the fund raisers. Reporters covering one of her events quoted Heather as saying, "It doesn't necessarily have to do with the money. It's the love and support shown by everyone. It's spiritually uplifting."

The money certainly didn't hurt though, and she took upward of $75,000 over the years. She spent it on renovations to her kitchen, new household appliances, and a new roof. There was also that dying wish for a trip to Walt Disney World.

For Heather, as with most perpetrators, it was hard to keep up the rouse of dying without actually dying or wasting away. Eventually, something has to give, and when death or diminished health doesn't happen, people start to get suspicious, which is what happened in Heather's case. Those who worked hard on her fund raisers became leery of her illness. They contacted the police, who did their due diligence on her case. She stuck to her story. She arranged for her physician to call the sheriff's detective and even had another physician write a letter in support of her and her condition. Both the phone call and letter were fraudulent; she never had cancer. Heather was arrested on three felony counts of false representation and was later sentenced to two years in prison in 2005.

If these few stories weren't bad enough, here come the tales about mothers claiming their children were dying of cancer and about their need to go to Disney with their terminally ill kids. All of the situations are very unfortunate, and it appears as though the mothers operated not only for attention but also for greed. Thankfully, the mothers didn't do any damage to their children physically, as the mental ramifications of their actions were more than enough. Without further ado, the story of the mother-of-the-year candidate number one:

In 2003, thirty-five-year-old Lisle from Chicago, Illinois, told family and friends her seven-year-old son was terminally ill with eye cancer that spread to his brain. People around the community donated thousands of dollars to her when she announced that she wanted to take her sick son to Walt Disney World for a long weekend and that the trip was going to be a treat in light of everything he was going through. Donations came in from jars placed around town with a picture of the little boy on it. Even his elementary school held fund raisers on his behalf. The story started to fall apart when the little guy went back to school, and his teachers started to prepare his coursework for an expected long absence. The teachers reached out to his physician, only to be told there was not a patient with that name under the doctor's care.

Once the State Department of Child Services contacted Lisle, she immediately confessed to her actions. Lisle was charged with theft by deception, seven felony charges, and one misdemeanor for theft of over $12,000. Lisle faced up to seven years in prison. She accepted a plea deal that put her on two years' probation; she had to attend counseling, write a letter of apology to her son's school, and pay back the money she accepted, all of which prosecutors believe she spent at Walt Disney World.

The next mother didn't fare as well in the legal department. Stephanie, twenty-two years old, of Wetumpka, Alabama, was sentenced to twenty years in prison; yes, that's two-followed-by-a-zero years. In 2010, Stephanie claimed that her five-year-old son had cancer. The usual fund raisers happened, along with collection jars set up at convenience stores and gas stations. Multiple businesses pitched in to specifically send her and her son on a trip to Walt Disney World; it was his dying wish. Who could say no to this, especially seeing Stephanie parading her son around in public in a wheelchair? Like all of the others, this story also started to fall apart.

In May of 2013, Stephanie pleaded guilty to theft of property by deception and attempted theft of property by deception, for which she was sentenced to ten years in prison on each account, with the sentences to run consecutively. The sentences were handed down despite her attorney's pleas that Stephanie was only fourteen years old when she gave birth to her son and was ill equipped to raise the child. The amount of money she pleaded guilty to stealing was a total of $1,400.

Saving what is the worst case for last—if you can quantify any of the horrific acts. This story happened across the pond in England. Thirty-six-year-old Emma from Stroud, Gloucestershire, convinced her husband, her son, community (she also announced it on Facebook), and government that her six-year-old boy was diagnosed with a fatal autoimmune disease, lymph proliferative syndrome—an often fatal blood disorder.

Emma told her husband about their son's condition and explained he didn't have long to live. The couple then sat their son down and revealed this to him; they told him his condition was fatal. The next thing the little guy knew, his mom shaved his head and eyebrows. She made him wear a bandanna to school and forced him to spend his days in public seated in a wheelchair. With her son being wheelchair bound even in school, Emma directed teachers to keep an eye on him, as his condition was very serious and dire, thus allowing him no freedom at all. Only when he was home and alone with just his mother could he leave his wheelchair.

The boy often wondered why he could move about at home on his feet, even play on the backyard trampoline, but in public this was not permitted. He asked his mom why he had to take the wheelchair in public. Her reply was his knees had serious problems and he should stay off them. Obviously, she even stayed her course when she took the young boy on his dream vacation to Walt Disney World. She forced the young boy to stay in his wheelchair at the parks so that she could jump to the head of the line (more on situations like this in chapter 7).

The government funded Emma's fraudulent trek to Walt Disney World. From October 2007 to February 2011, she milked England for over £85,000 and a handicapped-accessible vehicle to cart him around. She forged letter after letter to the government for disability claims, which were accepted. After several years the scheme started to collapse when she separated from her husband. One of the doctor's notes that Emma sent to school was sent home with the young boy when his father picked him up that day.

In what could be something out of a movie, her cover was blown on a simple spelling mistake. Some of the school officials were already a bit suspicious of the letters, but when Emma's husband read the letter, he noticed a very simple spelling mistake, a mistake Emma made often when she spelled. She wrote the word "too" when it should have been spelled "to." She did this so frequently that the two—father and son—joked that it was an "Emma-ism." In an effort to confirm his suspicions, the father took his son to see their family doctor.

The physician ran tests, and all was well medically with the boy. Emma was confronted by both the boy's father and eventually the police. She was arrested on child cruelty, fraud, and forgery, all of which she admitted to. Emma was sentenced to three years and nine months in prison. The young boy now exclusively lives with his father. Emma writes to her son from prison begging for forgiveness. Her son is not interested in maintaining a relationship with his "mum."

Again, the question of why people create this situation for themselves or their children is something obviously more complex and transcends a book about a different side of Disney. Over the years, the Disney Company, too, has had its own share of madness.

All the magical times in the world sometimes aren't enough to exonerate them from doing some dubious acts and creating their own mania.

Dubious Disney

Over the decades, the Walt Disney Company has won numerous awards spanning the spectrum of theatre, television, movies, and music. Today, Walt Disney still holds the Academy Award record with thirty-two Academy Awards. The company that bears his name is still racking up a bevy of business accolades for their business and customer-service practices. Disney received its most dubious award back in 2001. They were awarded a Sweatie. What's a Sweatie, you ask? Well, a Sweatie is an award given to the sweatshop retailer of the year.

The award was created by the Maquila Solidarity Network (MSN). The MSN is a labor and women's rights organization that supports the efforts of workers in global supply chains around the world. The group, founded in 1994, works to win improved wages and working conditions for workers around the world, most notably, in Mexico, in Central America, and throughout Asia.

So what did Disney do to earn their Sweatie in 2001? Apparently, the company was a repeat offender over the years and around the globe for a litany of things. They utilized or contracted with factories abroad that employed children as their labor force, paid pennies in wages, had deplorable working conditions, and had their employees work long hours.

The sweatshop claims for Disney started to mount in the mid-1990s, as it did for many companies in the United States. The trouble didn't stop with the new millennium. If anything, they increased (or the media coverage of it intensified). Disney wasn't just a repeat offender but an equal opportunity offender. Disney or their licensees were having their labor issues exposed in Haiti, Vietnam, China, and Bangladesh.

In 1996, Disney was accused of contracting with two US companies that produced Mickey Mouse and Pocahontas pajamas in sweatshops in Haiti. The report noted that some employees were only earning twelve cents an hour. Even worse, some of the employees were underage.

After the story broke, and Disney denied the claims, the conditions improved. Many employees were given raises, up to twenty-eight cents an hour, and a heck of a profit was still made on the pajamas, since they retailed back home for nearly eleven dollars. Interestingly, a writer covering the story figured out that Disney CEO Michael Eisner made roughly $97,600 an hour with his salary and stock options.

In Vietnam in 1997, Disney was accused of utilizing the Keyhinge toy factory. Employees there worked on average nine to ten hours a day, seven days a week, at six cents an hour. At the time, things in Bangladesh weren't much better. Factory workers there were paid eight to nineteen cents an hour and forced to work fourteen hours a day, seven days a week. The workplace was so high pressured that if they didn't meet their quota, they were threatened with beatings. The factory allegedly banned workers from speaking to each other, as it slowed production; however, when it came time for workers to speak to factory inspectors, they were permitted to speak with them but were coached on what to say and to lie.

Over the years China has been a big source of violations for Disney. These allegations exist as recent as 2012. Everything from Disney books to clothing and toys has come under the spotlight. Allegations against Disney in this country featured the hiring of thirteen- and fourteen-year-old junior-high-school students to work fifteen hours a day, for pennies an hour, in high-pressured environments where an average worker has a ninety-six-hour workweek. One worker allegedly committed suicide from the stress and pressure.

At the beginning of this controversy, Disney denied the allegations and maintained that they did not own or operate any of the factories; instead, they merely licensed with US companies that subcontract out work. Disney wasn't privy to all of the practices of their licensees.

As the media attention increased, Disney changed their stance. They started to acknowledge and accept some responsibility. Instead of merely stating that it was up to their licensees to inspect and authorize factories, Disney became more proactive. They joined an initiative called Project Kaleidoscope to promote better working conditions in Chinese plants that Disney often receives merchandise from. They even started to work with their licensees and contractors to inspect and audit the factories, not just with announced visits but with unannounced visits as well.

Next, Disney created and posted a code of conduct for manufacturers on their corporate website for companies looking to do business with Mickey. The website outlines what is expected from their partners and what won't be tolerated—child labor, involuntary labor, harassment, health and safety violations, and unfair wages. Many violations of these expectations, or the lack of interest in fulfilling them, came to an unfortunate end for hundreds of factory workers who died at factories Disney used abroad. A Bangladeshi factory fire in 2012 and building collapse in 2013 killed many hardworking people. Since these tragedies, Disney announced in May 2013 that they are phasing out all production of their products in Bangladesh, Pakistan, Belarus,

Ecuador, and Venezuela.

The subject of race has plagued Disney for decades, and it runs pretty deep. Many believe Disney has some racially insensitive character portrayals within their movies. Folks will cite *The Song of the South,* the crows from *Dumbo,* King Louie in the *Jungle Book,* Native Americans in *Peter Pan,* and the portrayals of Arabs in *Aladdin.* The list could go on, but seeing as this chapter is long enough, we will keep Disney and potential racial situations exclusive to their theme parks.

Two years before Disney introduced some diversity into their princess lineup with Princess Tiana, star of *The Princess and the Frog* in 2009, Walt Disney World was accused of profiling black teens at their Downtown Disney location. In June of 2007, the Orlando Sentinel ran a series of articles about Disney's crackdown on teens loitering at Downtown Disney. Disney claimed that the atmosphere of the area started to change in early 2005 after they stopped charging an entry fee to Pleasure Island.

Once they removed the turnstiles, the area started to see an influx of teens hanging out around the nightclubs. In an effort to curb the loitering and deter some of the wrong element from hanging around, Disney removed the projection screens and loud music to remove the party-like atmosphere for those not patronizing the clubs.

In 2007, Disney's concerns came to a head when two tourists from Connecticut reported they were robbed and abducted from Downtown's parking lot. With that, Disney bolstered their security and Orange County sheriff's presence. After a handful of arrests (including one of a fifteen-year-old carrying a gun and some marijuana) Disney began a late-night crackdown on Friday and Saturday, under the suspicion that some of the teens and young adults on site were members of street gangs. As Walt Disney World spokeswoman, Jacquee Polak stated the following:

> A gang-like presence was unfortunately identified at Downtown Disney. A lot of them were described as "wannabe gangbangers." And some of them were flat-out harassing and bothering other guests. And that is not going to be tolerated. So additional deputies were proactively assigned to patrol the area and that's going to go on as long as is needed.

The bigger police presence was on-site, and groups of teens were actively being screened. If some of the teens couldn't convince Disney security officers that they had a good reason to be in Downtown Disney late at night—for example, seeing a movie, eating dinner, and so forth—they were asked to leave. Those who refused were escorted off the property and issued trespass warnings banning them from Disney World for life.

This is exactly what happened over the course of two weekends. Security issued fifty trespass warnings during this time—the same number they issued in the first five months of 2006. Within this group of fifty warnings were four football prospects who were to attend Florida State University in the fall. Ironically, one young man's father happened to be a civil-rights attorney, and another's father was a Disney manager. The four teens were asked to leave by security guards, who claimed they were loitering for too long. The situation escalated when they were asked to leave and refused to oblige. The group was fingerprinted, photographed, and issued their lifetime ban from Walt Disney World.

The teens and their parents couldn't help but think it was because they were African Americans. The *Orlando Sentinel* did some digging and saw of the forty-eight trespass warnings the Orange County deputy sheriffs issued over these two weekends, forty-five out of the forty-six people receiving the trespass warning and lifetime ban were African Americans or Hispanics. When this story hit the media, Disney went on the defensive: everything that transpired over the two weekends was in an effort to maintain the safety in the area and all of the bans were justified.

Spokeswoman Jacquee Polak said, "Because of concerns about a rise in gang-like activity at Downtown Disney lately, loitering or 'any other inappropriate behavior' by groups of youths is not going to be tolerated. This group of young men was seen loitering for an extended period of time. When asked, sometime after 11:30 p.m., they produced a movie ticket for a film that had already started sometime earlier. Disney Security asked them to go to the movie or leave, and they failed to cooperate."

After speaking with some of the teens' parents, Disney decided to revise the trespass warnings for the four young men; they were now banned from only Downtown Disney and not the entire property for life. Disney was also quick to note that this was not racial profiling. Despite the story about the four teenage boys, the year prior in 2006 at Downtown Disney, officers handed out 296 warnings; of these, twenty-nine went to African Americans; forty-two, to Hispanics; and the rest, to white and Asian guests.

While on the subject of discrimination, how about a story maybe not so dubious, but perhaps just as sordid? The story begins in 1971 with the construction of Walt Disney World. People from all over the world recognize Walt Disney World's Cinderella Castle as not only the theme park's iconic structure but also as a trademark for all things Disney. If you've ever visited the park and made your way to the castle, you've certainly seen the five intricate and beautiful mosaic murals that adorn the inside of the castle and tell the story of Cinderella.

A former Nazi of the Third Reich, Hanns Scharff, created this mosaic. Scharff was called the "master interrogator" of the German Luftwaffe. Others said he was the most prolific military interrogator not just of the Nazi party but of the world.

Prior to World War II, Scharff studied art and was learning his family's textile business. The business took him out of his native Poland and around Europe. Living in Germany just before the war intensified, he was drafted into the German military. Being fluent in English made him an ideal candidate as an interrogator for the Nazi party. Scharff was tasked with interrogating US troops who had been shot down and captured in Germany, and his success rate was in the neighborhood of 90 percent. According to the stories of the day and his biography, his interrogations were all done without violence. Scharff excelled at his position, so much in fact that after the war, he came to the United States and lectured to the US military about the tactics he used to successfully interrogate prisoners.

Now living in this country permanently, he began his artistic conquest again, initially as a hobby. Scharff, interested in mosaics since childhood, started to create chests, desks, and lamps all inlaid with mosaic designs. The hobby eventually became a way to support himself. He opened a small studio in New York City, where he gained a following. By the mid-1950s he relocated across the country to Los Angeles and started selling his work commercially. Scharff created tables for Disneyland, fountains at Los Angeles City Hall and UCLA, and swimming pools in Vegas. His work continued not only through the state of California but also through the country.

In 1971, one of Scharff's masterpieces was created at Walt Disney World's Cinderella Castle. The five murals at the castle measure fifteen feet high by ten feet wide. They feature millions of pieces of hand-cut Italian glass with authentic gold and silver, all placed by hand. They capture several scenes from Cinderella and aren't the only works by Scharff at Walt Disney World. He created another mosaic for the Land Pavilion at EPCOT.

Hanns Scharff passed away in 1992, the same year a book came out that spoke of another piece of Nazi artwork that supposedly took up residence at Walt Disney World—the key word here is "supposedly."

In a mural at Walt Disney World's Grand Floridian Resort, there is a scene that is supposed to depict a Great Gatsby–type theme as the artist claims. It was about "rich people in the good old days;" the people were depicted as happy and prosperous. One of the scenes was a street scene, where a well-dressed couple is conversing in front of a hotel. On the balcony floor of the hotel above them in the background is a man who is dressed in a dark uniform. The artist claims this man is a Nazi SS storm trooper.

Supposedly the Nazi is the artist's comment on the state of the world during that time. Here are these folks living it up, while the Nazi party was running rough shod over Europe. Now, this story comes from a book named *Sabotage in the American Workplace: Anecdotes of Dissatisfaction, Mischief and Revenge.* The book is a collection of stories about people doing exactly what the title implies. The only problem is there is really no way to substantiate or verify just about anything in the book. The book tells stories and then merely puts the person's first name and their occupation. The above story about the Nazi mural was by "Harvey," a mural painter, not the most reliable source; nonetheless, it is an interesting story. Perhaps you can lump this tale into the other Disney urban legends of Walt Disney being cryogenically frozen and the hearse in front of Disneyland's Haunted Mansion belonging to Brigham Young.

Being an eternal optimist, I can't end the chapter with a group of negative stories; there's still an entire book left for that. So let me highlight a few good deeds and close out "Mickey Mania" with a few Disney-inspired stories that pull on the heartstrings a bit.

Five-year-old Bryce and four-year-old Dorothy met in 2012 at the University Medical Center in Tucson, Arizona. They were both undergoing chemotherapy for their leukemia. The two became instant buddies and shared a strong bond, beyond their illness. Bryce really wanted to go to Walt Disney World, so he asked the Make a Wish Foundation if he could go and bring his friend Dorothy along so that they could enjoy the trip together. In December of 2013, that wish came true, and the two took a trip down to Orlando to visit Mickey and had the time of their young lives.

In another story, if you can't get down to Disney to watch a parade, how about having the parade come to you? An even better option is to have the parade feature and honor you. This is what happened to five-year-old Claire, from Dickinson, Texas, who really got the royal treatment, and she deserved it.

Little Claire loves the Disney princesses. She received a surprise in February of 2014 when her town threw a princess parade to honor her. Claire has a rare form of cancer called alveolar rhabdomyosarcoma. The cancer causes malignant cells to form in muscle tissue, and there is no known cure.

Hundreds of people went out to honor the town's princess. Claire had no idea what was in store for her until women dressed as Cinderella and Snow White knocked on her front door. Next, she was whisked away by her father to see what the fuss was all about. Outside of her house she saw a red carpet, covered in rose petals, which led to a horse-drawn carriage. Claire and her parents threw on their royal attire (Claire dressed as Belle from *Beauty and the Beast*) and went on their parade. The Texas City High School's cheerleaders and marching band cheered them on, as nearly one thousand people lined the streets and participated in the two-hour parade. Claire was having such a good time she did several laps.

This is a touching story of a little girl who during her forty-two weeks of chemotherapy never cried or acted sad; she always maintained a positive attitude and even looked forward to seeing her doctors every week. "I haven't been feeling good," Claire told KHOU News in Houston about her cancer battle. "I have tubes in my sides. And I had my hair in a knot. But they gave me shots, and they have to give me some medicine. They were trying to just make me feel better, but it really hurt."

Not all Disney or real-life stories end happily ever after. But it certainly doesn't hurt to try.

CHAPTER 2

Lights, Camera, Accident!

In September of 2006, Disneyland adopted a six-year-old German shepherd/Labrador retriever mix named Hemmingway. The pooch was put to work at the Big Thunder Petting Zoo. Two weeks into his job, Hemmingway mauled the face of a two-year-old girl who was petting him. Disney settled out of court days before the trial.

The pilgrimage to Walt Disney World and Disneyland for millions of people around the world is a happy, relaxing, family-centric experience. There is, however, a very minute percentage of people who unfortunately have different views of the Happiest Place on Earth. For these folks, a Disney park is anything but a nostalgic or fantastic dreamland. Instead it's actually a nightmare, a place of sorrow, accidents, or negligence—not all of which are Disney's fault.

The tragedy and loss of life within the confines of a Disney theme park can't help but make you look at the wonderful world of Disney with a different perspective, which is certainly something that may happen to you after reading these next few chapters.

Unfortunately, no one is immune to an accident in his or her everyday life. People are not safe from accidents and incidents just because they are on vacation. As the top family-vacation destination in the world, no place has more of a focus on people than Disney, especially when it comes to accidents, crimes, and death.

In the heavily regulated society that we live in today, most people are surprised to learn that there are no uniform safety standards at the federal level in regards to the large theme parks across the country, and the parks would like to keep it that way. There is the Consumer Product Safety Commission that oversees traveling amusements like fairs and carnivals, but permanent theme and amusement parks are self-governing in regards to federal oversight. At the state level, things are different yet similar. California and Florida have state agencies. In California, it is the Department of Industrial Relations. In Florida, it's the Department of Agriculture—Bureau of Fair Rides Inspection.

The Florida agency inspects all rides of permanent or temporary nature, except for theme parks that have more than one thousand employees and their own full-time inspectors. Obviously Walt Disney World falls into the exempt category here; however, in 2002, Disney and the other major theme parks in the state entered into a Memorandum of Understanding (MOU) with the Florida Department of Agriculture. The MOU requires quarterly reporting of any serious ride-related injuries and immediate reporting of fatalities. The MOU also performs biannual site visits, consultations, and reviews of the safety programs at Florida's permanent amusement facilities.

Over in California, home to Disneyland, the park was also self-governing for safety from 1955 until 1999. In 2000, a Theme Park Inspection bill—California's Permanent Amusement Ride Safety Law—was enacted allowing for the state's Department of Industrial Relations to annually inspect permanent theme parks; thus, Disneyland is inspected by the California Division of Occupational Safety and Health that performs ride inspections, operational and documentation audits, along with maintaining public reports on any accident requiring more than first aid.

Regardless of the state or federal involvement, when it comes to safety, "the house of mouse's" reputation and business model relies heavily on safety. An accident or tragic event hits the media and, regardless of cause, brings unwanted publicity onto their theme parks; hence, Disney has a pretty thorough and detailed safety protocol for their attractions. According to Disney's executive vice president for facilities and operations management, "You take care of the attraction like your family goes on every ride."

With that in mind, Disney spends hours each night inspecting every ride after the park closes. Once the last guest is gone, maintenance crews descend on each attraction. The crews perform inspections of ride vehicles and tracks based upon Disney's daily, weekly, monthly, and yearly maintenance checklist.

They look for wear and potential mechanical problems. The ride engineers and maintenance workers perform their tasks, and by the end of their shift, just mere hours before thousands descend on the parks again, the attractions are powered up and run through their paces again before any guests can climb aboard. All of this preventive and corrective maintenance equates to roughly one thousand daily hours of inspection time, on all attractions.

Disney's diligences with safety, along with many of their cohorts in the industry are doing a commendable job. Just take a look at the numbers: you have a better chance of being seriously injured by a bee sting (one in 79,842), being struck by lightning (one in 34,906), or mauled by a dog (one in 144,899) than being seriously injured on a ride at a theme park.

According to the International Association of Amusement Parks and Attractions (IAAPA), the chance of being seriously injured on a ride at a fixed-site park in the United States is one in twenty-four million. In 2012, of the 1,415 ride-related injuries, sixty-one, or less than 5 percent, required some form of overnight treatment at a hospital. It's pretty remarkable if you think about how many millions upon millions of people attend amusement parks around the country every year.

As we know, accidents do happen, and not every accident at Disney has to do with vacationing. Many of the accidents on Disney property happen on the job. For many, and just ask a cast member the next time you're at a park, working for Disney is a dream come true. They love their job and the environment. Aside from being entertaining, the parks are complex, chaotic, and a mechanical labyrinth with many details to be aware of. Oftentimes people lose sight of this, things go awry, and accidents ensue, or shall I say, people sue.

When an employee gets hurt at a Disney park, it is national news. The same can't always be said for other workplace accidents, although injuries or fatalities do happen every day at work somewhere in this country. According to OSHA, in 2012, twelve deaths happen each workday in America; it's just much more newsworthy when things happen at Disney.

Many of the accidents, incidents, and deaths to guests on Disney property are not always Disney's fault. As history has revealed, there was often negligence or unknown preexisting medical conditions that unfortunately were exasperated by a ride. Before we dive in, first and foremost, condolences to the families affected.

Let's take a look at some of the accidents over the years. First stop, the place that started it all, Disneyland. Disneyland opened in Anaheim in 1955, fifteen years before the US government passed Occupational Safety and Health Act, known as OSHA. Just four years after the opening, another Disney innovation made its debut, the Matterhorn Bobsleds.

The Matterhorn was revolutionary for theme-park rides. Instead of using wooden tracks, as all roller-coaster rides had relied on for decades, the Matterhorn utilized metal tubes as the track. With metal being malleable, it allowed for a tighter, faster, and smoother ride. It set the standard for thousands of tubular steel coasters around the world. Unfortunately the Matterhorn also has the dubious distinction of being a part of the first fatality in Disneyland's history.

In May of 1964, Mark, a fifteen-year-old boy from Long Beach, California, was riding the Matterhorn. As his bobsled approached the apex, the young man stood up and was subsequently ejected from the sled he was riding in. Mark was found lying on a ledge about three feet from the coaster's track, about a third of the way down the mountain. Investigators determined that, for reasons unknown, Mark unfastened his seat belt and then stood up.

At the time, there was speculation that his actions were part of initiation into a private club or some sort of hazing. The other belief and more realistic one was that it was "horseplay," as Mark and his friends were quite rambunctious in the queue, joking around and screaming. Unfortunately, due to the injuries suffered, Mark passed away several days later in the hospital. The investigators deemed his death accidental.

Regretfully, the Matterhorn was the scene for another accident twenty years later in January of 1984. This time it took the life of a forty-eight-year-old woman, Dolly of Fremont, California. Dolly was riding the bobsled with her friends. They were in the front, and Dolly was in the back by herself. When her trip on the Matterhorn started, her seat belt was fastened. When police investigators witnessed the accident scene, her seat belt was open, obviously as she was ejected from the sled. When Dolly fell from the ride and landed on the tracks, she was hit by another sled and pinned underneath it. Dolly was pronounced dead at the scene, giving Disneyland their seventh fatality in nearly thirty years and 230 million visitors.

The same month and year the Matterhorn made its debut at Disneyland so did another legendary Disney attraction, the Disneyland Monorail in June of 1959. The first of its kind in North America, the futuristic transportation was one of Walt's favorites. Disney didn't invent the concept of the elevated train with rubber tires traversing a concrete beam, but Walt always had an affinity for anything having to do with trains. With the monorail concept, Walt envisioned this mode of transportation all over the country. Today, the concept is utilized all over the world, just not to the degree Walt believed it could be. Despite its overall lack of popularity around the globe, Walt's own monorail did gain worldwide notoriety.

In June of 1966, the Disneyland Monorail garnered much unwanted attention. Just before the beginning of Disneyland Grad Nite (an event Disneyland hosted for graduating high-school seniors in Southern California), nineteen-year-old Thomas from Northridge, California, scaled Disneyland's sixteen-foot fence at the northern portion of Harbor Boulevard in an effort to sneak into the park. Once over the fence, Thomas hopped on the monorail beam. Security guards noticed him and began shouting for him to "Jump, get out of the way, and get off there." Instead Thomas fell to a fiberglass canopy beneath the track, and the lower part of the monorail killed him instantly.

The Disneyland Monorail isn't known for its thrills and chills, and neither is the Disneyland PeopleMover. Just like the monorail, the PeopleMover claimed some young lives; two lives to be exact. The attraction was dubbed "Tomorrow's transportation today" when it debuted in Disneyland in 1967.

The technology and idea for the PeopleMover came from Disney's work in the 1964–1965 New York World's Fair. In the same vein that Walt viewed the monorail as an alternative way to "move people," so too was the PeopleMover. The trains of the PeopleMover don't use a motor to propel them down the track. The track itself uses electricity and rubber tires to move each train down the track at speeds ranging from two to seven miles per hour. This crowd favorite gave guests an aerial view of the Disneyland landscape below them.

For a handful of guests, the openness of the trains and their relatively slow speed was enticing enough for them to try and leave their train and hop into another adjacent train. This is exactly what happened to fifteen-year-old Rick of Hawthorne, California, in August of 1967. While attempting to change trains by hopping out of one and into another as the train was moving, Rick fell and got caught under the wheels of the PeopleMover and was dragged along. Unfortunately, this resulted in his death and the third death of a teenager in the 1960s at Disneyland. Rick's wasn't the last life the slow-moving PeopleMover would claim.

In nearly identical circumstances, in June of 1980 at another Grad Nite (there was a third death during a Grad Nite three years later when an eighteen-year-old boy drowned in the Rivers of America), Gerardo from San Diego was struck and killed around 1:30 a.m. by the PeopleMover. As Gerardo's train passed into the tunnel portion of the ride, he climbed out of his moving car in an attempt to hop into another. He lost his footing and landed on the track. The next train coming hit and dragged him until ride operators noticed and shut down the ride. Gerardo was pronounced dead at the scene of extreme internal injuries. Gerardo's death was the last casualty for this ride. The attraction closed in August of 1995.

When Walt Disney's Carousel of Progress left Disneyland and headed to Florida for Walt Disney World in 1973, a huge hole needed to be filled, figuratively and physically. Carousel's building featured a circular revolving theatre. The stage is stationary, and the guests seated in the theatre rotate around the central stages. To take the place of the Carousel of Progress, Disney created the attraction "America Sings" in June of 1974.

The show featured 114 audio animatronics singing and entertaining the masses with different medleys of American music—think "Yankee Doodle" and "Pop Goes the Weasel," some good patriotic stuff Walt would be proud of. Not even two weeks after the attraction debuted did tragedy strike. On July 8, 1974 (the attraction opened on June 29, 1974), Deborah, eighteen years old, of Santa Ana, got caught between a stationary wall and a moving wall as the theatre rotated. Deborah was pinned by the walls and crushed to death. Her death was the first employee casualty in the nearly twenty years the park was open. In an effort to avoid a similar situation in the future, Deborah's death prompted changes to the attraction with a warning system and modifications to the walls so that another accident wouldn't happen. In April of 1988, this attraction was shuttered.

The *Columbia Rediviva* was the first American ship to circumnavigate the globe in 1790. A replica of the ship dubbed the *Sailing Ship Columbia* is the first (and only—the *Mark Twain* which also cruises through the Rivers of America is a river boat) full-scale replica to circumnavigate the Rivers of America at Disneyland. The *Sailing Ship* is an enormous three-masted windjammer that is 84 feet tall and 2,310 feet long. The ship made its debut in 1958 and still operates today.

Much like the Disneyland Monorail or PeopleMover, a trip on the *Sailing Ship Columbia* is pretty mild in the world of theme-park attractions. As we've seen, even the mellowest of rides can be dangerous. On a fateful Christmas Eve, in 1998, Luan, a thirty-three-year-old man from Duvall, Washington, was visiting Disneyland with his wife, Lieu, their son, and grandson.

The family was set to take a ride on the ship and waited on the dock for the vessel to approach. As the ship approached, a cast member threw a mooring line around a cleat—for those less nautical, a cleat is a metal device used to wrap a rope (or mooring line) around to anchor a ship—on the still-moving ship, to secure it to the dock. As was just mentioned, the *Sailing Ship Columbia* was still moving, and this caused stress and strain on the bolts that secured the cleat. The bolts of the cleat snapped off and the eight-pound piece of cast iron went airborne into the crowd waiting to board the vessel.

The cleat hit the cast member trying to secure the boat; it shattered her foot and then proceeded to hit Luan and his wife, Lieu, both in their head and neck. Luan passed away from his injuries: brain hemorrhage and skull fractures. Lieu suffered severe facial trauma and paralysis. She underwent numerous surgeries over the course of a year.

California's OSHA quickly went to work on the scene to investigate the cause of this tragedy. When they closed out their investigation, they issued two serious citations as a result of the accident and a state-max penalty of $12,500, which revealed some troubling issues that were the primary cause of the accident.

The injured employee that was trying to dock the ship had not received proper and specific training to dock the vessel. She had never performed the docking procedure prior to the accident. As it turns out, due to a scheduling error, Christine, the cast member involved in the accident, was actually filling in for the person usually tasked with securing the Columbia. This was OSHA's first citation: lack of training.

The second citation was for the overloading of the cleat. The OSHA investigation determined that the accident occurred because the cleat on the ship was designed to hold the ship at the dock and was not strong enough to be used to brake the ship's forward motion and bring it to a stop and hold it there—something they determined happened several times, as the bolts securing the cleat were bent at the time of the accident.

The *Sailing Ship Columbia* was moving too fast, and an attempt shouldn't have been made to corral it. At the speed at which the vessel was traveling, the captain should have overshot the dock, reversed the ship, and moved it back to the dock at the proper speed. The investigation into the accident and its aftereffects loomed larger than just with Disney. The Anaheim Police Department (PD) also came under scrutiny. The claims involving the PD had to deal with their lack of response time. The first uniformed police officer didn't arrive at the park until an hour after the accident. The officer then waited in the security office for two hours until additional police investigators arrived, and they were all briefed. They eventually made it to the park's accident scene, four and a half hours later.

At that time, the PD wasn't able to investigate the original accident scene. Disney cleaned up the scene as quickly as they could. They washed away any blood or debris from the accident scene, as it was very "unsightly."

The aftershocks of this accident were far reaching. Obviously, and most importantly, was the loss of life of Luan and the devastating injuries to his wife and their family members who witnessed the atrocity. While money is no replacement for a loved one, or the mental and physical pain the family endured, Disney settled this case in October of 2000. The details of the case were not released but legal experts estimated the settlement was in the range of over $20 million.

Christine, the cast member who was also involved, underwent over ten operations to repair her foot and was walking with a cane. Unable to physically work in the park as she did before the accident, she eventually took a job with Disney, working from home.

An aftereffect of the accident helped give leverage to those looking to usher in more regulations and oversight from the state into theme-park safety. This came to fruition roughly a year later as discussed earlier in the chapter with the California Permanent Amusement Ride Safety Law implemented in 2000. As for the Anaheim PD, they set up a permanent station at the park, and Disney agreed to leave accident scenes undisturbed until police investigators arrive.

If you're the type of person who believes in curses, bad omens, or just plain bad luck, then the attraction "Big Thunder Mountain Railroad" may not be the attraction for you. The ride debuted in 1979 at a cost of nearly $16 million, almost as much as Disneyland itself in 1955. The roller-coaster attraction takes guests on an indoor and outdoor excursion through the setting of a mine-train operation during America's gold rush.

Since 1991, the attraction has been plagued with a myriad of accidents, a fatality, and was even the scene for a non-ride-related medical emergency. In June of 1991, Grigore from Romania was visiting Disneyland to celebrate his forty-fourth birthday. He took a ride on Big Thunder Mountain and the next thing he knew, he was lying in a hospital bed. Around 9:00 p.m., a cast member found Grigore on a catwalk next to the track of the ride. How he got there is the mystery, as he doesn't recall what happened, and no one witnessed him jump from the coaster.

Grigore, who didn't speak English, told a park mechanic at Disneyland who was fluent in Romanian that he felt faint on the ride and may have passed out. Others speculated that he might have suddenly tried to exit the train before it entered the mountain portion of the attraction; nevertheless, his injuries were not life threatening, and he was released from the hospital after a few days.

It was almost eight years before Big Thunder was the scene for another accident. This accident came only a few months before the tragedy involving the *Sailing Ship Columbia*. In March of 1998, young David, from La Jolla, California, just five years old at the time, set out on his first trip aboard Big Thunder Mountain.

As David's mom described the day, he was very excited for his ride. David was finally tall enough, at forty-six inches, for the real roller coasters, and he wanted to ride them over and over. At the end of the day, he talked his more cautious seven-year-old brother, Steven, into a last go at his favorite—Big Thunder Mountain. The boys piled into the car with their mother, Kathy, in the middle. They all loved the ride, screaming gleefully as it whipped along the track.

But as the roller coaster wound down and pulled up to the platform, it paused about twenty feet from where the passengers are supposed to disembark. Thinking the ride was over, David nonchalantly stuck his left foot out of the open-sided car, "as if he were trying to slow it down the way he does his bike," Kathy explained. "It was such a kid thing to do." When the ride slowly started up again, David's foot became wedged in the small gap between the car's running board and the edge of the platform.

Panicked, he grabbed his mother and the safety bar, which fit only loosely across his lap, and managed to keep his body in the car, but the friction against his foot virtually tore it in half. Kathy explained, "It was held together by just two tendons, and he had lost all soft tissue on the bottom, up to his heel; all of the pieces were there, in his tennis shoe."

The roller-coaster operator, who was on the opposite side of the track and thus unable to see what was happening, stopped the ride within seconds, but David remained caught. It took about a half hour for Disneyland employees to pry the running board off the car to release him and another twenty minutes or so for the paramedics to arrive. Later, all of his toes would be amputated, though his foot would eventually be salvaged with vein, muscle, and skin grafts.

Kathy considered suing Disneyland but was philosophically opposed to taking the company to court. "It was an accident, for God's sake," she says. Plus, she was worried that a trial would prolong her family's agony—and David's emotional recovery—so she settled privately with Disneyland in January 1999 and agreed not to discuss the details.

On January 21, 1999, Robert was walking through Disneyland by Big Thunder Mountain when he took a spill and struck his head on the ground. Paramedics rushed to the scene, where Robert was in the throes of a seizure.

He was transported to the hospital and admitted to the intensive care unit. This situation was the first accident or emergency after the accident involving the *Sailing Ship Columbia*.

The troubles in and around the Big Thunder Mountain came to a fatal climax in September 2003, with an accident that left a twenty-two-year-old man dead and ten other riders injured. On September 5, 2003, Marcelo of Gardena, California, was riding in the front car of Big Thunder Mountain Railroad when the locomotive became separated from the rest of the cars and derailed. Marcelo died on the scene from blunt-force trauma to the chest.

An accident report by California's OSHA faulted park maintenance workers, ride operators, and a mechanic. The report noted that operators heard loud clanking noises at least thirty minutes before the accident; however, they decided to keep the coaster running for twelve more rides before deciding to remove it from the track after one more run. The "one more" run was the fatal run. The train crashed on the thirteenth ride.

The mechanical cause of the crash happened when two bolts on the locomotive's left guide-wheel assembly fell off. This caused an axle to jam into the railroad's ties. The locomotive nosedived, and its rear hit the top of a tunnel. The force snapped a tow bar connecting the locomotive to the lead passenger car, which slammed into the locomotive's undercarriage.

The OSHA report faulted a mechanic who didn't tighten bolts and attach a safety wire on the wheel assembly that fell off, a manager who declared the ride safe without inspecting it, Disneyland's maintenance guidelines for allowing workers to sign for procedures done by others, and obviously the ride operators who heard suspicious noises but didn't stop the ride. With a mountain of evidence, Disney settled with Marcelo's family in their lawsuit against the park. The amount was undisclosed, and terms were confidential, but Disney did acknowledge the accident in a public statement.

"We all deeply regret that the tragic accident occurred and are terribly saddened by the grievous pain this caused the Torres family," said Disneyland spokesman Rob Doughty.

Unfortunately, we aren't done discussing Big Thunder Mountain and its plight with accidents. When the ride reopened, after the accident investigation, the empty trains crashed into each other after a dry run by cast members.

Then in July of 2004, one train bumped into another as it entered the loading station, leaving five people with minor injuries. OSHA investigators discovered mistakes made by an inexperienced ride operator (who was only on the job for three days and had performed procedures out of sequence), and a software glitch was to blame.

Indiana Jones Adventure debuted in Adventureland in March of 1995. The ride is the fourth successful collaboration between Disney and George Lucas. Guests to the attraction embark on an adventurous trek in a jeep-like vehicle that dips, veers, and careens through an archeological adventure. It is themed after the blockbuster movies that give the ride its name.

The ride vehicles that shuck and jive all over are what make this ride unique technologically. The ride vehicles have onboard computers that can deliver 160,000 different rider experiences as they move through the attraction. When the attraction first premiered, some of the movements the vehicles made were leading to minor injuries to riders and thus had to be reprogrammed with safety modifications. Apparently, for some riders on Indy, the modifications were not enough to avoid physical injury.

Just a few months after the attraction opened, on July 17, 1995, forty-two-year-old Zipora from Los Angeles was at Disneyland and took a ride on Indiana Jones Adventure. After leaving the ride, she felt as though her head was going to explode and began to projectile vomit. Less than three hours later, she fell into a coma. Surviving the coma and three brain surgeries (one of which was to insert a catheter that ran under her skin from the right side of her skull into her stomach to drain excess fluid) her physicians informed her that she had a hemorrhage, which is basically a stroke.

Zipora's physicians concluded that the hemorrhage was caused by extreme shaking, akin to what is known in infants as "shaken baby syndrome." In Zipora's case, the jerking and jarring movements on the attraction tore the brain tissue near the base of her skull. Prior to going to trial, in 1999, Disney settled Zipora's lawsuit with a confidential settlement.

In November of 1998, Deborah, a forty-six-year-old woman from Texas, suffered a dull throbbing headache after riding Indiana Jones Adventure. After passing out two times, she sought medical care, and she too was diagnosed with a brain hemorrhage. Deborah had to undergo surgery to resolve her medical issue. Disney settled this case out of court with an undisclosed, confidential settlement in June of 2001.

In June of 2000, tragedy struck again for a rider on Indiana Jones Adventure. Cristina, twenty-three, visited Disneyland on her honeymoon from Spain. Immediately after disembarking from the ride, she felt as though her "head was rolling around." Cristina and her husband went back to their hotel where she complained of a severe headache and subsequently lost consciousness.

She was then taken to Cedars-Sinai Medical Center where she was diagnosed with a brain hemorrhage. Cristina was then taken by air ambulance back to Spain, where she continued to be hospitalized for the next several months while she accrued over $1.3 million in medical bills. Cristina never regained consciousness and passed away on September 1, 2000. Her family filed a wrongful-death lawsuit against Disney. Nearly seven years later, in January of 2007, Disney agreed to a confidential settlement before the case was set to go to trial.

Despite these tragedies and subsequent lawsuits, Disney maintained that the ride was safe. The riders' injuries or deaths were unrelated to the attraction. After the settlement of Deborah's case, Disneyland spokesman Ray Gomez remarked that "settlements are routine at this stage of any case. Mediation is a costly endeavor for both sides. Disneyland officials continue to firmly believe that Indiana Jones Adventure is a safe attraction based on the fact that it carried more than forty million people since it opened more than six years ago."

The Academy Award–winning movie *Who Framed Roger Rabbit* inspired a ride at Disneyland. In 1994, Roger Rabbit's Car Toon Spin debuted in Mickey's Toontown. The attraction allows riders to control their own ride vehicles by spinning them 360 degrees around. The spinning takes place while tooling through the colorful set and following the adventures of Roger Rabbit and the gang.

In September of 2000, four-year-old Brandon was enjoying Disneyland with his family, celebrating his mother Victoria's fortieth birthday. The family proceeded to Roger Rabbit's Car Toon Spin. They planned this attraction for the last ride of the day. Brandon, his older brother, and his mother were in one car. The following car had his father and grandmother. As the family set out on their three-minute journey with Roger Rabbit, in a blink of an eye, their lives were devastatingly changed.

Brandon fell out of the spinning ride vehicle and was trapped under another vehicle—the ride vehicle his father and grandmother were riding in. The vehicle rolled over him, dragged him several feet, eventually crumpling and folding his forty-five-pound body in half. Brandon's father, David, leaped from his vehicle and ran out toward the beginning of the ride and implored cast members to stop the ride, as his son was trapped under a vehicle and being dragged. The ride stopped, the lights came on, but Brandon couldn't be freed right away.

David ran from the interior of the ride back to the queue where guests were waiting to depart on their adventure. He screamed and begged for help from cast members and the soon-to-be passengers of the ride. Several times imploring the folks around him to help, he screamed, "Please help! My son is going to die!" As he begged for help, the only response he received from cast members was, "Settle down, sir." They then advised the people who were willing to go help not to do so, instructing them to stay where they were.

As soon as the cast members disappeared, several people jumped over the fence to help David rescue his son from this horrible scene—a scene so horrible that one of the guests who tried to help was so shaken by the accident that he and his wife turned in their annual passes; the tragedy haunted them, and they didn't want to return to Disneyland for quite some time. Maintenance workers and paramedics ushered everyone away from the scene, and Brandon was eventually freed and rushed to the hospital. Brandon went into cardiac arrest; he had a collapsed left lung and broken pelvis, and his diaphragm, spleen, and liver were also torn. Brandon had global brain damage in addition to the internal injuries. Never again able to function physically or cognitively as he did before the ride, Brandon put up a fight for eight years both in and out of the hospital until he passed away in January of 2009, at age thirteen.

The state investigators from OSHA determined that Disneyland employees did not properly load Brandon into the ride. The smallest child should not be placed on the end; he should have been seated the farthest from the cutout entry of the vehicle. The Disney employee also failed to lower the lap bar properly. The investigators ordered significant changes to the ride. Doors were installed with a sensor-equipped guard around the bottom, along with skirts at the bottom of each car. The report also indicated that the ride operator first called a supervisor in a break room to explain the situation rather than 911.

In the months following the accident, Disney made the changes investigators required because, shockingly, Brandon's accident actually wasn't the first of this nature. A thirteen-year-old girl was injured on the ride in April of 2000, just a few months before Brandon. The young girl slipped underneath her lap bar and stepped out of her car in an attempt to retrieve a stuffed animal, which had fallen out of it. As she reached to grab the toy, her lower left leg got caught underneath her car. Paramedics were able to dislodge the girl's leg within minutes.

The ride's safety procedures also changed how paramedics would be staffed at the park, along with 911 being called directly and immediately. Prior to this implementation, cast members were instructed to call a central communications center first, where the center would contact the Anaheim Fire Department. In 2002, Brandon's family reached a confidential settlement with Disney over the accident.

Long before Roger Rabbit's Car Toon Spin, people were taking their bumps and bruises on Space Mountain. The legendary ride debuted in May of 1977 and takes guests on an intergalactic trip without ever leaving Anaheim. As with all trips aboard a rocket or space ship, the ride can be turbulent and bumpy.

Back in August of 1979, Sherill took a trip on Space Mountain and fell unconscious during the ride. After being rushed to the hospital for care, she passed away seven days later. Her family's lawsuit against Disney claimed Space Mountain caused this fatality. The coroner's office stated otherwise. They ruled she died of natural causes, as a portion of a heart tumor dislodged had traveled to her brain.

In 1983, James, a teenager at the time, was thrown out of his ride vehicle while taking a trip on Space Mountain. James suffered serious injuries—brain damage and partial paralysis. He sued Disney, and the case went to trial in 1985. His lawyers claimed that a defective design caused James to be ejected from the ride. They contended that the ring-type lap bar that was installed on the ride was defective and would permit a person to remove it, thus ejecting them from the ride. James's attorney even brought in a physicist to testify that the lap-bar design appeared to be defective. Adding to James's defense was the fact that Disney replaced the ring-type lap bar with a T-shaped bar; however, on cross-examination, the physicist concluded that gravity would most likely keep the rider in the seat should the bar design be defective or if the bar was raised.

Disney's lawyers contended that James actually wriggled out of his lap bar intentionally, and thus he was ejected. Jurors sided with Disney despite James being in the courtroom in a wheelchair and needing braces to help him walk.

Decades later, Space Mountain is still giving both Disney and guests some bumps. In August of 2000, a wheel on a Space Mountain's car became dislodged. The safety system kicked in, and the ride stopped abruptly; nine people suffered minor injuries. In April of 2013, Disney voluntarily shut down Space Mountain for one month. The shutdown was spurn by an OSHA safety review over an incident where a worker fell down the outside of Space Mountain and was injured.

Even today, Space Mountain leads the list of incidents at Southern California's theme parks. In a study of reported incidents and accidents (these could be as minor as feeling light-headed, vomiting, or someone having high blood pressure or a preexisting condition and shouldn't be on the ride anyway) from 2007 to 2012, utilizing data from the California Department of Industrial Relations, Space Mountain had more incidents than any other attraction—not just Disney but in all of Southern California—with over 120 incidents. With that being said, everything is relative, and a few numbers can put this into perspective. During this five-year period, the ride had over forty-four million riders. That equates to one incident in every 367,000 riders.

Overall, the topic of Disneyland and accidents must be looked at in the same way as we just looked at Space Mountain—on the macro level. Since 1955, and with billions upon billions of rides taken, there have been fewer than twenty deaths in and around the parks, hotels, and parking structures. Not every accident or tragedy at Disneyland was mentioned in this chapter, just some of the more noteworthy ones.

Obviously, Disneyland is the setting each year for some form of accident or incident. But what about a joyful accident—does this even exist?

Well, one does come to mind, joyful yet nerve wracking. How about giving birth at Disneyland? The first time this happened was on July 4, 1979. Rosa knew she was taking a chance by visiting Disneyland that day. By the time she boarded the submarine voyage, she knew the chance was now a sure thing. Several minutes later, she gave birth to a baby girl. Such a happy event has happened several times over the years, with the most recent one happening in March of 2012.

As many people know, the theme parks we see at Walt Disney World weren't Walt's original intentions. In his original "Florida Project," the theme park was going to be tertiary, a vehicle to lure folks down to his property to see his other marvels—which may have been less interesting to some people than a theme park. In an effort to keep this brief, Walt wanted to create a prototype community of tomorrow. Within this community would be a revolutionary place for people to work, reside, and live their day-to-day lives. A few aspects of what Walt originally planned to have on the property were implemented; obviously the theme park, Walt Disney World, was one of them.

Another one of Walt's plans was for an on-site airport of the future. We know this never came to fruition, but something in the vein of an airport did, at least for a brief time. In October 22, 1971, three weeks after Walt Disney World opened, Disney announced one of the nation's first STOLports (and Florida's first) was coming to Walt Disney World. You may ask, "What is a STOLport?" STOL stands for "short takeoff and landing."

Not too far from the entrance to the Magic Kingdom and the Ticket and Transportation Center is a two-thousand-foot runway (it can still be seen via car or monorail) that can handle the duties of smaller commuter planes, with average passenger capacities of around nineteen people. The STOLport was set to handle around twenty-six flights per day via Shawnee and Executive Airlines. These carriers would service the cities of Tampa, Miami, and Fort Lauderdale by way of Disney.

Disney's STOLport lasted almost as long as a flight over to Tampa. After a bit more than a year in service, flights ceased at the runway. Logistical and profitability issues doomed the enterprise. Despite not having a long track record, the STOLport in its brief stint at Walt Disney World (WDW) was accident-free, but the same couldn't be said for Walt Disney World, not even in reference to a deadly plane crash.

In 1984, Gary, Doreen, and their three children boarded a single-engine piper plane in Greer, South Carolina. They were flying to Kissimmee Airport to spend Thanksgiving with family members and then visit Walt Disney World. Ten miles short of Kissimmee Airport, FAA investigators believed the plane ran out of gas and crashed in the EPCOT parking lot hitting several unoccupied vehicles. The plane crashed just two hundred feet before a monorail beam and killed Gary, Doreen, and their year-old daughter, Stephanie. The family's other two children were initially hospitalized in critical condition but went on to survive the crash.

The monorail escaped damage in the accident with the plane crash, but less than a year later; Disney's unique form of transportation had an accident of its own. Today Walt Disney World's Monorail System boasts over fourteen miles of track and runs three lines to different areas of the property. Tens of millions of people travel the "highway in the sky" each year, with relatively pristine safety since it went online in 1971.

But on the evening of June 26, 1985, roughly 240 people were aboard a six-car monorail going from EPCOT to the Ticket and Transportation Center. Along their journey, the monorail driver noticed a warning light, stopped the train, and radioed in for help. People on the ground noticed the rear car had smoke billowing out and was obviously on fire. Stranded more than thirty feet in the air, the passengers had to kick out doors and windows in an effort to climb onto the roof for safety. Eventually, a cherry picker came to rescue the passengers as firefighters battled the blaze. The accident could have been a lot worse; most passengers escaped any real danger with only a few being treated for minor smoke inhalation and bumps and bruises.

The cause of the fire was due to a flat tire to both a primary and a backup tire that heated up too quickly, caused friction, and sparked a fire to the monorail. The tires were checked every other day, and thus the situation was deemed a fluke accident. The fire did bring safety changes to the monorail; each car now features an emergency exit that lifts out to the roof, in case a similar situation should arise.

The monorail had a minor crash in 1974 and another in 1991 during the filming of a commercial, but nothing major occurred. Fatefully, in 2009, all of this changed. On July 5, 2009, around 2:00 a.m., the Disney monorail was beginning to wind down for the evening. One of the trains in service was attempting to do a transfer from the EPCOT loop and onto a "switch beam" and then to the Magic Kingdom Express beam. This maneuver takes place at the Ticket and Transportation Center, where a track switch is activated, and the monorail needs to switch beams goes into reverse to accomplish the task. This fateful night, the track switch was never activated, and the train ended up reversing back down the EPCOT line and into a second stationary train. The stationary train's driver, twenty-one-year-old Austin of Kissimmee was killed when the monorails collided. The six passengers on Austin's monorail were unharmed.

During a two-and-a-half-year investigation, in October of 2011, the National Transportation and Safety Board (NTSB) determined that a lack of safety protocols contributed to the accident. Another factor was "Walt Disney World Resort's lack of standard operating procedures leading to an unsafe practice when reversing trains." The NTSB went further and agreed with an OSHA report that the employee at the monorail's maintenance shop, which controls the track switches, failed to adjust the switch beam properly. In addition, the shop manager was not in the control tower during the procedure. Had he been there, he may have caught the error.

The shop manager being in the control tower during this process was not a mandatory procedure at this time for Disney. Also, Disney did not require its employees to follow an operating guide by which monorail drivers were supposed to switch from the front cab of their trains to the back cab before driving in reverse, so they could operate the trains while in a forward-facing position. These two procedures were changed after the NTSB and OSHA accident investigation. In March of 2011, the mother of Austin settled her wrongful-death lawsuit against Disney for an undisclosed amount of money.

In keeping with the theme of transportation, the 1990s featured several fatal car accidents at Walt Disney World property. In April of 1995, nine-year-old Tyler from a town outside of Kalamazoo, Michigan, was with his family visiting Walt Disney World. The family was walking along the sidewalk that connects the Contemporary Hotel with the Magic Kingdom when Tyler was fatally struck by a car at the intersection connecting the two properties. The family claimed the intersection was an accident waiting to happen. There was no traffic light, there was a large amount of shrubbery along the walkway, the sidewalk was poorly lit, and there was no curb indicating a transition from the sidewalk into the street of the intersection.

The police deemed this fatality an accident and didn't charge the seventeen-year-old Disney employee with speeding or negligence. Today, there is a traffic light in the area where the buses pull in to drop guests off from and to the Magic Kingdom, and there are lights leading the way from the Magic Kingdom to the Contemporary.

A few years before the accident in front of the Contemporary, the Caribbean Beach Resort was the scene of a fatal accident. In July of 1990 four teenagers were visiting a friend working at the Swan hotel. Upon leaving the hotel, they got into Joseph's 1989 Mustang and set out on to Buena Vista Drive. At a high rate of speed, the Mustang crashed into the rear of a bus as it sat in the median waiting to turn into the Caribbean Beach Resort.

The car quickly burst into flames, ending the four young lives. Police investigators believe Joseph pressed down hard on the accelerator, and then couldn't handle the speed. When he realized that the rear of the bus was hanging out in his lane, it was too late. Instead of swerving, he locked up the brakes and skidded 250 feet before the impact. Joseph was driving on a suspended license and had several speeding tickets in the past. Investigators didn't fault the bus driver, who was the only occupant on board.

Ever wonder how the nearly three hundred buses in and around Walt Disney World (the fleet is the third largest in Florida behind Miami and Jacksonville and one of the largest private fleets in the country) know exactly where they are as the bus pulls into a resort or park and plays the appropriate message or music to correspond with the location? Is it Disney magic? Well, sort of—it's that good old global positioning system (GPS) and a computer program that Disney installed on all of their buses; it's called Magic in Motion.

Magic in Motion (MIM) was implemented in 2006. The MIM allows Disney to track in real time the position of all of their buses. The system also allows for real-time rerouting around the property to ease crowding at locations that may need additional buses. All sounds great, right? Especially if you've stood at a bus stop in ninety-degree heat and wondered if a bus was ever going to pick you up!

Well, in 2010 the system came under scrutiny during a few weeks in April when the Disney buses were involved in three accidents in two weeks; one was fatal involving a nine-year-old boy. Many of the bus drivers complained that the MIM was distracting and unsafe. Drivers said they should be focusing on the road and not dealing with a computer program. At that time, here's how the MIM worked: just before the driver completed one round-trip route, the driver radioed into their dispatcher for a new five-digit code. The five-digit code is their next destination and is then entered into the onboard computer. The code gives the driver the new route, updates the marquee on the bus, and changes the music and greeting. The problem for some drivers is that the process is distracting, with having to radio into dispatch and then type into a computer. In contrast, Disney officials think MIM has improved safety for drivers by relieving them of some responsibilities, such as making passenger announcements, and has cut down on waiting times for guests.

With the MIM on board, more than twelve hundred Disney bus drivers cart around millions of people each year. Before they can get behind the wheel, the drivers undergo a four-and-a-half-week training program. They sit for the state's licensing exam, drug testing, a physical exam, and Disney's on-site training. Despite all of this training on Magic in Motion, just as in any other bustling town with buses and heavy traffic at times, accidents are bound to happen.

Three accidents in the spring of 2010 spurred the publicity about MIM aside; Disney had had bus accidents before and will continue to have them despite advances in technology. Then in December of 2010, a bus killed a pedestrian as he walked in the parking lot of the Port Orleans resort, and as recently as August 2013, a bus hit a stationary car near EPCOT that resulted in another fatality.

Accidents at Walt Disney World aren't exclusive to just planes, trains, and automobiles; there are boats as well. From the resort hotels to within the parks themselves, boats and ferries are omnipresent at Walt Disney World. It is even a way to get to the illustrious Magic Kingdom. Before we get there, we have to traverse the Seven Seas Lagoon, and sometimes the waters are rough and troubled.

Walt Disney World's 185-acre Seven Seas Lagoon is one of the gateways to the Magic Kingdom. Ferries shuttle up to six hundred guests at a time from the boat launch at the Ticket and Transportation Center to "the house of the mouse." The lake is more than just a byway to the Kingdom. Guests can do a number of things from fishing, parasailing, to renting private boats at the lagoon. Sometimes things don't always go as planned in a boating environment.

In October of 1989, thirty-three-year-old Pat, from Glen Cove, New York, and her son rented a boat from the marina at their hotel along the lagoon. They were going to videotape friends and family waterskiing when tragedy struck. A ferry carrying about eighty people to the Magic Kingdom saw Pat's boat cross into the path of their ferry. The captain sounded a warning whistle and tried to throw the ship into reverse to avoid hitting them. The accident was unavoidable. The ferry hit the boat as Pat drove right into the front of the ferry. A crewmember and guest dove into the water from the ferry and was able to save only Pat's eight-year-old son, as Pat was killed in the accident. Investigators claim Disney was not held negligent in the accident, and a wrongful-death case was settled out of court.

In April of 2010, there was a similar boat-versus-ferry accident at Walt Disney World. This accident happened in the waterway near Disney Springs. Barbara, sixty-one years old, of Celebration, Florida, and Skipton, England, rented a two-person Sea Raycer boat with her husband at Cap'n Jack's Marina. As the couple set out, they steered into the path of a larger boat shuttling guests. Barbara's husband, commandeering the boat, said he turned away to avoid the other boat. When the ferry saw the boat coming toward them, the captain put the boat into reverse in an effort to avoid hitting them, but it was too late. The boat went under the ferry, and Barbara was wedged between the two vessels. She was knocked unconscious and suffered a collapsed lung, fractured ribs, and back pain.

Barbara and her husband filed suit against Disney and claimed that neither her nor her husband were given any instruction about piloting the boat and had no previous experience boating. Thusly, they should not have been allowed to rent the boat and use it in the waterway.

Boating accident aside, Barbara should feel somewhat lucky with the injuries she received. Barbara's accident could have been much more dire, considering the part of the country she was in and the climate. As the accident report detailed, Barbara was submerged into the water of a lake, a lake in Florida no less. In Florida—as with much of the South—during the summer months, a dip in a freshwater lake can be deadly. There is a single-celled amoeba called *Naegleria fowleri,* known in the media as the brain-eating amoeba that can do devastating things to people's neurological system.

These little buggers love warm freshwater lakes, something the Southeast of the United States is filled with. In the rare chance the amoeba is present in a body of water, and someone is exposed to it, usually by having the water go up their nose and introducing the water into their body, the results are almost always fatal. The *Naegleria fowleri* can invade the human nervous system and brain with a 95 percent mortality rate. Tragically this is exactly what happened to an eleven-year-old boy from New York who was swimming at Walt Disney World's River Country in 1980.

Not familiar with River Country, eh? Well, let's go back in time to June of 1976, the month the water park opened. Along the shores of Bay Lake (the lake next to the Seven Seas Lagoon) was a six-acre themed water park, Walt Disney World's first. The park was situated adjacent to the Fort Wilderness Campgrounds and had a rustic theme featuring an Ol' Swimmin' Hole, rapids, raft rides, rope swings, beaches, and water slides. River Country featured both a pool (chlorinated) and cove that was part of Bay Lake—although separated by a barrier. Disney utilized the water from the lake for the slides and attractions. It was filtered and monitored for quality, but that couldn't stop the amoeba incident from happening. Sadly, the last week of August 1980, the eleven-year-old boy passed away from *Naegleria fowleri* infection from his exposure at River Country during the first week of August. Brain-eating amoeba aside, calamity struck River Country two more times in the 1980s with the drowning of two teenage boys. Despite these deaths, River Country continued to entertain guests until the park closed in November 2001; however, swimming was banned at the lakes around Disney property in the 1990s.

The mecca of family entertainment for millions of people around the world is just beyond the Seven Seas Lagoon, and we are about to enter it and view it in a different light—if your views haven't been altered already. As we all have experienced at one time or another, accidents do happen at home. The East Coast version of Mickey's house is no different.

The land that encompasses Walt Disney World is roughly forty square miles. They have their own infrastructure like every other city in this country and in many ways more elaborate and technical. WDW has a nightly evening population of well over one hundred thousand people and a daytime population hovering around three hundred thousand people, roughly the population of the city of Pittsburgh, Pennsylvania.

To attempt to compare the accident frequency at Walt Disney World with Disneyland, or quite frankly any other amusement park, would be unjust and futile. Plain and simple, Walt Disney World is enormous, from the many theme parks to the over twenty-five on-site hotels and resorts. Feeding the masses and providing them with accommodations and comforts of home isn't easy, and accidents happen everywhere and in every imaginable situation.

There have been situations where over sixty people were made sick by salmonella poisoning from unpasteurized orange juice Disney served at their resorts in 1995, and warnings from state epidemiologists about an outbreak of mosquitoes carrying St. Louis encephalitis forced Disney to close resort pools and limit evening activities in an effort to limit guests' exposure to the buggers in August of 1997. There was even a woman in 2010 doing laundry at the Pop Century Resort who had her coins jam in the change machine, and in an effort to dislodge the coins, the machine fell on top of her and broke her leg.

Walt Disney World has seen it all: mechanical failure, suicide, a hostage situation, and random violence (chapter 3 details some of the latter). All of these situations are atrocious and painful both emotionally and mentally for those involved. With that being said, accidents are aplenty, but the focus of most of these are ones where Disney usually learns from these incidents and implements some sort of change, be it for ride safety or procedures for their cast members.

On August 11, 1977, four-year-old Joel from Dolton, Illinois, wandered away from his mother at the ice-cream shop on Main Street after 11:00 p.m. Once his mother, Marietta, realized he was gone, panic ensued and a search commenced to find the little boy. A child separated from his or her parents is a daily occurrence at the theme park, even today. This situation ended with more dire circumstances. Joel's body was found three hours later in the moat around Cinderella's Castle.

The little boy drowned in roughly five feet of water just a short distance from the ice-cream shop. There were no witnesses to Joel scaling the nearly three-foot fence that separated the pavement from the grass or of him entering the water. Joel's parents filed a wrongful-death suit against Disney that ensued for several years, taking almost a decade to settle. The initial $4 million case was originally dismissed in October of 1981 by the Orlando Circuit Courts.

The basis of the dismissal was Marietta failed in her duty to control and watch her child during the child's tender years, and that outweighed Disney's negligence. This ruling was appealed, and in 1982 the courts reversed that finding and sent the case back to the lower court for trial. A jury was unable to reach a verdict in 1984. A second trial was held in February 1985, where the family was awarded $2 million, one million for each parent. The award was based upon the family's attorney claiming that there were no fences around the moat, and the 3.1-foot fence separating the sidewalk from grass near the water was too low to prevent children from climbing it. Further, the four- to five-foot-deep moat was a potential hazard for children, yet there were no signs warning parents to keep their children away from the water.

However, the jury deemed that the parents should share in some of the negligence, and the award was reduced by $500,000 from each parent because they shared in half the negligence. In December of 1986, the case was finalized. The parents were awarded $1 million from Disney.

Unfortunately, this wouldn't be the last accidental drowning around the Magic Kingdom. Just two years later, in August of 1979, sixty-two-year-old Hattie from Baltimore was at Walt Disney World vacationing with her grandchildren when she suffered a diabetic seizure and fell into a drainage ditch at a Walt Disney World parking lot when looking for her car. Hattie's family sued Disney as well and eventually reached a confidential out-of-court settlement.

Not too far from the Magic Kingdom is the Fort Wilderness Campground. On May 23, 1987, six-year-old Miguel was visiting the campground with his grandparents and extended family members. The trip to Walt Disney World was something they did monthly for several years. That afternoon, Miguel's grandfather left him poolside under the supervision of other family members. By the time his grandfather returned to the pool, just mere minutes later, CPR was already being performed on Miguel in an attempt to revive him from drowning—their attempts were unsuccessful. Miguel's parents filed suit against Disney and, in June of 1989, the case settled for $250,000.

Accidents in pools still haunt Walt Disney World. As recently as March 2013, tragedy in a pool struck when thirteen-year-old Anthony from Missouri was swimming at the Pop Century Resort when he drowned. Lifeguards didn't staff the pool Anthony was swimming in at the time. At the Pop Century, as with many other pools on Disney's property, the lifeguards were only on duty until 8:00 p.m.; Anthony's accident occurred at 9:30 p.m.. There were signs posted that warned swimmers that they are swimming at their own risk. In the months after the accident, Disney changed their swimming policy.

Property wide, the Disney resorts feature more than two dozen pools. In late 2013, they announced that lifeguards will now be stationed at each resort's largest pools during operating hours, meaning early morning to late at night. Traditionally, when the lifeguards stopped watching the pools, the rule was "swim at your own risk," as in young Anthony's case. The new rule changes will not permit swimming after hours when no lifeguards are on duty at each resort's main pool. The smaller, or "quiet" pools as Disney calls them, will continue to open as they previously were.

The abovementioned accidents and incidents happened away from the attractions at Walt Disney World. It wasn't until nearly thirty years after opening day that Disney experienced their first ride-related fatality with a guest. Splash Mountain opened in 1992 and features a log flume ride based upon the story from the Disney movie *Song of the South*. Ironically, this hugely popular ride is based on a movie most Disney fans have never watched, and Disney wants to keep it that way, due to some racially insensitive issues. The ride takes passengers on a ten-minute trip that ends with a fifty-two-foot drop at a forty-five-degree angle.

On November 5, 2000, William, a thirty-seven-year-old annual pass holder from the St. Petersburg, Florida, area, was enjoying a day at the park with two friends. Around 2:00 p.m. in the afternoon, William was the last passenger in his boat at the attraction. More than halfway through the ride, at a slow point before the thrilling drop, he got out of his boat and informed his passing friends that he was feeling sick and wanted to leave. With the ride at a lull, William hopped out and stood on one side of the attraction, the side opposite an emergency exit door.

In order to exit the attraction, he would need to get across the canal the boats traverse. In an attempt to get to the other side, William tried to use one of the boats in the canal as a bridge to the other side with the exit. As William was trying to cross on the boats, the movement of the ride started to pick up speed again, and William slipped. He fell into the canal and was pinned between the left side of a boat and the canal wall. Lodged by the boat, William was impeding the canal's movement. Quickly, each boat, in a chain reaction, continued to ram into the boat crushing William. William's actions proved fatal; he was killed from blunt-force trauma to the chest. In the eight years prior to William's accident, Disney remarked that sixty-four million riders enjoyed the attraction without a fatality or serious accident. William's incident did not result from any mechanical issues with the attraction.

EPCOT and Hollywood Studios are no different from the Magic Kingdom with their ability to give out Disney bumps and bruises. In fact, some of their attractions may bring to the forefront preexisting physiological conditions riders are unaware of, usually to the rider's detriment.

Walt Disney World's Hollywood Studios gives guests a taste of Walt's Hollywood during the town's golden age. Many die-hard Disney fans dub this park a "half-day" park, as there isn't enough to do there. Whether Hollywood Studios is lacking attractions for an entire-day trip is up for debate. What isn't debatable is the fact that a couple of Walt Disney World's most thrilling rides are located there: Rock 'n' Roller Coaster Starring Aerosmith and the Twilight Zone Tower of Terror. The coaster and tower satisfy thrill seekers from all over the world who need a little adventure and adrenaline when visiting Mickey. The two attractions made headlines when they debuted in 1994 and 1999, giving Disney some bona fide thrill rides. Unfortunately, the two rides made headlines for different reasons in the summers of 2005 and 2006.

Sixteen-year-old Leanne of Kibworth, England, rode the Tower of Terror six times in one week during her vacation at Walt Disney World in July of 2005. The thrill ride is themed after the 1960s television hit *The Twilight Zone* and takes riders on a haunted elevator ride that ascends and descends quickly over the course of a few minutes.

On July 12, 2005, at 9:50 a.m., Leanne exited the ride shaking and light-headed. She sat for a few minutes with her mother in an air-conditioned room. Not too long after, she lost consciousness and was rushed to the hospital. Along the way there, her heart stopped beating. Paramedics were able to revive her and, once in the hospital, it was determined she had a stroke and required immediate surgery.

After more surgeries and months in the hospital, Leanne has permanent brain damage. She is unable to speak and care for herself. Disney investigated and found no problems with the attraction during the times Leanne was on the ride. Leanne's mother, blaming Disney and the attraction for Leanne's stoke and subsequent heart attacks, filed a lawsuit. The $15 million suit was settled in December of 2012 out of court for an undisclosed amount.

The Rock 'n' Roller Coaster at Hollywood Studios features over three thousand feet of track and sends guests traveling at speeds close to sixty miles an hour in under three seconds. If that isn't thrilling enough, the ride features a corkscrew turn and a rollover, all set to some rock and roll.

On June 29, 2006, twelve-year-old Michael, of Fort Campbell, Kentucky, rode Rock 'n' Roller Coaster with his parents and younger brother. When the family's ride was over, Michael's father noticed his son was slumped over and limp in his seat. He immediately began to perform CPR. Paramedics were notified, and they transported Michael to the hospital where he was pronounced dead. Disney closed the ride for an investigation by the Florida Bureau of Fair Rides Inspection. The closure found no evidence of ride malfunction. Upon performing the autopsy on Michael, the medical examiner's office found he suffered congenital heart abnormalities that caused his death.

Just a brisk scenic walk from Hollywood Studios and through Disney's BoardWalk Inn resort will lead you to EPCOT. Entering the park from the World Showcase, a quick trip around the World Showcase lagoon and into Future World will lead you to the attraction Mission: Space.

The $100 million ride opened in August of 2003 and takes guests on a trip to Mars. The ride is meant to simulate the training and experiences NASA astronauts undergo. Disney consulted with former astronauts in addition to NASA granting Disney permission to reference some of their training methods for the attraction.

A trip to space, let alone Mars, albeit a simulated one, isn't easy. The original version of Mission: Space (there are two now, we will get to that in a minute) at its core is based on a military flight simulator. The simulator plays with your senses (primarily your brain and your inner ear, which help gauge movement) with projected video and audio, along with sudden bursts of movement. These actions tend to give people motion sickness (even military pilots and astronauts have been known to suffer from a trip in a simulator); in fact this attraction was Disney's first attraction to provide sickness bags, a.k.a. barf bags!

The first year (and still today) Disney's ride received stellar reviews. It is an incredible experience for many people. For other folks, the ride is a bit too intense and makes them sick. In its first year alone, three million guests went aboard Mission: Space. Of those millions, six people were hospitalized with chest pains and severe nausea after their trip into space. Interesting, though, are the demographics of those hospitalized. All were over the age of fifty-five and four of six had preexisting conditions, something the signs at the attraction warn guests about.

Disney, and obviously their crack legal team, has warning signs posted on most of their attractions. Mission: Space is no different; throughout the attraction, warnings advise folks with high blood pressure, back problems, anxiety, and the like to think twice about the ride. Despite the warning, many soldier on, oftentimes with health conditions they are unaware of. This was the case twice in 2005 and 2006, and unfortunately both events ended in fatalities.

In June of 2005, four-year-old Daudi of Pennsylvania rode Mission: Space with his mother and sister. At the end of the five-minute ride, Daudi was rigid and unresponsive in his seat. His mother promptly picked him up and ran to a cast member who called paramedics. Two hours later at nearby Celebration Hospital he was pronounced dead.

Daudi's autopsy revealed he had suffered from a rare undiagnosed condition in which his heart was enlarged and the walls were thickened with scar tissue. This condition left him susceptible to a cardiac arrhythmia (the heart contracting out of coordination) and led to his death. The coroner also stated that the risk of sudden death could be increased under physical or emotional stressful situations. The family filed a wrongful-death suit against Disney, which was settled in January of 2007 and, as usual for Disney, terms were not disclosed.

A similar fate awaited forty-nine-year-old Hiltrud, visiting Walt Disney World from Germany. When Hiltrud exited Mission: Space in April of 2006, she felt sick and was subsequently taken to the hospital. Tests revealed Hiltrud suffered from a brain hemorrhage after her ride. She passed away in the hospital the next day. Hiltrud's autopsy revealed she suffered from long-standing and severe high blood pressure, and no direct trauma attributed from the ride.

Mission: Space and simulators in general make certain people sick and have for a long time. The military and NASA have studied the physiological effects of simulators for over fifty years; they dubbed the effects on some riders "simulator sickness" and don't have any predictors as to who may get sick on them, but they do know underlying health problems don't help the situation.

Despite the deaths, tens of millions of people enjoy the attraction, and Disney stands by its safety. Disney standing by it and people being wary of riding it are two different things. The weeks after each of these deaths made headlines, the ride attendance did seem to drop a bit as judged by the wait times for the ride.

In May of 2006, Disney revealed a less intense version of the ride, claiming the tame version had nothing to do with the two rider deaths; Kim Prunty, a Disney spokeswoman, said, "At least one of the four centrifuges that now spin riders to simulate the approach and landing of a spaceship on Mars will be shut off. The new version is intended for those subject to motion illnesses. While it gives the illusion of a space ride, by offering a second adventure, we hope to broaden the appeal of Mission: Space and enable even more guests to experience the attraction."

Less spinning on the attraction means a better trip for many guests and additional ride exposure for Disney. Mission: Space still shows up in the voluntary accident reports that Disney submits to the state of Florida; then again, so has the Prince Charming Regal Carrousel. Luckily there have been no further deaths or major accidents, just the usual nausea and light-headedness.

In 2002, the Disney theme parks completed one of the largest private and proactive deployments of automated external defibrillators (AED) across their theme parks, resorts, and cruise ships. If used correctly and in the appropriate situation, defibrillators shock the heart in hopes of restoring a normal heartbeat in someone under duress.

In the years from 1998 through 2002, Disney's on-site AEDs saved six lives between the two properties in California and Florida. At the time, Disney had four thousand cast members trained as "designated responders" to operate the roughly 650 machines at Disneyland, Walt Disney World, and their cruise lines. By 2007, the number of people saved across Disney property with an AED had jumped to over forty lives. Operating such a successful program had Disney announce in November of 2007 that Walt Disney World would install another two hundred AEDs on premises. Unfortunately, just a month later, one of those life-saving AEDs was needed at Disney's Animal Kingdom Park but was not in the vicinity.

In December of 2007, forty-four-year-old Jeffrey was visiting Walt Disney World from the Florida panhandle with his family. Around 11:30 a.m., Jeffrey boarded the Animal Kingdom's roller coaster, Expedition Everest. The roller coaster features speeds up to fifty miles an hour and an intense eighty-foot drop, along with traveling both forward and backward in a creative setting themed around the Yeti and Mount Everest.

Less than a minute before the ride concluded, Disney's security cameras at the attraction showed Jeffrey conscious on the ride. Seconds later, as he pulled in to the platform to exit the ride, he was unconscious and unresponsive in his seat. Disney employees and a nurse visiting the park immediately performed CPR and 911 was called. The operator answering the 911 call asked if an AED was on-site; there wasn't one—at the time, the Animal Kingdom was home to only three AEDs out of five hundred on the entire Disney property. Paramedics came, and Jeffery was rushed to the hospital where he passed away. The autopsy performed indicated that Jeffrey died of dilated cardiomyopathy or an enlarged heart, which had no known cause, and this was deemed his cause of death.

In 2009, Disney announced additional AEDs were coming to the park. This time, they would be installed at many of their high-speed and most popular rides: Expedition Everest, Mission: Space, and The Twilight Zone Tower of Terror. This announcement brought Walt Disney World's total to nearly eight hundred on-site defibrillators, which are now indicated on maps of the parks and at guest services (Animal Kingdom now has upward of fourteen) and over five thousand cast members trained in operating the equipment.

The Disney parks and their AEDs couldn't operate without the cast members that run the show. At Walt Disney World, there are over seventy thousand workers to spread the magic. There is nothing more magical for children than to meet their favorite Disney character in person, face-to-face. However, working as a costumed character at a Disney Park is a tougher gig than one would think.

Sure, the job brings smiles to the millions of children that pine for their attention, but within that costume, there is another tale playing out, a tale of both physical and mental stress. One can imagine the mental stress of things—overly excited children who jump, hit, and pull at the character. The physical component of working as a costumed character is a much larger issue. For many cast members, the costumes are hot, heavy, and horrible, and the accident reports support their claims.

Almost two thousand cast members go "under cover" portraying nearly three hundred different Disney characters for a combined 350,000 working shifts a year. Many of these costumes, primarily the head, can weigh up to forty-seven pounds. It is obviously no surprise that some cast members donning the costumes end up having back, neck, and shoulder injuries to the tune of several hundred incidents each year. In recent years Disney has turned to NASA to help create lighter, more efficient suits for their characters. They even took it one step further by offering training classes to show the actors in costume how to bend down, pick things up, and move ergonomically.

The actors partake in a stretching and warm-up session led by sports-medicine professionals about a half hour before putting on their costumes. All of these measures are in an effort to cut down on and prevent injuries. Disney is constantly looking to refine and improve their costumes. Always looking to improve the functionality but not compromise on the aesthetics, the company spends upward of $100,000 on certain costumes. Yet with all of this work, accidents are often unavoidable.

In February of 2004, an eight-year veteran employee of Walt Disney World was accidentally run over by a parade float when he was in costume as Pluto. Javier, thirty-eight years old, was about to exit a backstage area and play his role of Pluto in the Share a Dream Come True parade. As the three-part float rolled past Javier, his right foot got caught between the second and third sections of the float. Javier fell to the ground and was fatally run over by the third portion. The float weighed over six thousand pounds and was moving no faster than the speed of someone walking. Unfortunately, the accident still happened, and

OSHA investigated. They issued a serious citation and fined Disney $6,300 for the accident. Disney paid for the funeral and for travel arrangements for family members needing to fly in for his funeral.

Prior to and since Javier's accident, many of the employee fatalities on Disney property were exclusive to contractors or construction workers helping to build the parks. In 1974, a carpenter died when glue fumes ignited around him. In 1981, another fatality happened with construction at EPCOT, when a welder fell and was hit by a steel beam that fell from a crane. In 1988, a construction worker on site at the future Typhoon Lagoon was killed when a pipe burst.

But in February of 1999, part-time cast member Raymond, sixty-five years old, was working at the Skyway gondola lift ride in the Fantasyland section of the Magic Kingdom. Raymond was cleaning and sweeping around the attraction platform just minutes before the park's opening. Tragically, a cast member switched on the ride unaware that Raymond was there. Raymond quickly grabbed onto the gondola, which was now off the platform. Raymond unsuccessfully tried to pull himself into the gondola. He fell forty feet into a flower bed near the Dumbo ride. He was airlifted to the hospital where he died a short time later. Raymond and his wife had retired to Florida from St. Paul, Minnesota, after he worked for thirty years at the water department. Raymond had only been working for Disney as a part-time cast member since September of 1998. OSHA ruled his death accidental and fined Disney $4,500.

As the years progressed, employee fatalities weren't exclusive to the Magic Kingdom. Over the years, employee tragedy struck both Disney's Hollywood Studios and The Animal Kingdom. In May 1989, Disney's MGM Studios, now known as Hollywood Studios, debuted at Walt Disney World. One of the attractions that opened in the park's first year was the Indiana Jones Epic Stunt Spectacular!

The show recreates several stunt scenes from the *Indiana Jones* movies, eight times a day, in front of a crowd of twenty-five hundred people. Within the first several months of the attraction's debut, there were three accidents to the performers of the show; all three were equipment failures. The first incident happened when one stunt man fell thirty feet onto concrete, after the rope he was utilizing failed to lower him slowly down as designed. Another performer fell twenty-five feet and landed on crates when a trick ladder collapsed before it was planned to do so. In December of 1989, another performer was injured when he was squeezed by a trapdoor that malfunctioned, pinning him against the wall.

OSHA investigated each of these accidents and fined the company $1,000 for failure to protect their performers. In March of 1990, after the accident investigation, Disney changed some of the procedures and installed additional safety equipment and padding to safeguard the performers. All was okay safety-wise for the attraction for nearly twenty years; the ride even received a makeover in 2000. Then came the year 2009, which was a deadly year for Walt Disney World cast members. We already discussed the monorail accident that claimed the life of Austin in July that year. On August 10, Mark, a forty-seven-year-old cast member, died from an onstage fall during a mock sword fight during Captain Jack's Pirate Tutorial. A little more than a week after Mark's accident, Anislav was rehearsing for the Indiana Jones Epic Stunt Spectacular. Anislav, only on the job about a week, suffered a head injury while doing a tumbling roll; witnesses say he landed awkwardly on his neck. Two hours after his injury, he passed away at the hospital. OSHA investigated the incident and cleared Disney of any wrongdoing.

On Earth Day, April 22, 1998, Disney opened their fourth theme park at Walt Disney World, the Animal Kingdom. As the name explains, the park is centered on animals and their conservation. The Association of Zoos and Aquariums and the World Association of Zoos and Aquariums accredit the park; however, as Disney is also quick to point out, the Animal Kingdom is anything but a zoo.

Featuring six themed lands, the park is home to more than seventeen hundred animals across 250 species. The park's underlying theme is Walt Disney's dedication to conservation, animal care, education, and research. In 1998, when the over $800 million park was coming together, things got off to a bumpy start for some of their future cast members, those of the mostly four-legged variety.

In the months leading up to the opening of the park, Disney had over ten animals die on their watch; two West African crowned cranes were run over by safari vehicles on two separate occasions; four cheetah cubs died from kidney failure after ingesting ethylene glycol (a toxic chemical found in antifreeze and other industrial solvents); a female hippo died of blood poisoning from multiple infections; a white rhinoceros succumbed to anesthesia during what was to be a routine medical exam; a black rhinoceros swallowed an eighteen-inch stick which punctured its intestine; and two Asian small-clawed otters died after eating the seeds of a loquat, a citrus fruit that is not normally part of their diet. These accidental deaths were certainly not the attention or publicity Disney was interested in receiving. They were already under an intense spotlight from animal-rights groups, not just because of their planned park but also because of an animal-cruelty incident back in September of 1989 at Discovery Island in Walt Disney World.

From 1974 to 1999, Walt Disney World had an attraction near the Magic Kingdom in Bay Lake, called Discovery Island. The island was a place for guests to explore wild plants, animals, and birds. In 1989, it was uncovered that Disney workers beat vultures to death; held dozens of vultures in a small, overheated shed with little food and water; and shot at hawks and falcons. Employees of Discovery Island did these cruel acts in an attempt to control wild birds that were attacking the island's animals, stealing their food, making too much noise, and defecating all over. After a state investigation, Disney settled sixteen animal-cruelty charges and paid a near-six-figure fine in an agreement with the state. Ten years later, with the opening of an enormous animal-themed park, you can understand the skepticism and concern.

With the Animal Kingdom nearing its second decade of operation, it has thrived. In addition to breeding many of the rhinos, giraffes, and elephants, Disney has donated over $20 million from their worldwide conservation fund for grants, research, and of course conservation efforts around the globe. The park has had minimal animal casualties since it opened (an animal casualty happened in July of 2003 with a freak lightning strike killing a giraffe), and the animals have safely entertained the masses without fatal accidents. The same hasn't always been true for some of the people working at this park.

Back in March of 2002, in the Dino Land section of the Animal Kingdom, a new roller coaster premiered, the Primeval Whirl. Primeval Whirl is a very un-Disney-like ride. The ride is a type of roller coaster known as a "wild mouse" or "mad mouse"; the term mouse has nothing to do with Mickey. This type of coaster has been featured in amusement parks all over the world since the

1960s. The ride itself features small cars that are usually much wider than the track itself. The small cars usually seat four or fewer people and take riders on very tight, flat turns without banks or huge drops, at speeds under thirty miles per hour. The wild-mouse track designs are usually in amusement parks because they are cheap to introduce and require minimal square footage—something unusual for Disney, as they usually don't offer many "industry-standard" attractions that guests can ride in other places.

Even industry-standard amusement rides that have been in existence for fifty-plus years can be the scene of accidents. In November of 2007, sixty-three-year-old Karen was working as a ride attendant at the Primeval Whirl. On that fateful day, Karen stepped onto a restricted area to assist some guests on the ride platform. Seconds later, the ride started again and another car came by. The car struck Karen and pushed her ten feet. She fell nearly three feet to the ground where she hit her head. Karen was rushed to the hospital, where she passed away a few days later.

In the months after her accident, changes were made to the ride, primarily to the entry and exit platforms. The platforms received sensor mats in the restricted areas that will shut the ride down if someone walks in the area. These changes were done proactively before the completion of the OSHA's accident investigation. In May of 2008, OSHA concluded their investigation and charged Disney with five safety violations, three serious violations, a repeat violation that wasn't fixed from an earlier inspection, and a paperwork violation and fined the company $21,500.

Three years after OSHA's investigation, the government agency was back on-site investigating another employee death at the Primeval Whirl, in March 2011. This fatality resulted in a $69,000 fine against the park from OSHA.

Back in April of 1998, before Disney's Animal Kingdom opened, when the park was dealing with the negative publicity regarding the deaths of numerous animals, their spokesman, Rick Sylvain, released an interesting statement: "Because it's Disney, people think animals shouldn't die. But deaths happen. It saddens us." This is applicable for the employee and guest fatalities too, a hundredfold.

Not to trivialize or compare the death of an animal to the death of a person—a father, mother, son or daughter, and so forth—but accidents do happen. Many of the early catastrophes in Disney history were with guests displaying reckless behavior. The other accidents probably could have been avoided had certain safety measures been implemented, most notably with small children and Disney employees. Regardless of all that, Rick Sylvain's statement is very true.

People do die at Disney theme parks; however, people have been trained to not expect bad things to happen in the utopian and fantasy worlds Disney works so hard to present and maintain. Their name is synonymous with happiness and capturing fantastic dreams and not with a Disney death tour. This is not how the world wants to view their Disney. After all, people go there to escape from the real world. When the real world encroaches and starts to seep into their Disney dreams, people have trouble dealing with it.

Again, millions of people visit these parks each year and ride these attractions multiple times during their stay. This translates into hundreds of millions of rides each year multiplied by the amount of years the parks have been open. Compare that to the amount of deaths over the years. Translation: visiting their parks is safe.

As for the employee fatalities, where according to OSHA, Disney seems to be a bit more negligent in things, think about all the shifts worked and upward of one hundred thousand cast members that work every day across all of the theme parks. Many parks and resorts actually have a staff working twenty-four hours a day.

The accidents leading to fatalities can be one of those freak things, but it seems there is a good share of blame with rider error and operator error. The theme-park industry in general says the odds are 1 in 24 million of being seriously injured and 1 in 750 million of being fatally injured at a theme park; that sounds great, unless you are that one.

I'll take my chances at riding an attraction at Disney. I do just about every year. But I'd be lying if I didn't say some of these stories have resonated a bit and will probably linger in my thought process as I'm standing in a queue at some point. With decades in the theme-park business and billions of rides, the Disney death tour stands in the very low double digits.

CHAPTER 3

Peter Pan's Fight

In July of 2004, Ronald Iden, a former FBI agent and California's director of Homeland Security, left the public sector and joined Disney as the head of worldwide security for the Walt Disney Company.

Over the years, Disneyland and Walt Disney World have been the target of violent threats. On February 3, 1972, the Walt Disney World's telephone-switchboard operator received a troubling call. The man on the line demanded $90,000 in twenty-dollar bills or else a bomb would go off at the park. The caller told the operator, "If you don't think I can blow up the place, just look in the utility shed." The call became much more serious when a timed bomb was in fact discovered near a utility shed in Frontierland. Luckily, it was discovered three hours before the timer would set it off.

A bit more than a month later on March 13, another bomb threat was phoned in, and the same caller demanded $250,000. On this day, no bomb was found, and no money ever exchanged hands. A courier was sent with the ransom, but no one ever came to pick it up. Roughly three months went by without any additional threats or leads in the case. Then in June of 1972, police arrested a former Walt Disney World employee and charged him with the threats.

Robert was that employee. He was twenty-three years old at the time (and son of the president of Tupperware Home Products) and worked at Disney World from December of 1971 through March of 1972. He was arrested on an eight-count indictment of charges of planting a live bomb at Walt Disney World and extortion.

In January of 1973, the case took an interesting turn. The federal charges that were pending against Robert were suddenly dropped. A US district court judge had dismissed the charges on a motion by US Attorney John Briggs. Briggs stated he acted at the request of the US Justice Department in Washington, but that was all he would divulge. Perhaps daddy's money or clout had some influence over this situation.

A year later and over twenty-five hundred miles away, in December of 1974, twenty-four-year-old Craig, a transient living at a motel in Santa Barbara, phoned into Disneyland security and informed them a letter had been left at the Santa Barbara bus station detailing plans to blow up both Disneyland and Walt Disney World. Disney contacted police, who then picked up the letter. The letter claimed seven bombs would be detonated over a fifteen-day period at both parks unless Disney paid a $3 million ransom.

If Disney left $1.5 million at a location the bomber specified in Santa Barbara and another $1.5 million at a location in Orlando, they could avoid any tragedies. Disney agreed, and with help from the FBI, they placed a box with the ransom at the specified location in Santa Barbara. Craig pulled up on a motorcycle, retrieved the box, and was promptly arrested by the Santa Barbara police and FBI for extortion.

The previous stories ended without harm. The same can't be said for the next one. This story made news headlines around the country and was featured on an episode of *Dateline NBC* in 2006. In April of 1996, teens Kevin Foster, Pete Magnotti, and Chris Black from Fort Meyers, Florida, went on a crime spree of arson, destruction, and eventually murder.

The crew dubbed themselves the Lords of Chaos and started on their path of crimes and arson by setting on fire a supermarket-construction trailer, a Baptist church, a restaurant, and then a historic Coca-Cola bottling plant. They next moved on to armed robbery and carjacking. Another component of their crime spree was set for Walt Disney World and Grad Nite. The crew planned for their "ultimate crime of chaos" on that evening.

The plan was for the thugs to enter the park, assault a few staff members costumed as Disney characters, and steal their outfits. They would then reenter the park and shoot and kill any African American or minority guests in the park.

In the days leading up to Grad Nite, they set out to rob a Dillard's department store for clothing to wear for that evening. The crew planned to enter the department store and set off a homemade smoke grenade. When the store filled with smoke, they would grab clothing and run out. The smoke grenade never went off, and they abandoned that plan. Instead they headed over to their high school to vandalize and burn the school auditorium. After breaking into the school and stealing latex gloves, a fire extinguisher, two staplers, and a bag of canned peaches, they were approached on school grounds by a music teacher, Mark. Mark confronted the boys and told them to go home and expect a visit from the school's deputy the next day. Before the next school day came, Kevin Foster, Chris Black, Pete Magnotti, and Derek Shields found Mark's home address and went over to his house at 11:30 p.m.

The thugs rang the doorbell, Mark answered, and Foster pulled out a shotgun and murdered him in cold blood. All of this was over the possibility of Mark informing authorities about the minor vandalism they did at the school. The teens were arrested and charged with murder and arson. Foster was sentenced to death; and the other teens, to life in prison. By a snafu in their plans at the department store, police determined that lives of numerous people might have been saved, as their plot to terrorize Walt Disney World would have ended, as sheriffs put it, in a "blood bath." Had the teens met any resistance, they wouldn't have hesitated to kill anyone in their path or crosshairs. When police searched the teens' homes, they found a large stash of firearms and ammunition. Tragically, Mark was on the other side of the department store snafu.

Fortunately, all of the major plots on Disney's parks never came to fruition, but tempers do flare from time to time in the land of the mouse. The family-centric environment and happiness oftentimes isn't enough to deter violence within the parks. The wall-to-wall crowds, hot Florida or SoCal sun, combined with some unruly kids can definitely take its toll on people, sometimes in a more detrimental way than others. Let's dive in to the fisticuffs Disney style, routinely just minor squabbles and fights. Although there have been some very violent confrontations at both Disney properties, they're just very infrequent. Let's start with Disneyland and then head across the country to Walt Disney World.

Long before Downtown Disney in Florida increased their security presence back in 2007 due to suspected gang activity, Disneyland had their own violent brush with gangs in January of 1975. On a Saturday night in the Tomorrowland section of the park, two rival gangs from San Gabriel, California, faced off in a brawl just before midnight. That evening, the park was closed to the general public but still had an evening attendance of over seven thousand guests. A Junior Chamber of Commerce group (who knew the chamber of commerce had any gang affiliations!) rented out the park.

As the melee broke out, a seventeen-year-old gang member whipped out a .22 caliber gun and began firing indiscriminately. Two males, aged fifteen and seventeen, respectively, as well as a twelve-year-old girl, were hit. The three were taken to the hospital, and they survived their injuries. The seventeen-year-old was apprehended and charged with attempted murder. Thankfully, no one lost his or her life during this shootout; however, Tomorrowland was the scene for another violent confrontation a few years later that did end in death.

Disneyland's first death stemming from violence was in March of 1981. In an odd similarity to the gang shootout, on the evening of March 7, Disneyland was again rented out for a private party, this time by the Rohr Corporation. Eighteen-year-old Mel went to the park that evening with a few friends; some stories indicate that Mel may have been intoxicated. Their evening of joking around and having fun near the Matterhorn escalated to a dangerous apex when Mel supposedly pinched the rear end of a woman walking by him. The woman, twenty-five-year-old Julie, told her boyfriend, twenty-eight-year-old James, who confronted Mel. A fight between the two men ensued. After an exchange of punches, the two men ended up on the ground, where the two pummeled each other and rolled on the ground. Mel eventually rolled off James. His shirt was covered in blood; he had been stabbed with an 8.5-inch buck knife.

The knife pierced his heart, diaphragm, and liver. As Mel lay in Tomorrowland, bleeding to death, James fled the scene.

As security scoured the park for James, he was found hiding in a bush in Adventureland. He told police Mel was choking him on the ground, and he must have fell onto his knife repeatedly when the two were tussling around on the ground. James was arrested and convicted of second-degree murder charges. He received a sentence of sixteen years to life in prison. While James was hiding in a bush, Mel was dying. A nurse who happened to be visiting the park that evening saw him on the ground bleeding and immediately started to work on him. She was trying to stop the bleeding from his wounds by applying pressure with her hands, hoping an ambulance was on its way.

Instead, and this is where some of the stories get fuzzy and play out in years of long court cases, the park nurse employed by Disney came on the scene. She determined that Mel must be transported to the hospital. Rather than call paramedics, she would accompany Mel, as he was bleeding to death, in the Disney first-aid van on a trip to the hospital. The trip to the hospital took over ten minutes, as the ride was in a first-aid van—basically just a regular old van, driven by a Disney security guard. There were no flashing lights or medical equipment. They encountered traffic along the way and obeyed all the rules of the road by stopping at traffic lights on the two-plus-mile trip. When Mel arrived at the hospital, he was already dead. Mel's family filed a $60 million wrongful-death suit against Disney. The lawyers for Mel's family said Disney was ill equipped to handle the situation. Rather than loading him into the first-aid van, paramedics should have been called, and perhaps his life could have been saved.

Mel's legal case bounced around the court system for several years. The Disneyland nurse testified in court that the park's unwritten policy was to never call paramedics, as it may bring the wrong kind of attention to the park, a.k.a. ruin the fantasy and Disney magic. Disney's lawyers insisted their nurse did the right thing and had trauma surgeons testify that even under perfect conditions, Mel would only have had a 50 percent chance of surviving his injuries. The best course would be to immediately take him to hospital for care. The lawyers for Mel argued otherwise.

An ambulance with oxygen and appropriate equipment and training could have expedited the process, as hospital records indicated it took Disney nearly twenty-five minutes to just get him to the hospital after the decision was made to transport him.

Disney was adamant that they were not at fault. Jack Lindquist, senior vice president of Walt Disney Productions at the time, announced at a news conference, "We're not going to settle out of court. We're going to take this as far as we can." Disney never did settle, but the case came to a conclusion in July of 1986 when a jury found Disney negligent in treating Mel in the situation. They were ordered to pay $600,000—and, oh yeah, in April of 1981, just a month after Mel's stabbing, Disneyland did hire an ambulance to stay on-site.

The next story is from August of 1983, when twenty-six-year-old Joseph was working as a security guard at Disneyland. One evening when he was on patrol, he said he saw a man attempting to break into a car. When he approached the man, the suspect pulled out a gun and shot him in the chest. Luckily, he was wearing a bulletproof vest that night, which stopped the bullet before it entered his body. Joseph radioed Disney security, who in turn called Anaheim police, and he was transported to the hospital.

Even after repeated questioning, Joseph didn't waver in his story; however, things weren't quite matching up for police. First, no one in the area heard a shot fired, and second, the spent shell casing that was found on scene was that of a gun found at his brother-in-law's house. The biggest "smoking gun," if you will, was that there was absolutely no injury to Joseph—no bruising, no abrasions, nothing, which is something obviously highly unusual for someone who takes a direct hit from a .22 at close range.

Police suspected he actually shot the vest and his shirt at home prior to coming to work and then made up the story. Police arrested him on claims of filing a false police report. When Joseph's case went to trial in April of 1985, he was acquitted on charges. The jury told attorneys after the verdict that they didn't know if he faked the shooting or not but said there was enough evidence to show he could have been telling the truth.

If you think that last story was a bit crazy, get ready for this one. In February of 1990, eight-year-old Nayeli of Downey, California, was taking a ride aboard the Disneyland Railroad with her parents. At just after 6:00 p.m., the train pulled into the station near Videopolis with Nayeli sitting in the last row of the car. As the train stopped, she complained to her family that she had pain in her back. Her father notified the conductor, who then called for the park nurse. The nurse noticed the girl was bleeding, and off she went to the hospital—this time in an ambulance. At the hospital, physicians discovered she had been shot in the back.

Nayeli was rushed into surgery where surgeons removed a medium-caliber bullet from the lower right portion of her back. Over at Disneyland, the train was shut down and inspected. Sure enough, a bullet hole was found in the canvas roof near Nayeli's seat.

After a few days in the hospital, she made a full recovery. Disney offered to help pay for any medical expenses the family incurred. As for the origins of the bullet, police were never able to exactly determine where it came from. They were certain the bullet originated outside of the park based on its trajectory. They determined it came from the north or northwest, in the area of Ball Road and West Street. The surrounding area has many homes, businesses, and hotels/motels, so it could have come from virtually anybody.

"This is a modern world. It's an urban world, and Disney is not responsible if a crime takes place." That is the quote from Disney's lawyers during a lawsuit involving a grandmother who was robbed at Disneyland's parking lot. This grandmother was not just *any* grandmother; she was Billie Jean Matay, also known as Mouseketeer Billie from the first season of *The Mickey Mouse Club*.

In August of 1995, Billie, her daughter, and her grandkids enjoyed a free day at the park; one free trip a year was a perk from her days as a Mouseketeer. As Billie and the family were leaving the park and in their car, she claims a man put a gun to her neck and robbed her of over $1,600 in cash, credit cards, and jewelry.

After the crime she sought help from Disney security. Billie claims the security team was less than helpful; they illegally detained her in a back room at the park and badgered her. Anaheim PD was called, and a police report was taken, but the damage was already done. Billie was traumatized, and so were her grandkids, aged five to eleven. While backstage, the children saw Mickey and pals out of costume, wandering around the area with costumes on their bodies but not on their heads. The secret was out; the characters were just people, and the kids were horrified—or so the lawsuit said.

Billie filed suit against Disney for negligence, false imprisonment, and emotional distress. In August of 1997, Disney tried to settle out of court, but Billie wouldn't consent, off to trial they went. After a week in the courtroom, Billie's lawyers presented their case and handed it off to Disney's legal eagles. They in turn asked the judge to dismiss the suit, as there was a lack of evidence. The judge did just that.

Oftentimes, in confrontational situations, a person or group of people needs to be controlled by nonlethal means. One of the great immobilizers in these scenarios is the utilization of pepper spray. Law enforcement uses it frequently.

In the early to mid-1990s, it wasn't uncommon to see your everyday person wielding a little canister on their key ring. The next two stories are situations where pepper spray was used—one, where it was used for its intended purpose, and the other, well, where it went a bit awry.

In February of 2012, fifty-three-year-old Glenn caused a major scene at Disney's California Adventure. It appears as though Glenn may have had a bit too much to drink. He was slurring his words and showing some hostile erratic behavior, judging from the video—it went viral on YouTube; a quick search can retrieve it. After a few obscenity-filled minutes and physically challenging and then assaulting some Disney cast members and guests, it was time for Glenn to go down, and down he went in a scuffle after a good dose of pepper spray to the face. Glenn was arrested for assault and battery.

Long before Glenn was sprayed at California Adventure, Marcello was in line with his family at Disneyland's Haunted Mansion in March of 1993. Apparently, Marcello didn't take too kindly to a person cutting in front of him in line, and a confrontation ensued. Feeling threatened and in need of some self-defense, he reached for his trusty pepper-spray bottle and sprayed the alleged line jumper. It must have been a windy day in New Orleans Square, or he must have used the entire can, as eighty people in the queue felt the wrath of the spray as it spread through the area. Most guests who felt the effects of the spray were treated at Disneyland, but eight others were taken to the hospital.

The tales of dissidence and disturbing behavior Disney style now continue in Florida at Walt Disney World. Regrettably, much like the subject of accidents, WDW has had its share of violent outburst and deaths. Even the artist formerly known as Mr. Whitney Houston got into a fracas in Florida while visiting Mickey; stay tuned for that one.

In July of 1992, thirty-seven-year-old Allen got into a fight with his girlfriend, thirty-three-year-old Barbara. After the spat, Barbara decided it would be best if they split up, and Allen moved back to New York. This decision was devastating to Allen. After the breakup, he tried to take his life by slitting his wrists. His actions frightened Barbara so much that she received a protective order against him. A few weeks went by, and Allen wanted to talk with his ex. He was unsuccessful in his attempts from New York, so he decided to go back down to Florida in an effort to communicate with her. Allen headed over to EPCOT where Barbara worked as a security guard.

The park was closing, and he was told to head to the exit and leave the park. Instead he continued to linger around the area near the Journey into Imagination pavilion. When security approached him again about leaving, he got hostile. He told them he wanted to speak with Barbara and wasn't leaving. Allen then pulled a sawed-off twelve-gauge shotgun from his bag and fired four shots at the guards. Luckily, the guards weren't hit, but the situation escalated when he took two of them hostage into the bathroom at the pavilion. After ten minutes, he released the hostages to the sheriff's deputies that were now armed and surrounding the pavilion. After their release, Allen too made his way out from the pavilion. He started walking out with his shotgun pointed at his chest. Deputies repeatedly shouted and encouraged him to put the gun down; his response was, "No, just shoot me; shoot me. You're going to have to kill me." Deputies continued to try to verbally disarm Allen, but it didn't work. Allen put the shotgun to his head and pulled the trigger. Deputies tried first aid on him, but even then he was combative toward them. Allen was rushed to the hospital via helicopter where he was declared dead on arrival.

In a case of tourist-on-tourist crime in August of 1994, thirty-year-old Michael R. allegedly bumped into thirty-year-old Michael T.'s baby stroller, and some words were exchanged between the two men. After the heated confrontation, the two men went their separate ways. At the end of the evening, they encountered each other again at the monorail station. Their previous argument resumed, and this time, more family members were present. As the argument became more heated, Michael T. started to feel threatened by Michael R. and his family members, particularly one of his brothers. Michael T. pulled out a pocketknife and stabbed Michael R. three times, claiming self-defense. Michael R. was treated at the hospital and recovered from his wounds. Michael T. was arrested on aggravated battery charges, to which he pleaded no contest. He was sentenced to sixty days in Orange County Jail along with four years' probation, in addition to paying $5,800 in restitution to Michael R.

The next story takes us out of the parks in Florida and into Disney's planned community, Celebration. The town was created and developed by Disney in the 1990s. The neighborhood is adjacent to the Disney theme parks and utilizes some of the park's creativity to harken back to the days of white picket fences and small-town feelings. For many residents of Celebration, the community is the closest thing to living in the past, when life was less complicated. It's almost like owning a piece of a utopian community.

However, utopian communities aren't usually the settings for violent deaths; they don't fit, and neither does losing your home to foreclosure. In 2010, Celebration was plagued with both of these issues. That year, one in twenty homes in the community went into foreclosure, as compared with one in forty-eight in the rest of the state. The planned community was also the scene for two violent deaths only days apart.

The tragic events started to unfold over Thanksgiving weekend 2010, when fifty-eight-year-old retired schoolteacher, Matteo, befriended a twenty-eight-year-old homeless man, David. David claimed he went to Matteo's house in Celebration to earn money by washing his Corvette and doing work around his house. After he finished with the work, he went into Matteo's home and fell asleep. During his nap, David claims Matteo sexually assaulted him in his sleep.

David awoke to Matteo touching him and became infuriated. He repeatedly struck Matteo in the back of the head with a hatchet. He smashed his face into the floor and then strangled him with a shoelace to ensure he was dead. The reason for such violence? Self-defense. He claims he was drugged and could have been raped. David claimed he was actually the victim, a victim of a sexual predator who took advantage of him, as he was merely looking for work.

However, over the next several days after killing Matteo, he ransacked his house and sold some of his possessions. He stole his laptop, Corvette, and rare-coin collection, which he sold. David was arrested in early December of 2010 and charged with murder. A jury in January of 2013 convicted him of second-degree murder, and he was subsequently sentenced to life in prison.

Just days after Matteo's murder, Celebration had another violent situation play out in their community. On December 2, 2010, fifty-two-year-old Craig, a former American Airlines pilot, barricaded himself in his home at Celebration. Craig was in the midst of a divorce from his wife and a foreclosure on his home. A distraught man, he called his wife the day before and told her he was armed and going to kill himself. She immediately called authorities. The Osceola County sheriff's deputies arrived at Craig's house, but he wasn't home. They waited two hours for him to return but left after not encountering him.

The next day, authorities arrived at the home again after learning Craig was back and barricaded himself with at least one firearm. As the deputies approached his front door, he opened fire with several shots; luckily nobody was hit.

They didn't return fire, as they didn't have a visual on him or anyone else who might have been behind the door. They retreated and called in reinforcements. A short time later, the SWAT team arrived, along with a negotiator. The negotiator tried to coax Craig out of the house and into put down his weapon. Ultimately, they were unsuccessful. The situation escalated when they launched tear gas into his home to help defuse the situation. After gassing the house, they lost communication with him. Their next plan was for the SWAT team to storm the house. They deployed a robot into the home to survey the situation before they entered. Craig's body was found; he had taken his life.

Just a few miles away, back over at Walt Disney World, this next story gives a new meaning to the Disney ride, Mad Tea Party. Two moms got spinning mad when waiting in line for the teacups. The accusations of cutting in line led to a fight, an arrest, and supposed neurological issues. In May of 2007, fifty-one-year-old Victoria of Anniston, Alabama, was in line with her eleven-year-old daughter, as was thirty-four-year-old Aimee with her children, aged six and seven, and two of her friend's children.

The dispute ensued when Victoria accused Aimee of jumping ahead and cutting the line. As the story goes from Victoria's testimony, a ride attendant let several people in front of her and her daughter at the Mad Tea Party ride. Victoria said she tried to get back to her original place, and as she did, so did Aimee with the four children in her group. Victoria claims that as Aimee tried to push her way through the line, she elbowed, bumped, and kicked backward as she passed Victoria and cut ahead. Aimee denied this and said that Victoria was the violent one. As the two women made their way onto the ride, Victoria continued to voice her displeasure toward Aimee, quite loudly. She allegedly started yelling and cursing and even shoved Aimee's seven-year-old daughter (Victoria was at Walt Disney World with her church group, mind you). As the two bruisers took their "teacups," they continued to argue. They were allowed to enter the ride, only after a cast member separated them.

Aimee put a pair of her children into the teacup, and then Victoria allegedly kicked her from behind and grabbed the back of her hair. Next thing Aimee said was that Victoria was pummeling her. She hit her in the head with her purse, and then she started using her fists and slammed her head into the ride. The beating continued until Victoria was finally separated from Aimee. Disney Security was called and so were the police.

After filing the police report, authorities originally let Victoria go back home to Alabama, as they thought it was a minor scuffle. After Aimee went to the doctor and was diagnosed with a concussion, a herniated disk in her cervical spine, and posttraumatic seizures, police issued a felony warrant for Victoria's arrest. Authorities had her brought back to Florida to face the charges. In April of 2008, the case went to trial. Victoria was facing a charge of felony aggravated battery and battery. The trial had both sides denying any wrongdoing. Victoria said she didn't push Aimee's child, curse, or even strike Aimee. She claimed she only grabbed her hair, as she was trying to get her attention. The defense claimed Aimee exaggerated her medical claims in an effort to eventually sue Disney and score a payday—something she did and subsequently lost.

Victoria's team said that Aimee was actually the aggressor and provoked the attack. She is the one with a history of aggressive behavior, particularly at her child's school. As the trial progressed, witnesses for both sides painted two different scenarios of the same scene. In a typical "she said, she said" case—or David v. Goliath case—the prosecution emphasized Victoria was five feet ten inches tall and weighed 230 pounds, and Aimee was five feet five inches tall. When it was all said and done, the jury found Victoria guilty of the lesser charge, battery, a misdemeanor. Victoria was sentenced to ninety days in jail (she received credit for thirty-two days served), nine months of probation, community service, and anger-management courses.

In 1988, Bobby Brown (the entertainer and former Mr. Whitney Houston, not the cosmetics company mogul) released an ubersuccessful album entitled *Don't Be Cruel*. In April of 1995, he didn't heed his own advice and was arrested for aggravated battery and disorderly conduct at Walt Disney World's Pleasure Island.

Twenty-six-year-old Bobby and his entourage were at the nightclub Mannequin one evening. He, along with another patron, was vying for a young lady's attention when things got out of control.

Bobby told the other suitor, thirty-seven-year-old Neil, to scram, as he was talking with this tenderoni (a song also featured in his album from 1988).

Words were exchanged and eventually so were punches. The next thing Neil remembers, he was hit in the face. He dropped to the ground and was repeatedly beaten, even hit in the head with a glass bottle while he lay helpless on the club floor. Police arrived, as did an ambulance to take Neil to the hospital where he received six staples to close a head wound and another eight stitches to reattach his ear.

With the situation under control, police told Bobby, his bodyguard, Gary, and his publicist, Travis, to have a seat outside the club so that they could get a handle on the situation. The entourage took a seat, but Bobby would not; he became hostile and belligerent with police. The police placed him in the back of their police car to try and keep him under control. Once inside the car, he started to hit his head against the window in an act of defiance.

He next asked police if he could go to the bathroom. They were in the process of taking his two buddies into custody and informed him that once they were finished escorting his pals into another car, he could go. Well, Bobby must have really needed to go, as he proceeded to pee all over the back of the police car—the seat, the floor, and all over the cage that separates the front of the car from the back. He also gave the police a little autograph to remember him by. He wrote the word "fuck" on the back seat—something he clearly wasn't going to be doing that night, as his antics just earned him a trip to jail. The three men posted bail and went back to spend another two days at the Yacht Club resort under assumed names, as the three of them were banned from Disney property after their incident.

November of 1996 rolled around, and the three men were set to go on trial. At the last minute, Bobby's charges were dropped. Neil refused to testify against Bobby, as the two men came to terms on a settlement deal. Neil originally sued Bobby for $6.6 million, and in the end, Bobby paid roughly $2 million to settle and be free from the case (his two friends pleaded no contest and were fined for their actions). That was an expensive trip to Disney, especially for a married man who didn't bring his family.

The EPCOT food-and-wine festival treats Disney guests to a unique and tasty tour of culinary cuisines and libations from around the globe. In 2013, one of the event's attendees appeared to have enjoyed the alcohol portion a bit more than your average person. Twenty-three-year-old Austin, from Pensacola,

Florida, a 2012 Naval Academy graduate, went on a tour of his own. A tour that became a mobile assault of EPCOT cast members.

Austin, already feeling the effects of some of that festival booze, entered a backstage office area near Innoventions in Future World. He encountered Michael, who was on the receiving end of a punch to the face from Austin. As he worked his way through the area, Austin then came upon a cart to move merchandise around with. He commandeered the cart; when Timothy tried to stop him, Timothy too received a punch in the face. Being an equal opportunity offender, Austin next grabbed a three-foot PVC pipe and struck Jessica in the face and neck with it. After his third assault, he was apprehended not initially by Disney security but by two other servicemen. Thomas, a navy airman, and Jay, a marine private, were at EPCOT separately from Austin but saw him, and the two immediately tackled him to the ground.

After a few more squabbles with the duo, and a continuing stream of drunken rants, sheriff's deputies arrested him in front of Club Cool in Future World. Austin was charged with battery, aggravated battery, and felony battery. Austin's case is still pending.

The next few stories certainly don't feature people's most prudent or logical behavior. In October of 1982, Justin of York, Pennsylvania, was arrested for playing with a hand grenade at the entrance to Walt Disney World. When approached by deputies, he informed them the grenade was deactivated. He said he bought the dummy grenade at an army/navy store. Taking no precautions, the bomb squad seized the grenade and dismantled it. Inside, they found it was filled with sodium chloride tablets. With the addition of another chemical, it could have become live. Justin was promptly arrested.

Another tale of danger happened in May of 2013, when a Floridian left his loaded gun on a ride at the Animal Kingdom.

Forty-four-year-old Angelo realized after he left the Dinosaur ride that he was without his heat. He went back to the ride and learned that a woman and her grandson got on the ride and found the .38 semiautomatic on the seat and turned it in to Disney. Angelo did have a permit for his weapon, but obviously Disney has a no-weapons policy on premises. When interviewed by authorities, he said he thought the security checkpoints at the entrance to the parks were only for bombs.

Bombs at Disney are no laughing matter. For a German tourist, he figured it would just be easier to notify the bag checkers at the front of the park that he was in possession of a bomb—two, actually. In November 2009, thirty-seven-year-old Jochen from Leipzig, Germany, told employees very casually that he had two bombs in his backpack. The cast members questioned him again about his statement to make sure they (and he) understood what he was saying to them; he reiterated it. In came the deputies and the bomb-sniffing dog. Turns out there were no explosives, and Jochen got his trip to the United States extended with a stay in Orange County Jail.

The Disney bomb-and-gun brigade isn't exclusive to men; sometimes even grandma gets in on the action. Sixty-three-year-old grandmother Mary Ann of Nickelson, Pennsylvania, was arrested in December of 2007. It appears back home, she lives alone, and she keeps her .32 Berretta with her at all times. She didn't realize she was still packing when she tried to enter the Magic Kingdom with her loaded gun, locked blade knife, and a pair of scissors in her bag. Mary Ann was arrested and charged with carrying a concealed weapon inside the theme park.

As most visitors to Walt Disney World or Disneyland know, Disney's security officers don't carry guns. In this instance, it was probably a good thing a Disney security guard didn't have access to a firearm. Parl worked as a security guard at Walt Disney World from 1996 until late 2004. He probably would have worked there longer, except he devised a plan and reached out to an illegal gun dealer to have his current wife's ex-husband murdered over a child-custody battle.

The murder-for-hire plot started to unravel as the ex-con Parl got involved with was being investigated for illegal gun sales. Parl paid $2,000 upfront and after the ex-husband was killed, he would pay another $2,000. If it wasn't for the ongoing federal investigation into the movement of illegal guns, authorities said this killing would have happened.

One afternoon, shortly after the initial payment was made, the federal Bureau of Alcohol, Tobacco, Firearms, and Explosives; the Osceola County Sheriff's Office; and Disney security went over to Disney's Fort Wilderness

Campground and arrested Parl. In 2005, Parl's murder for hire got him a conviction on first-degree premeditated murder, and he was sentenced to seven years in prison.

Another story of creative police work with Disney security in tow happened in August of 1995. Jerry, forty-nine years old and from Brick, New Jersey, entered his ex-girlfriend's house while she was on the treadmill. He snuck up behind her and shot her in cold blood. Leaving her for dead, he then fled the state and eventually landed at Walt Disney World's All-Star Resort. Jerry stayed for a few days and registered the room under his real name.

After a few days of odd behavior and suspicious conversations with some of the cast members at the hotel, Disney security alerted the sheriff's department about their shady guest. The sheriff's department thought Jerry was in fact the suspect wanted in New Jersey on a homicide. Two sheriff's detectives went undercover and dressed as maintenance workers for the resort. They approached their man and arrested him on the charges back in New Jersey.

Grandmothers, moms, celebrities, military men, and Disney employees have all lost control at Mickey's house. So it's not surprising when kids do as well. The last two stories are some of the more notable scuffles with some underage parkgoers.

The Wide World of Sports Complex at Walt Disney World features numerous sports fields, clubhouses, and stadiums for just about every sport imaginable. The facility has been the spring training home of the Atlanta Braves and Tampa Bay Buccaneers. When the pros aren't suiting up at the facility, the amateurs are. Various amateur youth teams descend on the facility for tournaments and championships throughout the year. Each December, the Pop Warner youth football Super Bowl is held at the Wide World of Sports Complex.

In 2007, three teams didn't get in enough hitting on the field, so they started to hit each other off the field. The teams, two from Hawaii and one from Baltimore, were staying at the same resort. Late one evening, a brawl between the three teams broke out around 1:00 a.m. in a resort arcade. The Orange County Sheriff's Department sent six units to the scene along with Disney security. By around 2:20 a.m., the situation was under control with one boy taken to the hospital with a broken nose.

No arrests were made, but about thirty minutes later, over seventy families were given the boot from their hotels. Each family received written notice from Disney that they were to immediately vacate their rooms and the premises. The families had twenty minutes to pack up and leave, as Disney has a zero-tolerance policy for violence. If they didn't leave the premises, the sheriff's office would be called again to remove them. Begrudgingly, all the families met in the parking lot to leave. Most thought Disney handled the eviction poorly and rashly. Through a cavalry of taxicabs, the families made their way over to a local Holiday Inn at 4:15 a.m.

Disney explained as follows: "This was unfortunate, but with thousands of guests staying at the resort, we have to maintain a safe environment for everyone," said Jacob DiPietre, a spokesman for Walt Disney World. "All participants were made aware of our strict zero-tolerance policy regarding any physical disturbances. Any teams involved in fighting are subject to disqualification and eviction. We were in direct consultation with both Pop Warner officials and law enforcement throughout the course of the event."

As the Disney website outlines, group packages include a provision that if "one or more person(s)" in a party takes part in a violent act, everyone will be forced to leave.

The last story to close out a tumultuous chapter didn't feature a youth sports team but a few youths who assaulted guests and police like it was a sport. If you were in the vicinity of Space Mountain at Walt Disney World on Sunday, May 20, 2007, hopefully you didn't encounter the five knuckleheads from Long Island that went around spitting on and cursing at anyone within their reach.

The crew from Shirley, New York, ranging in age from fourteen to twenty (four siblings and a girlfriend to the oldest brother) weren't happy enough assaulting innocent parkgoers; they took it up a notch and assaulted an Orange County deputy sheriff.

After many complaints by guests around Space Mountain, Disney security gathered the group, and escorted them down to the Disney security office. When the sheriff entered the office, nineteen-year-old Brian became belligerent and started to make threats to Disney security. The deputy intervened, and the four other kids pounced on the officer.

As the deputy noted in his report after the incident, "I was punched in the face with closed fists several times by all the defendants. I defended myself by throwing counter punches in their faces and bodies in an attempt to break free. The suspects surrounded me and intermittently attacked me as I turned." The deputy eventually used his stun gun on a seventeen-year-old girl after she continued to throw punches. Once the stun gun was used, the crew retreated, and all five were arrested on charges of battery on a law-enforcement officer and of resisting arrest with violence.

You can probably add this family to the list of people who are currently banned from Walt Disney World. As the decades progress, it's apparent Disneyland and Walt Disney World don't have quite enough pixie dust to sprinkle on everyone who passes through their gates.

The Disney theme parks are no different than any other large public place where a very small percentage of people can't play well with others. Most often, things go off without a hitch, but here and there some people prefer their Disney a bit more violent with a sprinkle of attitude and violence rather than pixie dust.

CHAPTER 4

Disney Debauchery

In 2012, Disney cut ties with three-time Olympian Suzy Favor Hamilton after she was exposed as a high-priced Las Vegas escort. Favor Hamilton was a featured speaker at both Disneyland and Walt Disney World's marathons.

There is an old saying in the world: sex sells. This notion is applied daily to advertising, news reporting, and entertainment. There is another thing that sells almost as well, and that is Disney. The two subjects couldn't be more antagonistic, but here and there these two topics intersect, and usually not in a good way. Disney tries their best to avoid anything salacious, be it on the big screen or in their theme parks, yet sometimes things of a sexual nature occur that they can't sweep under Aladdin's magic carpet.

Since ancient times, sex has been a deviant motivator for people from all socioeconomic backgrounds and professions; today it's no different. By nature, the subject finds its way into everything we do, either consciously or subconsciously. Sex and sexuality are primeval acts and traits; they transcend and unify. Unfortunately, they often corrupt and harm many in a perverse and twisted way. As society has revealed, people can force their will upon others in an unscrupulous and damaging way, especially onto those weaker or younger.

Then there are the vast majority who like to dabble in sex and sexuality, be it for occupation, novelty, thrill, or harmless fun. All of these aspects have worked their way into Disney in one form or another. Most notably it has been in an unacceptable and illicit way at their theme parks involving children; however, a few frisky, or shall we say consenting adults, do make Disney their adult playground. Welcome to the chapter of Disney debauchery.

Before Splash Mountain opened at Walt Disney World in 1992 and gained its nickname "Flash Mountain" (a nod to the ladies who lift their shirts as they take the plunge down the mountain and have their "screams" captured, wink, wink, by Disney's cameras), men could get a different kind of thrill ride a few miles away.

In October of 1982, as Disney was putting the final touches on EPCOT, an influx of prostitutes started to descend upon Disney from as far away as New York and Philadelphia. The ladies of the night came into town looking to capitalize on the large crowds expected for EPCOT's grand opening. During the first twelve days of October 1982, sheriff's deputies arrested forty-two women on prostitution charges. An average month usually sees twenty-five arrests in thirty days. This increase was no coincidence or speculation; it was the truth. After the arrests were made, the ladies flat-out said they were there to "commemorate the opening of EPCOT."

Not to worry, ladies—all the extracurricular Disney excitement wasn't just exclusive to men. In April of 1999, a man claimed he was abducted from a Hilton Hotel at Walt Disney World across from Disney Springs, and was held captive as a sex slave. In all seriousness, at the time, forty-year-old Anthony, of Sausalito, California, told police his story was 100 percent accurate, and he had no reason to make it up. Anthony was a telecommunications salesman visiting Orlando for a business conference in September of 1998. When he didn't check out of his room, board his flight back home, or contact his sixty-five-year-old wife back in California, she called the police and reported him missing. Six months later, he turned up in Georgia and told police he was kidnapped and held as a sex slave.

Anthony said he was abducted by a group of Middle Eastern men and held prisoner in a dark dirt-filled room where he spent every day naked and tied to a cot. His kidnappers, at least three men and two women, abused him daily. They always wore masks, so he was never able to see their faces. Only one spoke to him in English; everyone else conversed in a language Anthony couldn't understand.

During the course of his captivity, the women would taunt him, and the men would abuse him. He claimed he was injected daily with a drug that paralyzed him physically so that they could have their way with him, but the drug kept his thoughts clear. If he was unable to "perform," he was injected with something else to restore his vigor. In his own words from the police report, Anthony said he was the group's "love toy." Despite their abuse, they fed him well. He ate sandwiches and stews that were filled with curry.

Eventually, his captors freed him in April of 1999. They left him with two peanut-butter-and-jelly sandwiches, two bottles of water, two packs of Marlboro cigarettes, a lighter, and a five-dollar bill and dropped him in the woods. Anthony eventually made his way to the police and was examined at a hospital in Augusta, Georgia. He showed no signs of drug abuse, needle injections, or rape. He was in good health and apparently weighed the same 185 pounds as he did before his kidnapping.

State investigators as well as the FBI were skeptical of Anthony's story. When he was found in the woods, he claimed he couldn't recall his date of birth, home address, or other personal information but managed to remember he was abducted on September 25. He also claimed he had to wander around the woods for a day and a half before he could get out of the woods, something police also found hard to believe, as a half a day's walk in any direction would get him out of there.

In today's voyeuristic society with borderline obsessive behavior for some folks when it pertains to reality television and social media, many people feel the need to chronicle every act, thought, or compulsion and share for the world to see. Even their intimate times are leaked out in sex tapes and nude photos. Over in Disneyland Paris, a few of everyone's favorite Disney characters had their own exploitations and fornications caught on camera, albeit simulated.

Minutes before costumed characters set out to entertain the masses, they had a little fun of their own backstage, in what was dubbed the "Disney Orgy" and released on the Internet. The video showed the costumed crew in some compromising situations. Mickey had a gay tryst with a snowman; Goofy grabbed Minnie's breasts and then had a ménage à trois with Chip 'n' Dale. The faux orgy was recorded by another cast member and eventually hit the Internet in October of 2006. When reached for comment, Disney said, "The behavior shown on the video is unacceptable and inexcusable. The video was taken in the backstage area not accessible to guests. Appropriate action has been taken to deal with the cast members involved."

While the cast members at Paris Disneyland may have been acting out their fantasies, their depraved acts with Disney characters are nothing novel. Ward Kimball, a cornerstone of animation at the Walt Disney Studios beginning in 1934, also spoke of some perverted Disney antics over the years. Ward was a colorful and eccentric man and one of the few employees Walt socialized with outside of his studio, for they both shared a love of trains. What they didn't share a love for were crude, crass, sexualized depictions of Disney characters. As Ward explained in the book from 1975, *You Must Remember This,* Ward talked about how, at times, cartooning can be monotonous and boring:

"So to relieve the monotony, we'd do things like, well, on *Snow White,* we'd draw porno things. That happened all the time. Here is this beautiful, saccharine sweet girl in the story and after making so many drawings of her during the day, our impulse was to draw her naked with one of the dwarfs standing there with a giant erection. A lot of these drawings found their way out of the studio. During the war, I think every guy on the assembly line at Lockheed had a copy of a booklet somebody put together. It was called *Snow White and the Seven Truck Drivers.* Snow White is sitting on a little chair with her dress up, and the dwarfs are all standing in line with their cocks out. The cocks of the dwarfs varied in size. Old Grumpy had one that looked about three feet long.

I've seen drawings of Dumbo flying through the air dropping elephant turds on everybody with Mickey Mouse in the foreground with a week's stubble of beard giving himself a fix or jerking off. There was one with Goofy buffing Minnie Mouse. So far as I know, Walt never saw any of those drawings. He was a funny guy. His humor was quite different than that of the man in the street. You could never tell Walt a dirty joke. The word got around quickly to new employees not to try and ingratiate yourself with Walt by telling him an off-color story. He thought dirty jokes were terrible, and he was embarrassed by them."

If watching Disney characters fornicate isn't your thing, then perhaps you would like to do *it* yourself, in the mouse's house. Many people over the years have sought out the thrill of having sex in and around Walt Disney World and Disneyland. Cast members on both coasts have been witness to just about everything you can imagine. From naughty time at Tom Sawyer's Island to quickies at the Haunted Mansion or Pirates of the Caribbean, apparently, nothing is off limits for some people. Need some suggestions on a safe place?

Turn to the Internet; there are numerous websites and blogs that provide sights for Disney "safe sex."

All kidding aside, adults and children visit Disneyland and Walt Disney World to have fun. Their parks are the most visible family entertainment places in the world. Families from around the globe come to them in droves, and Disney attracts all kinds—young and old, rich and poor, and 99.9 percent of them are at Disney with honest ambitions of seeing Mickey, but there is that infinitesimally small percentage of deceitful, calculating predators who rob children and adults of their innocence and disrupt an otherwise happy vacation and life.

Regrettably, this chapter discusses these disturbing tales. Unfortunately, I wish this chapter was nonexistent, or even much smaller with an isolated incident or two, but that is not the case. The Disney parks have been the place for some heinous sex crimes involving both guests and cast members; unfortunately, there have also been quite a few sex crimes perpetrated away from Disney property by some miscreants on the Disney payroll.

We know Disney is family centric, and therefore most people let their guard down when visiting and rightfully so. During a three-year spat with one of their unions, Unite Here Local 11, representing Disneyland's hotel workers, reminded guests of what may be lurking in the shadows. The union handed out flyers at Disneyland in 2010 that read "Keep Your Children Close! Places Like Disneyland Are Magnets For Pedophiles."

The possibility of pedophiles visiting a Disney park puts Disney in a situation that requires them to be more diligent and proactive. Disney certainly tries to keep the parks safe and free from sexual predators, but sometimes their best isn't good enough or someone or something slips by them. Beginning in October of 1998, newly hired employees started to undergo background checks as part of their hiring process. Previously, only cast members receiving background checks were those dealing directly with cash or overseeing children.

In 2013, some of Disney's background checks were extended to their guests at Walt Disney World. A local news station in Orlando ran a story indicating Disney actually started to screen potential guests against a sex-offender database. Walt Disney World was already doing this each year for their employees, since at least 2007.

As the story goes, guests, many of them annual pass holders, went to enter the park and were denied. When they swiped their cards to enter, they were pulled aside and told they were not allowed in. They were then issued a trespass warning, effectively banning them from Disney property for life. The news station did additional research with the Orange County Sheriff's office and noted over the previous six months that more than seventy-five trespass warnings were given to guests looking to enter the park; all of them were registered sex offenders.

Despite these proactive efforts, situations still happen, even from some unlikely people. A quick glance at the cast members at any Disney park shows a cross section of the world. From folks just starting out in the working world to others recently retired and working at Disney part time during their golden years, everyone has a story to tell. Some stories are better than others, and a handful can be absolutely dreadful.

In June of 2002, sixty-three-year-old Hugh was working as a greeter at Walt Disney World's Ticket and Transportation Center. He worked there for nearly two years and had a spotless employee file. His life before working at the Happiest Place on Earth was vastly different. Hugh was a prominent priest from Missouri. He worked as the editor of the official newspaper of the dioceses of Jefferson City, Missouri, the *Catholic Missourian*. He was also the chaplain to death row inmates and the Missouri Legislature and even the star of his own television show.

In January of 1999, the diocese suspended Hugh for allegedly sexually abusing prepubescent girls and teens dating all the way back to 1971. The diocese announced he was taking a leave of absence. He had privately gone through many treatment programs for his problem, but a recent incident involving an eighteen-year-old woman resulted in a suspension. No criminal or civil charges were ever filed but when asked about the allegations, he didn't deny them. When another allegation came up, this time involving a ten-year-old girl, the Missouri diocese felt compelled to reach out to the Orlando diocese and inform them about Hugh and his employment at Walt Disney World. The Orlando diocese called Disney, and Disney called the Missouri diocese to verify the allegations. By the next day, Hugh was gone. When interviewed by local media, he indicated he resigned for health reasons.

Forty-nine-year-old Cedric was another man of the cloth working at Walt Disney World. He worked the overnight shift at the Port Orleans Resort for seven years. He was also a revered pastor in Sanford, Florida, at the historic Saint James African Methodist Episcopal Church. One evening Cedric was at work and went onto the resort computer to prepare his Easter Sunday church sermon. Cedric was working on John, chapter 13, verses 1–35 and Psalm 14 for his service. He was also viewing porn from YouTube that featured underage teenage girls. Unfortunately for Cedric, more than just the "man upstairs" was watching over him—so was Disney. The resort's computer system monitors every keystroke; the computers take screenshots every three seconds of each employee's computer.

This wasn't his only unholy offense; Disney managers were notified that he had previously tried to visit websites that Disney had blocked. He also tried to engage young girls on YouTube by sending them private messages. He told the girls he enjoyed their videos, was a big fan, and encouraged them to send him a longer video privately.

Cedric was arrested in May of 2013 on the possession-of-child-pornography charges, and soliciting a child for unlawful sexual conduct. The case piqued the FBI's interest and, with another investigation in October of 2013, Cedric was arrested again on an additional twenty-one counts of child pornography. Needless to say, he lost his job with Disney and was relieved of his pastoral duties. Cedric's case is still pending.

Another story from 2013 involving a Disney cast member and possession of child pornography is that of forty-six-year-old Thomas, a retired Air Force Master Sergeant working as a security guard at Walt Disney World's Animal Kingdom. The Polk County Sheriff's department worked in coordination with the Internet Crimes Against Children agency to apprehend Thomas. Deputies went to his home with a search warrant and found numerous images he collected over a span of several years. He was arrested and charged with seven counts of possessing and distributing child pornography. Thomas told deputies he enjoyed looking at the images of nine- to eleven-year-olds because of their innocence.

In 2007, twenty-year-old Matthew was working five days a week at Walt Disney World as a costumed character. He would hug children and pose for photographs with them as either Goofy or the Beast, from *Beauty and the Beast*. One day at work, he received a surprise visit; sheriff's deputies were waiting to speak with him about a collection of photographs he may have at home. Deputies accompanied him home and found over one thousand images of child pornography. The new father of a sixteen-month-old baby, by his sixteen-year-old girlfriend, showed no remorse and told deputies there was no difference between looking at pornography of adults and children, as they were just bodies. Matthew was arrested on fifty-one felony counts of child pornography. His roommate had tipped off the police.

The next situation sounds like something that could be featured on NBC's show *To Catch a Predator*. The case made headlines nationwide not only because it featured a Disney executive but also because the case utilized a new defense in court. Patrick, thirty-four years old at the time, was on top of the world. He was a rising star in the field of Internet technology.

Patrick helped launch the computer-software platform Java when he was an engineer with Sun Microsystems. He partied with movie stars and earned $183,000 a year with vested stock options of $15 million as the executive vice president of the Disney-owned Infoseek Company.

Infoseek was a crucial part of Disney's Go.com Internet branding, which still exists today. In September of 1999, things started to unravel for Patrick. Living in Seattle at the time with his college sweetheart in a $2.4 million house, he hopped a flight aboard the Disney private jet to Southern California. He headed over to a Santa Monica pier to meet a friend—a friend who was a thirteen-year-old girl whom he met on an Internet chat room entitled "Dads & Daughters Sex." In the chat room, his screen name was HotSeattle; her name was KrisLA.

KrisLA said she was thirteen years old, was five feet tall, and had blond hair. She was game for whatever Patrick suggested. He told her he wanted to have his way with her in his hotel, among other things. She was enamored with him, as he sent her links to articles about himself and a few pictures, some graphic. Patrick *really* impressed this thirteen-year-old girl, and the two agreed to meet up at the pier.

HotSeattle went to the pier, as did KrisLA. Patrick was who he said he was; however, KrisLA wasn't a thirteen-year-old girl but an FBI agent. Patrick was arrested and charged with traveling interstate with the intent to have sex with a minor. The laptop he had in his possession was also seized and contained images of child pornography. In a matter of days, he lost his job, his wife, and his house. The case went to trial in October of 1999, and Patrick pleaded not guilty. In what became his entire legal strategy, he insisted that the whole situation was a fantasy scenario that he concocted in his mind (he did work for Disney, right?). Patrick may have engaged in online sexual fantasies about young girls, but that was it, just fantasy, and the Internet is filled with them. Apparently Disney theme parks aren't the only fantasylands; the Internet is one too.

Patrick claimed the entire Internet could be "one large masquerade ball." He never thought he would actually meet a minor in a sex chat room; despite the theme of them being adult men with sexual fetishes toward underage females, it was all a different sort of virtual reality. Well, Patrick's defense basically worked. The jury was deadlocked on his case. Normally the FBI claims a 99 percent conviction rate on similar cases, and in an effort to make a very long legal story short, Patrick basically walked on all charges.

Because his first case was deadlocked, he was retried two months later, and Patrick pleaded guilty under a plea deal. He received no jail time; instead he developed several computer programs for the FBI to streamline their online sting investigations; rather ironic.

He received nine months house arrest, was put on five years' probation, and paid a $20,000 fine. The child-pornography charges that stemmed from the photos on his laptop were also tossed out, as a portion of the federal law applicable to his case was found unconstitutional. In the end, he still maintained that he wasn't out to solicit sex from a minor. He didn't feel like a sexual predator, although through his plea, he would now have to register as one.

What do a Walt Disney World costume designer, security guard, and jungle-cruise operator all have in common? Well, they were all arrested in Florida during sex stings that began with chats online to underage children. The Disney edition of online sex stings didn't just end with Patrick; over the years cast members have been well represented to the Central Florida ICAC (Internet Crimes Against Children) task force.

Luckily, many of the sex stings or crimes that caught Disney workers operated entirely online, and no children were abused; however, that wasn't always the case. Sad to say, things did escalate from time to time, and innocent children became victims at the hands of a few repulsive and revolting people.

In January of 1996, a British family was on holiday at Walt Disney World. As the family entered Disney's MGM Studios (now known as Hollywood Studios), they were approached by a puppeteer, Jeffrey, who worked for a company licensed to sell puppets at Disney parks and was not directly employed by Disney. Jeffrey approached the seven-year-old girl with her family and pretended to wrap the legs of his puppet around the young girl's waist. While he did this, he placed his hand up her dress. Jeffrey was arrested, and in September of 1998, he was found guilty of lewd and lascivious behavior and sentenced to twenty-one months in prison.

In 1994, forty-seven-year-old David was arrested while he worked at Walt Disney World's Fort Wilderness campground. Two guests witnessed him improperly touch two girls. Prior to working at Disney, he was a substitute teacher in Osceola, Florida. That was until he was fired for excessively touching, hugging, and kissing elementary school students. David was also a Girl Scout Troop leader. After his arrest at Disney, other victims stepped forward, and he was eventually sentenced to fifteen years in prison.

In a story that shows the wheels of justice never stop turning, forty-five-year-old Bryan was working at Disneyland in 2013 as a ride mechanic when police arrived to arrest him for sexually assaulting young girls. Bryan's sexual assaults on young girls began in several towns in southern New Jersey beginning in 1992 and continued until he was arrested in December 2013. All together he abused four victims, all under the age of thirteen at the time, and often on multiple occasions. Bryan was also in possession of child pornography. He was indicted on charges of aggravated sexual assault, endangering the welfare of a child, sexual assault of a victim who is more than four years younger, and sexual assault through coercion.

In 2011, another Disney tradesman was arrested, this time, an electrician for Walt Disney World. Edgar, thirty-three years old, was arrested for indecent exposure and lewdness. He was caught in his car near a school and community center, watching pornography and exposing himself.

Somehow back in 1992, Richard was fired from Disney for indecent exposure but was never charged for his behavior. From 1990 to 1992, Richard worked in Walt Disney World's florist division. Over the course of two years, Richard admitted to Disney that he routinely exposed his genitals to guests.

In 1990, Disney security suspected him of exposing himself to guests who were walking along Disney's Caribbean Beach Resort. After more than one suspicious act, Disney security approached him, and in a sworn statement he said he repeatedly exposed his genitals to guests over nearly three years; subsequently, his employment was terminated. Prior to his employment at Disney, Richard had been arrested four times on similar actions. He admitted in court that he exposed himself in public over 250 times and served 120 days in jail back in 1986 for his lewd acts.

In July of 1998, a Walt Disney World employee sexually assaulted a sixteen-year-old teenager visiting Walt Disney World with her grandparents from Colorado. At the time, seventeen-year-old Daneal was working as a cook at Chef Mickey at the Contemporary Resort at Walt Disney World. The victim and Daneal met near the pool; after a brief conversation, he offered to take the young lady on a tour of the hotel.

Unfortunately, she agreed and ended up in a second floor men's room where she was raped as she feared for her life. That evening she reported the attack to the front desk, and the police worked the case. After initially denying the story ever happened, further questioning led Daneal to speak about the situation, and an arrest followed. When the case went to trial, in December of 1999, he maintained that the sex was consensual. The jury found him guilty of sexual battery, and he was sentenced to nearly sixteen years in prison.

Another alleged case of rape happened at Walt Disney World's Caribbean Beach Resort in February of 2011, this time with a different outcome. A woman called into Walt Disney World Reservations to inquire about reserving a room and theme-park tickets for herself and her two children. The cast member taking the call was engaging and through their conversation learned the woman was unemployed and using her tax return to take her children on vacation.

After the phone conversation, the cast member sent the woman a text message and told her not to book a room, as he would help her out and book the room under his "friends and family" discount. He informed her he was a product of growing up with a single mother and was looking to help her out with "no strings." The woman accepted his offer also under the guise of "no funny business."

The woman and her children checked into the room and were met by the cast member. He then took her and her kids to the Magic Kingdom to celebrate her birthday. After some time at the park, she wanted to go back to the room, complaining she hurt her back on Space Mountain. They all went back to the room where the woman allegedly dropped many hints indicating she wanted her new buddy to leave. The woman claims he never left, but she fell asleep anyway. She slept until she felt the cast member trying to pull her pants down. She told him to stop and leave, which he didn't do, and eventually she fell asleep again. She claimed at this point that she woke up again with the cast member sexually assaulting her. She pushed him off and demanded he leave, which he did. He told her he would see her tomorrow. After he left, the woman noticed her debit card was missing, along with forty dollars.

The next day the cast member returned to her hotel room and dropped off her debit card and said he found it in his car. He then escorted her and her children to EPCOT, signing her in for free and then leaving them at the park. Later in the day she called police accusing the man of both rape and theft. The cast member was subsequently arrested and charged with sexual battery involving a physically helpless person, theft of a credit card, and petty theft.

In November of 2011, the case went to trial. The defense stated that the sex was consensual and that the woman obviously continued to speak with cast member after the alleged attack and didn't call 911 after the assault. The jury agreed, and the cast member was acquitted on all charges, though he did lose his job with Disney.

That case was solved; however, there are two unsolved cases of rape against cast members working at Walt Disney World in the 1990s. The first case reported on April 1, 1990, happened when a woman was leaving work at the Caribbean Beach Resort after midnight. As she approached her car, a man with a knife forced her into the woods and raped her. Her attacker wasn't apprehended.

In May of 1999, a security guard working the overnight shift at the Magic Kingdom heard an alarm sounding as she was underground walking through the Utilidors. Around 5:00 a.m., she responded to the storage area beneath Pecos Bill's restaurant in Frontierland. The thirty-two-year-old woman found nothing suspicious in the area. She proceeded to the ladies restroom where a man threatened her with an object. She was unable to get a description of the rapist as the lights were off in the bathroom. Police believed it to be a fellow employee, as the park was closed, and it took place in an employees-only area.

Heading back to the Caribbean Beach Resort, a twenty-year-old woman from Maine was staying at the resort on Halloween of 1992. Wanda claimed she checked into the hotel with her ten-month-old baby, ordered a crib to be delivered to her room, and then went out to meet up with family members. When she returned that evening, the crib was in her room, as was a man. The man, dressed as Dracula, proceeded to duct-tape her eyes and mouth and then taped her to the bed, where she was raped and beaten. She was able to free herself and call 911.

In June of 1993, Wanda sued Disney. She claimed Disney was negligent in her rape. They had an inadequate 911 system (her call didn't go to Orange County Sheriff; it went to Disney security first, and then the Orange County sheriff was dispatched, but they didn't find out about her rape until over thirty minutes after she called), ineffective security patrols, poor screening of employees, poor accounting of room keys, and insufficient maintenance of guest-room locks. Disney tried to settle the case for $200,000; she declined, insisting on $1.2 million.

The woman's experience sounded horrendous, and her suit should have been justified, if only it really happened. It turns out Wanda faked the whole thing. The hoax was an effort to scam Disney out of money. She and her brother, thirty-three-year-old James, concocted the whole scenario. Wanda, not really from Maine, had sex with a friend before she went to her room (in case tests were performed), had her brother tie her to the bed, and then had him beat her with a stick.

The deputies were initially a little wary of her story, as there were some minor inconsistencies. The tape on her mouth and other parts of her body was perfectly smooth, and there were no signs of struggle, but this wasn't enough for them to totally disregard what she was saying. It wasn't until an anonymous call came in to police (from her half sister) telling them the hoax was money driven. The brother and sister team hatched the plot one night over dinner at an Orlando restaurant. The half sister dropped the dime after becoming angry at the duo in October of 1993.

In December of 1993, Wanda was arrested in Tennessee. In May of 1994, she pleaded guilty to grand theft and falsely reporting a crime. Under her plea agreement, she was sentenced to three and a half years in prison and had to make restitution in the amount of $24,000 to Disney and the sheriff's department for investigative costs. Her brother James died in March of 1994 before his sentencing.

Believe it or not, Walt Disney World has two rape hoaxes in its history. In February of 2006, nineteen-year-old cast member Elizabeth told police four French men raped her at her apartment complex. Elizabeth claimed around 4:00 a.m,. she was outside her apartment building when she was approached and then physically grabbed by four men. The men took her to another apartment where she was gang raped.

Elizabeth said she eventually got free from them and returned home to her apartment. She put in a full day's work at Walt Disney World and then called the police to report the assault when she got home. She told the police the four men took turns raping her as she begged and pleaded with them to stop. Police identified the men as members of the Disney International Program, a program that employs foreign workers at EPCOT's World Showcase. The men were fully cooperative with police and told authorities the sex was consensual, and they had proof; one of the participants videotaped the tryst. Authorities watched the video and saw nothing factual about Elizabeth's rape claims. Elizabeth was then arrested and charged with filing a false police report and making false statements in addition to a possession charge of a small amount of marijuana.

Another story at Walt Disney World that involved a Disney cast member utilizing a video recorder also culminated in an arrest in January of 1992. This time, the recorded evidence wasn't used to exonerate the cast member but to prosecute him. Twenty-one-year-old John, a wardrobe assistant, recorded female cast members getting changed into their costumes for work at a dressing room inside of Cinderella's Castle.

In May of 1991, Disney security was investigating thefts from the female cast members' dressing room. During the investigation, they learned holes had been drilled around the dressing room and bathroom so that someone could see in while the ladies changed. The female cast members had been notified of the situation and were assured the holes would be filled in, but they were not. In June of 1991, John developed an elaborate scheme to not only peep on the girls in various stages of undress but also to videotape them. Through the holes drilled into the wall, John arranged numerous mirrors, ran extension cords for electricity, and utilized an unlocked dumbwaiter to make videos of the girls. All told, he made three videos and shared them not only with his friends but also with other Disney employees as part of the entertainment for a Disney employee bachelor party.

By January, another employee tipped off Disney security about John's peeping. Security planned a sting operation and installed their own video equipment to tape John taping the girls. Sure enough, January 8 came, and he went to his spot to start filming the girls and pleasuring himself. Disney security moved in and caught him with his pants down. John was arrested and obviously fired from Disney. He pleaded no contest to the criminal charges against him and was sentenced to four years' probation. The dancers, six in all, filed a $40 million lawsuit against Disney for emotional distress, an invasion of privacy, and sexual harassment. In December of 1995, the suit was settled out of court, and terms were not disclosed.

With the employee docket complete for now, the attention turns to situations involving Disney guests—not in an effort to quantify the magnitude of each of these stories, as they are all terrible, but let's get one of the most horrible ones out of the way first. In 1998, forty-one-year-old Matthew Mancuso was living outside of Pittsburgh, Pennsylvania. He was an educated, prosperous, divorced dad. Matthew contacted a New Jersey adoption agency and began the process of adopting a young girl from Russia; let's just call her Angel for our purposes. Angel was five years old and already had a tough go at things despite being so young. She was born to an alcoholic mother, who tried to kill her by stabbing her with a knife in the neck. This happened just a year before Michael went to Russia to officially adopt his baby girl.

At last, perhaps she received a break in life; she was moving to the United States and could have a fresh start with her new adoptive father.

Unfortunately, this was not the case. Life became hell living with him. From her first night in this country, Michael sexually abused her. He abused her daily:

physically, sexually, and mentally (I'll try to spare most of the horrific details), and aside from the sexual abuse, he kept her isolated from the world, oftentimes locking her up in a basement. He starved her so that she wouldn't mature. This despicable man was a serial pedophile and shared his exploits with the world as he traded hundreds of sick photos of Angel with other child pornographers in the world.

In late 2004 and early 2005, Canadian investigators in the sex-crimes unit of Toronto repeatedly came across a series of child-pornography images on different pedophiles' computers. Authorities saw the same photos over and over of a young girl in a hotel room, hot tub, arcade, elevator, in a warm-weather climate. Along with these images were others of the girl being abused. The Canadian authorities did an unusual move and released six of the photos to the public with the girl's face obstructed. They wanted to find the setting of these photos in an effort to perhaps track her down.

The public reacted and identified the location. The photos were taken at Walt Disney World's Port Orleans Resort. Angel was just eight years old at the time of the photos and, without knowing anything about her, people dubbed her "Disney Girl." With this clue, the search intensified, and investigators were making headway into the identity of the young girl. As it turns out, from a different situation, the police already knew of Angel; they just didn't know she was "Disney Girl."

In May of 2003, federal agents raided Michael's house after he shared an explicit chat with a fellow pedophile online. This chat was actually with a law-enforcement officer. The raid uncovered a trove of child porn. Michael was arrested and sentenced to fifteen years and eight months in jail. With her adoptive father incarcerated, another family in Pittsburgh, whom she calls her dream family, adopted Angel.

After his arrest and the new information of Disney girl, authorities started to piece things together. The federal government charged Michael with additional child-pornography and abuse charges for his acts on Angel.

He pleaded guilty and was sentenced to another thirty-five to seventy years in prison. As it turns out, authorities believe Michael solely adopted her for his perverse and sick intentions of abusing and producing child pornography with her. As the details of the story unraveled, the agency did little in the way of a background check or interviews of his family members, let alone any sort of exhaustive search into who they are letting to adopt a child. Had they done their due diligence, perhaps they could have learned that Michael abused his own biological daughter throughout her adolescence.

Over Memorial Day weekend in 2009, at the Fort Wilderness Campground, twenty-nine-year-old Jean struck up a conversation with a twelve-year-old girl at the campground's pool. A short time later, he was having sex with her at a nearby laundry facility. The girl was fearful; she was pregnant and didn't tell her foster family about the rape until later in June. The only information she had about the man was a business card he gave her. The girl's family contacted police about the sexual assault. The police then set up a sting operation and contacted Jean. The police, pretending to be the girl, told Jean she wanted to meet him again at Fort Wilderness. In September, Jean showed up, as did the police. He was immediately arrested and charged with sexual battery and lewd or lascivious battery. Jean was found guilty of his charges in 2011 and currently resides in Florida state prison.

Also occurring in 2009, David of Mountlake Terrace, Washington, was visiting Walt Disney World in July with a friend's fifteen-year-old son whom he was caring for. The two of them went over to the wave pool at Typhoon Lagoon. While in the pool, a lifeguard and a boy's father witnessed David inappropriately touch more than five young boys in the pool. Most of boys didn't file a report with deputies, but one thirteen-year-old boy's father did, and David was arrested on charges of lewd molestation. In October of 2011, he was found guilty and sentenced to twenty-four months in prison.

It was the same park, same year, same week, and same outcome for a pedophile visiting Typhoon Lagoon. Robert, a fifty-one-year-old youth minister visiting from Victor, New York, groped more than one young girl at the wave pool. Robert would swim up to unsuspecting young girls; as the waves would come crashing in, he would pull their bathing suits down and fondle them. Robert did this repeatedly and on multiple girls. He claimed he only accidentally collided into them. Employees witnessed him pulling his stunt on no less than five girls, as did the park's security cameras. After complaints from a fifteen-year-old girl and her family, security and deputies were called in. Once they were able to identify him in the sea of people, he was arrested on molestation charges.

The youth pastor earned himself a new title after his trip to Walt Disney World: registered sex offender.

In August of 2011, a convicted violent sex offender was arrested for lewd punching on three young girls' genital areas while he swam at Typhoon Lagoon with his wife and children; sometimes, even adults are victims. A thirty-year-old woman was the victim of groping by a nineteen-year-old man. He was charged with battery and banned from Disney for life.

The wave pools seem to challenge certain people's moral behavior and self-control. Disney poolside sex crimes continue to surface at not only water parks but also resort pools. In 2012, a sixty-eight-year-old man was arrested for flashing his genitals to little girls at the Animal Kingdom Lodge pool. There are a few more stories that could be added to this part of the chapter, but you get the picture here.

Unfortunately, these crimes don't complete the stories Disney doesn't want you to hear. There are more from the past and will be more in the future. In our ever-changing society, even the Happiest Place on Earth isn't completely sex offender–free. As with accidents and other incidents covered in this book, these atrocities occur out of the tens of millions of visits. By and large, the two "towns" of Disney are probably safer than the towns you and I live in.

A quick sampling of the evening news reveals our local tales of woe—stories pertaining to corruption and crimes of our neighbors, friends, and family at the hands of strangers, civic and religious leaders, teachers, politicians, and law-enforcement officials. The same acts happen everywhere; it is the unfortunate part of life. Due to Disney's prominent role and reputation over the decades, these tales seem much worse and unexpected as pieces of reality seep into our fantasy.

CHAPTER 5

Making a Mint Off the Mouse

In February of 1985, Disney and the video-rental chain the Wherehouse paid two toddlers a combined $10,000 after the boys watched the Disney video *Silly Simplicities* and hardcore pornography had been spliced into the video.

One of the responsibilities of being a homeowner is accountability. If someone slips at your house or your dog bites them, there's a good chance you're going to be sued. Mickey's house is no different. Theme-park owners have a tremendous amount of liability and responsibility. Inviting the public onto private property that can be the setting for thrills and spills is also an invitation for lawsuits. Naturally, Disney has seen their share of spills, as much of this book has outlined. Spills usually lead to the courtroom, and no one has been there in respect to theme parks and entertainment, more than Disney.

Some of the lawsuits over the years have been more than justified as seen in chapter 2. Others have been quite frivolous, and Disney has experienced them all. There was once a lawsuit at Disneyland in 1959 by a woman who sued the park over her traumatic experience riding the Matterhorn. The woman claimed she would have never gone on the ride if she knew it was a roller coaster, as roller coasters scare her. There was another lawsuit filed in the 1970s when a person taking a seat on the Pirates of the Caribbean ride got wet. Then there was the case from 2004 when someone sued Disneyland for discrimination because they offered cheaper tickets to nearby residents (the Resident Salute Program gave locals an eight- to ten-dollar discount).

As you can well imagine, these lawsuits didn't get very far in the legal system. In fact, many lawsuits against Disney don't advance to the courtroom, and when they do, Disney is usually victorious. Disney's high winning percentage has to do with many factors. Sometimes they win because they aren't negligent, and other times it's because Disney is detailed, efficient, and diligent with their cases. And here and there, well, it's because some jurors love Disney. There was one case where a juror commented that her fellow jurors were very pro-Disney. During their deliberations, her fellow jurors commented that it would be terrible to ruin the park's pristine safety record, despite a man losing his finger.

Disney apparently feels they need to be proactive and diligent legally. Our society can be quite litigious and they need to protect Mickey's deep pockets. The diligence and attention to detail the company has mastered in providing entertainment to billions of people for nearly eighty years is also seen with their legal team. Disney has admitted they do maintain accountability for their incidents and accidents, under certain situations. "When a complaint has merit, the Walt Disney Company often settles the case but the company will very assertively fight cases it views as frivolous," said Disney spokesman, Ray Gomez.

Sometimes those settlements have been as cheap as a few theme-park tickets or Mickey memorabilia. Participants in cases that aren't settled out of court can expect to be followed, taped, and thoroughly investigated by Disney. In certain cases Disney has interviewed parents, children, family members, employees, coworkers, and anyone else they can get access to; depositions aplenty! Combine those interviews with a top-tier legal team and bevy of experts or physicians and Disney will bring the case to a conclusion, or as one attorney who battled Disney in the courtroom noted, "It's like suing God in the Vatican."

On the off chance that Disney does lose a case, they are trying to work with lawmakers to curb their awards to victims, at least in Florida anyway. In 2013, Disney teamed up with supermarket behemoth, Publix, to lobby lawmakers in the state to cut the size of civil-lawsuit awards. The companies are hoping lawmakers will rewrite the way medical damages are determined, if a business in the state is found responsible for an accident.

As a global powerhouse with a portfolio as diverse as Disney's, their countless brands, enterprises and profitability make them a great target and constant participant in the United States legal system. Some of Disney's time spent in the courtroom is unrelated to their theme parks. The company is sued on a myriad of levels, white-collar issues, harassment, copyright infringement, shorting royalty checks; if you can dream it, they've been a part of it. This chapter chronicles some of the more interesting lawsuits brought against Disney over the years, across their entertainment spectrum.

When Michael Eisner stepped down as Disney's head mouse in 2005, he amassed over $1 billion in salary, stock options and bonuses during his twenty-one-year tenure. During his time, he was the catalyst for Disney's revenue increase of $1.5 billion in 1984 to $30.75 billion in 2004, by way of adding seven new theme parks, a television network, radio stations, hotels, cable channels, a cruise line, and a slew of other enterprises. Eisner's personal wealth paralleled his companies and in the world of big business, it seemed justified.

During his reign, it appeared as though Eisner had the golden touch. His successes far outweighed his failures; at least financially. There was one fiduciary move, however, that caught the eye of not only the media but of Disney shareholders. The Eisner golden touch felt the sting of a golden parachute.

In 1995, superagent Michael Ovitz was one of the biggest names in Hollywood, and Eisner wanted him to work for Disney. Ovitz resigned from the talent agency he founded and joined Disney as president of the Walt Disney Company. Ovitz was Eisner's right-hand man and second in charge. After a tumultuous year working together, it was clear the two men couldn't helm the company together.

Clearly Eisner wasn't going anywhere, so the other Michael would have to go. Ovitz was relieved of his duties as of January 2007 and took with him a parting gift of roughly $140 million for fourteen months of employment. Pretty good work if you can get it.

Disney shareholders were outraged. Seventeen of them filed suit against both Disney and Eisner. They claimed Disney and their directors should have never hired Ovitz and then fired him so quickly. The golden parachute he received was excessive and they demanded the money be returned to the company; roughly $38 million in cash and another $100 million in stock.

The case bounced around the legal system, and by 2005, just a few months before Eisner left the company, judges ruled Ovitz could keep the money. It was determined that the money was in place and part of the initial contract he signed to come aboard. One hundred and forty million dollars for fourteen months work. It certainly makes Eisner's $1 billion for twenty-one years seem well deserved.

In April of 2000, Disney faced another multimillion-dollar lawsuit involving a former executive of their company, this time from the ex-employee's estate. Robert was a senior vice president at Disney Motion Pictures and Television. He was responsible for overseeing the creation of trailers for movies and television advertisements.

In May of 1994, Robert died from AIDS-related complications. Three weeks before his passing, while in the hospital, a Disney executive paid him a visit and asked him to sign away his pension, stock options and any deferred bonuses, worth roughly $2.8 million. Some of the higher-ups at Disney believed Robert was taking kickbacks from vendors and allowing them to overbill for services. This mismanagement was to the tune of $5.7 million. Sanford Litvack, Disney's chief of corporate operations, approached Robert on his suspicions. Litvack claimed Robert admitted, in 1993, that he took $60,000 in payoffs. There was a second claim from another vendor that Robert was paid over $160,000 to secure more work from Disney. Litvack knew Robert was dying and decided not to fire him or expose him to authorities for taking kickbacks.

He allowed him to keep his job and stay on the payroll so he could maintain his company health-care benefits. In the effort to keep his benefits and not be exposed to the police and public, Disney sent someone to Robert to have him waive his rights to future money, which he did. After his death, Robert's estate, led by his father, sued Disney for their actions.

The estate claimed Robert was a dying man, was unsure of what he was signing, and was pressured into the situation. There were no witnesses and they had no rights to ask him to waive away his rights to future monies. In April of 2000, a jury in California agreed with Robert's family's claims. The waiver Disney had him sign on his deathbed was deemed invalid.

Walt Disney World's Animal Kingdom features the popular attraction It's Tough to Be a Bug! The attraction, inspired by the Disney movie *A Bug's Life*, describes the arduous task of living as an insect. In the mid-1990s, bugs weren't the only ones having trouble in their day-to-day lives at Walt Disney World. It was also tough to be a firefighter for the park, male or female.

The 1990s saw the Reedy Creek Fire Department (Reedy Creek is basically the governing body of the land in and around the Walt Disney World property that Disney set up back in the 1960s) hit with three sexual harassment lawsuits from their firefighters, two cases from men and one case from women. The first case on the Disney docket was known around Florida courts as the "Sphincter Case"—lovely name, I know.

In 1996 and 1997, two male firefighters filed nearly identical sexual harassment cases against Disney's Reedy Creek Fire Department. The men, John and Ernest were veteran firefighters. At the time, John was a member of the fire department since 1988 and Ernest since 1982. The two men claimed that for years, they were subjected to hazing and harassment by their fellow firefighters.

The two men claimed the abuse persisted for over a decade at three different firehouses. The abuse came in the form of sphinctering or sphincter viewing and pancaking or fullering. So what do these lovely terms entail? Well, sphinctering was when the two men were physically restrained, often times handcuffed, had their pants and underwear pulled down and had their anus exposed to a group of their peers that would watch and cheer on the abuse. After they were paraded around like this in front of their coworkers, they then had pens, pencils, pocketknives, or penlights inserted into their anus. If the men fought or resisted this torture, the objects would be forced in.

Pancaking or fullering was when the victims were forced to the ground and the firehouse's largest firefighter would jump on top of them. The rest of the firehouse would then follow and jump on top of him; hopefully all foreign objects were removed prior to this act.

In all seriousness, the pancaking oftentimes would cause injury to the men at the bottom of the pile. Each of the men complained repeatedly to various leaders in the fire department and even to Reedy Creek officials. Very little was done to stop the harassment, in some cases, the harassment got worse after the men were reprimanded.

In 1995, Disney and Reedy Creek finally acknowledged the issue. They hired an investigator from the Orlando Fire Department to interview firefighters in the various houses to see if these allegations were true, although later in court, they would deny they hired the investigator for this specific purpose.

After interviewing thirty-five witnesses, the independent investigator concluded that the two men were subjected to this abuse, along with three other men. Multimillion-dollar lawsuits ensued from both men. Before the cases went to trial, settlements were reached, and in typical Disney fashion no terms were released.

The last sexual harassment case with Walt Disney World's firefighters involved three women. The ladies claimed that some of the male firefighters put up vulgar and nude pictures of women throughout the firehouses. They would even go as far as making vulgar comments about their genitals and would obstruct them from receiving proper training. They were routinely chastised by the men, telling them their place should be in the kitchen or barefoot and pregnant. When the women would complain to the fire department managers, nothing was done to curb it and at times they felt the managers actually encouraged the behavior.

The three women filed a sexual harassment lawsuit highlighting all the low points of their days at Reedy Creek Fire Department. They claimed that the environment was hostile and very much antiwoman.

In October of 1996, as the jury was selected on a Friday before the case was to commence on Monday, Disney settled out of court with the three women; they were seeking $5 million in their case.

A handful of the lawsuits Disney battled within the past twenty years or so actually originated with the big cheese himself, Walt. In June of 1955, Disney released the animated movie *Lady and the Tramp*. The romantic cartoon about a couple of pooches featured the voice of popular actress and singer Peggy Lee.

Peggy voiced the characters Darling, Si and Am, and Peg. Peggy also contributed to writing some of the songs featured in the movie. Her royalty for songwriting was a split of $1,000 with the other writer. Her voice work and singing earned her another $3,500—not bad for a contract signed back in 1952. Fast-forward thirty-five-plus years, and enter the popularity of the home VCR. In 1987, Disney released the movie on videocassette. The movie sold millions of copies in its first year, and Peggy wanted her cut.

In November of 1988, she sued Disney for $25 million. She claimed her contract entitled her to a portion of the proceeds. In her contract, it stated

Disney does not have the right to make "phonograph recordings and/or transcriptions for sale to the public, thus the movie was released without her consent and Disney is in breach of contract." The case went to court and in April of 1991, a jury ruled in Peggy's favor. They awarded her $3.8 million, almost 10 percent of what Disney made in sales from the videocassette.

About a year after the *Lady and the Tramp* case was filed, Mary Costa, an opera singer and voice of Princess Aurora in Disney's 1959 release of *Sleeping Beauty* filed a nearly exact court case. This one they settled out of court days before the start of the trial, but not before Disney tried to pull a legal fast one. Mary, too, signed her contract in 1952. She was paid $100 a day for her work on the film. In 1986, Disney released *Sleeping Beauty* on home video; her lawyers estimated Disney grossed $60 million with the videotape's release, and Mary was due a cut under the same argument Peggy's legal team utilized.

When the case was filed, Mary filed it in her home state of Florida. Disney countered and moved to have the case tried in California. If they could get the case into California's legal system, it could sit there for years as the courts are notoriously backed up. Disney's argument, and it is certainly an interesting one, was that they don't conduct business in Florida. They are based in California and, therefore, the case should be tried there. Disney contended that the film was produced under a different corporation. The theme park in Florida is under the umbrella of Walt Disney World Company, which is different from the film company based in California. This tactic didn't work, the courts denied their motion and allowed for the case to proceed in Florida. Days before the trial started, Disney settled the case out of court for undisclosed terms.

At the time, both women made a couple of interesting statements to the media about their cases. Peggy Lee was quoted as saying, "You know, they always say, don't mess with the mouse. I'm glad that my rights were vindicated." Mary's view was a bit more nostalgic or maybe naïve: "None of this would be happening if Walt were still alive." As Mary indicated, many of the folks Walt employed were fiercely loyal to him. They envisioned him as a father figure and held him in the highest of regard.

The lawsuits Peggy and Mary filed led to a similar lawsuit from a contract Walt signed with the Philadelphia Orchestra for their work on *Fantasia*. The orchestra received a flat fee of $2,500 for their work on the Disney film. They confirmed that they received royalties annually for records, cassette tapes, and compact discs that were sold over the years but received zero royalties for the video of the film released in 1991. The orchestra's lawyers estimated the gross sales of the video surpassed $350 million and the orchestra should be entitled to 10 percent. They filed a suit seeking $35 million, which was subsequently settled out of court in October of 1994; no terms were disclosed.

The last lawsuit, with origins back to the time of Walt, deals with that honey lover, Winnie the Pooh. Remarkably, this case went on for nearly twenty-one years. It all started when Disney agreed to license Pooh back in 1961, and again in 1983, from the family of Stephen Slesinger. Stephen had bought the rights of Winnie back in 1930 from the original creator A. A. Milne.

Disney featured Winnie the Pooh in a variety of movies, cartoons, and endless merchandising. At one point, the bear franchise was grossing more money than the mouse franchise. In 1991, the Slesingers filed a $700 million lawsuit against Disney claiming they were shorted on their annual royalty checks. The family's lawsuit claimed Disney lumped Pooh's earning into the earnings of other characters and weren't disclosing accurate royalty figures. By doing this, they were in breach of contract. The family also sued for copyright and trademark infringement.

Over the years, actually, over the decades, there were repeated dismissals and appeals on this never-ending case. There was even a libel suit by a reporter caught in the crossfire. Nikki Finke, a reporter for the New York Post, claimed she lost her job with the Post after writing articles covering the ongoing Pooh case. Nikki wrote a series of articles about the original royalty case filed in 1991. This case was ultimately thrown out in 2004 when a judge found misconduct on behalf of the Slesinger family. As it turned out, the family hired a private investigator to uncover "hidden" Disney documents that would outline Disney's theft of royalties. The investigator was accused of breaking into Disney corporate offices, rummaging through trash bins and into a garbage disposal center to find the damning papers. The judge said the family illegally obtained evidence and their investigator trespassed at Disney, case dismissed.

However, all was not holy for Disney after this. The judge fined Disney $90,000 for destroying documents that could have been very pertinent to the case. These stories were covered by Nikki (and other news agencies) and published in the *New York Post*. Her stories apparently infuriated Michael Eisner so much that he had his right-hand man, Bob Iger, write a letter to the Post stating Nikki's story had "serious misrepresentations clearly designed to injure the Walt Disney Company." Nikki claimed this letter got her fired from the *Post*. She filed a wrongful termination suit against her former employer and a libelous suit against Disney, and her lawsuits were settled out of court.

Now back to the original case, as stated above, the original 1991 case dealt with royalties was dismissed in 2004, due to the shady behavior by both parties. After several rulings and appeals on the copyright and trademark case in 2003, 2007 and 2009, a court finally ruled in December of 2012 that Disney does ultimately control the copyrights and trademarks to Winnie when the Slesinger family ultimately transferred all rights to Disney in 2009. And the case was closed.

Lawsuits claiming discrepancies over royalty payments continued on productions that were created long after Walt had passed away. The writer of *Who Framed Roger Rabbit* and the family members of the man who wrote the catchy tune "the lion sleeps tonight" that was featured in the *Lion King*, both went after Disney in court through the 1990s and 2000s. By the way, this is a notorious practice in Hollywood. Writers file cases seeking transparency in accounting and royalty payments all the time. The situation isn't exclusive to Disney. Neither is the challenge by writers and producers that a studio stole their idea or script for a movie.

Over the years, Disney has been accused more than once of stealing an idea about a hit movie or television show. These accusations are something Disney has gone to court for several times, leaving the courtroom with their usual high winning percentage.

A popular movie from 1992 was Disney's *Sister Act* starring Whoopi Goldberg (no relation to the author!). The hit movie went on to gross over $200 million and led to a sequel and Broadway musicals. In June 1993, Donna Douglas, former star of *The Beverly Hillbillies*, sued Disney for $200 million, claiming their film was based on a book Donna owned the rights to, "A Nun in the Closet." Donna said she bought the rights to the book and developed it into a screenplay, which she claimed had over one hundred similarities to Disney's *Sister Act*. Douglas said she submitted the script three times to Disney in 1987 and 1988 and they outright plagiarized the movie from her screenplay. The case went to court, but in 1994, a federal jury didn't find enough similarities between the two works and Donna lost her case.

Twenty years later, Disney's *Sister Act* was the focus of another lawsuit. Queen Mother Dr. Delois Blakely of the Franciscan Handmaids of Mary Covenant in Harlem, New York, claimed the movie, the sequel, and anything else having to do with the nun-centric movies were based on her life. She claimed many of the scenes in the movie are based on things that actually happened to her. The Queen Mother claimed her 1987 biography "The Harlem Street Nun" was the basis for the *Sister Act* movies. In September of 2012, she filed a breach of contract among other claims, seeking $1 billion in damages. Makes you wonder why it took her twenty years to file this lawsuit, maybe she took a vow of silence.

A few of the more recent Disney/Pixar movies have also been subject to plagiarism and copyright infringement lawsuits. In April 2001, Deborah Thomas submitted her script called "Squisher the Fish" for Disney to review in hopes of having it made into a movie. Two months later, her script was returned to her, with Disney informing her they do not accept unsolicited stories, and thus rejected her story.

When Deborah went to the movies and watched *Finding Nemo* in 2003, she claimed much of the plot line was similar to the story she submitted to Disney two years earlier. She filed suit against Disney claiming they stole parts of her story and worked them into *Nemo*. Instead of merely returning her script, they in fact copied it before returning it to her. In February 2008, a judge ruled against Deborah's copyright infringement claim. There weren't enough similarities between the two stories. Both stories dealt with young fish in the ocean that are captured, and that was about it.

This next case almost made it to the United States Supreme Court. In 2006, Disney released the hugely successful movie *Cars*. A sequel ensued, as did the thousands of products that flooded the marketplace. The movie even made its way into the Disney theme parks and resort hotels. Plain and simple, it was another Disney cash cow.

In 2011, Jake Mandeville-Anthony filed a lawsuit against Disney, claiming they infringed on his copyrighted material and incorporated it into their *Cars* movies. Jake claimed he created very similar anthropomorphic cars in his works called *Cookie and Co.* and *Cars/Auto-Excess/Cars Chaos* back in 1992. Jake claims he sent copies of his work to Disney years before *Cars* debuted, and Disney incorporated his ideas into their smash hit.

There were a few small problems with Jake's case. Disney's attorneys pointed out that Jake didn't register his works with the US Copyright Office until 2010, which was five years after *Cars* was released. The court ruled the two works weren't similar enough to warrant infringement, in addition to Disney's claim about the copyright being filed years after the movie was released to the public. Jake took the case up to the United States Court of Appeals for the Ninth Circuit and even attempted to get his appeal heard by the Supreme Court. In April of 2013, the court declined and all of Jake's copyright appeals were denied.

This next case could bring a little shock and disbelief to a Disney cowboy, a cowboy known for his honesty and humility, none other than Woody from the *Toy Story* franchise. In February of 2014, Diece-Lisa Industries (DL) sued Disney for copyright infringement. DL is a toy manufacturer that produces, markets, and licenses a stuffed teddy bear known as Lots of Hugs.

DL claims that Disney stole their idea for the devious Lots-O'-Huggin' Bear, (a.k.a. Lotso) costar of *Toy Story 3* from DL's trademarked Lots of Hugs bear, that the company has marketed since 1997. *Toy Story 3* is an enormous revenue generator for Disney. According to the lawsuit, Disney sought copyright and trademark protection for certain *Toy Story* characters but not Lotso. DL further claimed that the enormous success of the movie and notoriety of the Disney character Lotso has damaged the worth of DL's Lots of Hugs trademarked characters.

The company noted that firms they do business with, and that eventually, the consumer may confuse their bears with Lotso. They cited an example of a licensing agreement they entered into with a firm willing to market and sell their Lots of Hugs bear. After the success of *Toy Story 3*, the licensee was reluctant to move forward with their bears and asked for the trademarked name to be changed to "hugalots" instead of the traditional Lots of Hugs bear. This case is still pending.

The Walt Disney Company isn't just the target of trademark and copyright infringement of scripts and toys. Their supposed theft and plagiarism runs deeper. Disney has faced some tough lawsuits from a few folks that went right after the heart of the mouse. The lawsuits claimed Disney plundered their ideas for theme parks. How would you feel if someone told you Disney stole the idea for EPCOT?

Most folks that follow Disney know the story about Walt's creation of Disneyland. To this day, the Disney-marketing machine still spins the black-and-white interview with Walt explaining about how he took his daughters to a park; a filthy park. Something else was needed, a place where adults and kids could enjoy their day together and have fun. Presto, Disneyland was born.

The creation of Walt Disney World and Walt's original ideas for EPCOT and the City of Tomorrow have also been chronicled. But what about the EPCOT that did come to fruition? Was Disney actually the originator or did they steal this idea from someone else? A lawsuit from November 2002 challenged Disney on their authenticity of the world famous park. According to Orrin Corwin, a painting he inherited from his neighbor was the inspiration for EPCOT.

Orrin's deceased neighbor, Mark Waters, painted something titled, Miniature Worlds. The picture featured many miniature villages representing different areas around the world. The concept showed villages and landscapes representing nineteen nations and six continents. Each nation would feature an iconic symbol such as Big Ben for London or the Coliseum in Rome. There would also be a train circling the area. Throw in the lake and a large globe at the entrance, and there you have it, EPCOT; at least in Orrin's eyes.

Mark painted this for Robert Jaffray in the early 1960s. Apparently, Robert was a former intelligence employee at the Pentagon. He commissioned Mark to put his thoughts and ideas down on canvas as "a way to foster world understanding during the Cold War." Robert's family claimed he showed the picture to Disney in 1963 to see if they would be interested in investing in his Miniature World. Disney allegedly declined, there is actually no tangible proof Robert ever met with Disney or sent them his work. Fast-forward four decades, Orrin received the painting and heard the story from Robert's widow and daughter, he moved to have the artwork copyrighted and then sued Disney for copyright infringement. He claimed they took the idea for EPCOT from Miniature Worlds.

In 2007, the case was officially dismissed. A judged ruled that the painting and EPCOT were not strikingly similar. While the picture did have a large globe at the front of the park, EPCOT had a silver sphere with no world map on it. The train in the picture ran along the entire perimeter of the park; EPCOT's monorail only cuts through a portion of the park. While the park and picture did have similar ideas, both works expressed these ideas dissimilarly, therefore case dismissed. As we know from a myriad of interviews and books, including his own published in 2013, legendary imagineer Marty Sklar detailed the creation of EPCOT with influences from previous World's Fairs, along with other Disney-based ideas.

In the next theme park theft case, Disney didn't fare as well. While most people around the world are familiar with EPCOT, many may not be with Walt Disney World's ESPN Wide World of Sports Complex. As briefly touched on back in chapter 3, with some of the fighting at WDW, the sports complex in Florida is an all-in-one stop for playing sports. The complex is home to 230 acres of professionally run fields, courts and clubhouses. The facility can host up to sixty sporting events and thousands of spectators.

In March of 1997, Disney's $100 million sports complex debuted to the public. For a couple of folks, the concept looked awfully familiar. Nicholas Stracick, a former baseball umpire, and his business partner Edward Russell, an architect, claimed the sports complex was their idea. They called it Sports Island when the duo presented it to Disney back in 1987. When Nicholas and Edward left their presentation pitching their idea, they were confident Disney had an interest in it.

The men were shocked two years later when the company passed on their idea. The two were even more shocked in 1997 when they saw Disney opened their own sports complex. The business partners immediately filed suit in court claiming fraud, misappropriation of trade secrets, and breach of confidentiality. This time, Disney wasn't the only one that could bring in a shrewd and cunning legal team. The partners brought big legal guns to the courtroom to represent them. Not too long removed from the O. J. Simpson case, Johnnie Cochran was one of the attorneys representing the men in their David vs. Goliath case.

With the case underway, Cochran and his team deposed just about everyone and their uncle at Disney, except for Walt himself. Michael Eisner, Al Weiss, then president of Walt Disney World, Disney architect Wing Chao, no executive was immune. Eisner actually said he didn't initially like the idea and said it wouldn't make money. Despite his feelings, Disney moved forward with the idea.

The crux of Disney's legal defense, depositions and testimony all stated the same thing. The complex is nothing unique, and anyone could have created it. There are ballparks and complexes featuring more than one sports field all over the world. What is unique is the way Disney designs, creates, and executes things, and that is something the two men didn't create.

In August of 2000, a jury in Florida ruled in favor of Nicholas and Edward. They found Disney guilty on the counts of misappropriated trade secrets, making fraudulent and negligent misrepresentations and breached confidential relationships. The two men were seeking $1.6 billion in damages; they were instead awarded $240 million in damages. Disney immediately filed an appeal. In September of 2002, they dropped their appeal and announced a confidential settlement with the two men.

Throughout all this Disney discourse and legal wrangling, right or wrong, ethical or unethical, the one underlying theme within these tales is that the company is fiercely diligent and protective of their image, and we haven't discussed some of the cases where they were the ones initiating the lawsuits; that's in the next chapter.

Disney trademarks or copyrights anything and everything. Seriously, this is the company that attempted to trademark Seal Team 6, you remember those guys, actually scratch that, national heroes, who killed Osama Bin Laden. Well, two days after the news broke of their amazing conquest, Disney submitted a trademark for their name.

Now, what they were going to do with it, anyone knows. They listed games, toys and merchandise on their application. Once word got out, Disney dropped their application and relented out of respect to the Navy.

In order to appreciate the next few stories, you need to use your imagination. It's about a make-believe place. Where things allegedly happen, let's call this make-believe place, Disney Discrimination Land or World; depends if you're in California or Florida. Judgmental things aren't supposed to happen in our beloved Disney parks. They can happen everywhere else in the world but not in our dreamlands. Ah, whom are we kidding? Deaths, suicide, and sex crimes already infiltrated it. Welcome to the stories of alleged discrimination involving both guests and cast members.

In February of 2013, an African American family filed a lawsuit against Disneyland claiming they were discriminated against because they weren't white. Jason and Annelia of San Diego visited the theme park with their son Elijah. The family encountered the White Rabbit character from Alice in Wonderland, and young Elijah wanted to get close to the character. The person in the costume allegedly refused to hug or touch Jason and Annelia's children. The rabbit was also impatient with the other African American kids; however, when a white family approached the hare, he acted entirely differently.

The rabbit showered the white kids with hugs and kisses, posed for pictures, and was very playful. Jason, Annelia, and their kids witnessed this and were upset. They took a trip over to guest services and lodged a formal complaint. The family said Disney offered them VIP tickets; when they declined them, they were offered $500 with the caveat of signing a confidentiality agreement.

The family declined that as well, in favor of a lawsuit, which was settled out of court in July of 2013. A hauntingly similar case also allegedly happened in 2013, but this time Donald Duck was the offender. Nastasia retained the same lawyer as Jason and Annelia in their case against Disneyland. This one is still pending.

Over the years both Disneyland and Walt Disney World have been sued for age discrimination and lack of diversity through their work force. Today, Disney has several programs through their human resources department, outlining the company's plan and commitment to culture and diversity. Entire web pages are dedicated to the subject on their careers website. In addition to the company's Corporate Responsibility Report, the company even has a chief diversity officer. Despite this proactive campaign, discrimination cases still happen here and there in the Disney work force.

In April 1994, Jo-Ann obtained her dream job. The forty-nine-year-old veteran private investigator was hired by Disney as a security hostess for Walt

Disney World. After Jo-Ann finished the training and orientation programs, she headed over to pick up her employee uniform. This is where her dream job turned into a nightmare. Jo-Ann couldn't fit into the regulation uniforms for female security hostesses.

None of Disney's uniforms would fit her five-foot-six, 190-pound body. She inquired if she could wear the uniform designed for men or go out and purchase garments that would fit. She would go ahead and sew or tailor them to fit her appropriately. Disney said no to both of her inquiries. Jo-Ann was then informed if she can't fit into their uniforms, she couldn't work in security. She was eventually transferred to another department. She went to work at the communications center, a position for which she was ill equipped. She claimed she wasn't trained properly for the position and her supervisors and coworkers were abusive.

The stress of her communications position, and grief over being denied employment at her desired position because of her size, made her ill and sent her to the hospital for care. After leaving the hospital, she filed a complaint with the Equal Employment Opportunity Commission. They granted her permission to sue Disney for discrimination and a lawsuit was filed in July of 1996. Jo-Ann's suit was settled before it went to court.

In October of 2005, Sukhbir was a twenty-four-year-old trumpet player seeking seasonal employment at Walt Disney World. Sukhbir had previous Disney show experience. The music major from the University of South Florida worked for the mouse as a trumpet player, dressing as a toy soldier during Christmas time. Sukhbir returned to Disney and applied for another band position. This time, he would be working without a head-to-toe costume.

Sukhbir is a practicing Sikh; his religious beliefs require him to wear a turban and grow a beard. During his employment interview, a Disney human resources employee probed Sukhbir about both his beard and turban; HR was initially skeptical about hiring him due to his appearance. After a phone call to another person in HR, he was informed that he could work in the band, but only if he wore a red turban as the other band members were wearing crimson-colored berets.

All seemed well for Sukhbir—that is, until Disney asked him to shave his beard, as it didn't fit the "Disney image." He refused to shave his beard and therefore didn't get the job. He tried for a similar position in 2006 and was met with the same requirements.

After two rounds of rejection, Sukhbir filed a lawsuit against Disney in 2008 for $1 million. The suit claimed he was denied his religious rights and a job at the park. He was told repeatedly he was a great musician, but he just didn't fit the look. After the suit was filed, Disney denied the claims. They insisted that Disney does not discriminate, and that the company makes accommodations that allow Sikhs and others with different needs to work at the giant resort. "We value and respect diversity in our cast members and treat each request [for an accommodation] individually. The type of accommodation varies with the type of request, job and location." This case was settled out of court.

A similar case happened across the country at Disneyland in August of 2012 when Imane, a Muslim woman, was working as a hostess at a restaurant in Disneyland's Grand Californian hotel. Imane's story started to surface in the news in the summer of 2010.

The trouble happened for her a year after she started working for Disney. She wanted to wear a hijab to work; a veil that covers the head. When she made her request to Disney to wear it as part of her uniform, they denied it. She even offered to wear something with matching colors and a Disney logo in an effort to have it match the rest of her uniform. Her suggestions were declined and she was informed that if she wore the hijab to work, she would be sent to work in the back of the restaurant so guests couldn't see her.

The other option for her was to wear a hat and scarf combination that Disney would create for her. Imane said that the hat and bonnet type combination Disney suggested was an insult to her religion, whereas Disney said the accommodation was a compromise to help appease all parties in the situation. The combination would cover her head, neck and chest and would be in line with Disney's costume guidelines for workers. Imane declined and went to work several times wearing her hijab. The restaurant's management asked her to work in the back of the restaurant, out of sight of the public. She refused that other position, and was sent home without pay.

Her situation became worse when she claimed that coworkers started calling her names like "terrorist" and "camel." She claimed that she informed management about this as well, and they did nothing to stop the situation.

Finally, in August of 2012, Imane filed a federal lawsuit against Disney, with help from the American Civil Liberties Union of Southern California. The case is still pending and was filed on the grounds of religious discrimination and harassment.

Everyone enjoys seeing their favorite Disney character roaming around the Disney parks, greeting one and all. They press the flesh like the mayors of Disney town. According to a few Disney guests over the years, some of the characters got a little carried away and pressed too much flesh. They claimed that their chance to embrace a Disney character evolved into a downright assault, either groping or physical abuse. These sensational, and often unfounded claims, happened at both Disneyland and WDW.

A case in 1976 at Disneyland had claims of assault and battery, false imprisonment and humiliation. A woman claimed a character dressed as a pig ran up to her, grabbed her breasts, and started squealing "mommy." The woman later dropped the case when she was shown a photo of the pig she accused; the costume didn't have working arms.

Five years later, also at Disneyland, a nine-year-old girl claimed she was beaten up by Winnie the Pooh. The claims were that Pooh had slapped her in the face so hard she suffered from constant headaches, bruising, and possible brain damage. Disney took this one right to court. They presented exhibit A; the costume and the man wearing the costume at the time. The man put the costume on and did the dance he was doing when the nine-year-old girl pulled his tail. Donning the costume for all to see, the jury noticed his arms were too low to the ground and he couldn't connect with the girl's face with his hands; case dismissed.

A similar case went to court back in 2004 after an incident at Walt Disney World. A mother and daughter claimed that while posing for a picture with the character, Tigger, the character touched each of their breasts. The character was arrested and charged with one count of lewd and lascivious molestation of a child between twelve and fifteen and one count of simple battery. The family didn't immediately sue Disney in civil court. Instead, they proceeded with the criminal charges against the person in the costume to help build a better civil suit. The accused employee was even offered a plea, which he denied. The case went to trial and Tigger was acquitted, after he put on his character costume and showed the court the inflexibility and lack of sight lines while portraying Tigger.

It wasn't only Mickey's pals who were accused of improper behavior. Mickey himself battled a charge back in 1983. Paula of New Jersey claimed that during a visit to the Magic Kingdom, a drunken Mickey assaulted and attacked her four-year-old son. Paula claimed that after her son grabbed Mickey's tail outside of Cinderella's castle, the mouse snapped and grabbed her son and threw him against an iron railing. The boy was not only physically injured but needed psychological therapy. She sued Disney and the person playing Mickey for $3 million each. She claimed that the actor in the costume was drunk. Six years later, in July of 1989, her case was dismissed and Mickey was exonerated.

Each day in this country, $35 million of merchandise is shoplifted out of retail stores, a practice 1 in 11 people in America are guilty of. The Disney parks are obviously no different. During the early to mid-1990s, Disney had a 95 percent success rate at prosecuting guests with "sticky fingers." From 1994 to 1996, Walt Disney World alone had over 1,200 guest arrests for the petty crime.

Obviously, Disney security is watching you, especially around their merchandise. Sometimes their diligence crosses the line and encroaches on being overzealous or outright criminal. This is exactly the case for a handful of guests that filed lawsuits against Mickey when they were accused of shoplifting, despite still being in possession of their purchase receipts.

In October 1989, Lonnie and Karen of Idaho took their five-year-old daughter to Disneyland. The family won a trip to the park after their daughter took first prize in a contest held by their local television station. After enjoying much of their day at the park, the family stopped to buy a character piggy bank. The cashier rung up the purchase without bagging it and their little daughter played with the bank while she was pushed in her stroller. Once the family rolled out of the store, a Disney security guard flashed a badge and said, "Your little girl in the stroller has removed an item from the store without paying for it. That makes her a shoplifter."

Karen offered to show the receipt, but the guard refused and told Karen she was an accessory to her daughter's crime. He then proceeded to tell her to stop crying and making a scene. He escorted them into the security office for questioning. Two and a half hours later, after being questioned about the shoplifting, a supervisor finally examined the receipt she offered up initially. Not only did Karen purchase the bank, but she was overcharged for it as well.

Oh yeah, while the security supervisor was checking out her receipt, he noticed in her handbag that she had packed dried fruit and nuts for her daughter. He scolded her for that as well, as it was against park rules to bring food into the park. Finally realizing their mistake, security let the family go, refunded the cost of their tickets and drove them back to their hotel in a nice Cadillac. A spin in a luxury car wouldn't be enough for the family. They filed a $1 million lawsuit against the park, which was settled out of court in September of 1992.

Also at Disneyland, Denise took her son to the park to celebrate his third birthday in February of 1996. She purchased her son a twenty-one-inch Mickey Mouse doll at a souvenir stand. Hours later, she said she was approached by a plainclothes security guard, who informed her that he had watched her steal the doll minutes earlier at the Star Trader store near Space Mountain—ironically, the same store where Karen was accused of stealing.

Denise and her fiancé denied the charges and told security they purchased it and had the receipt. Security didn't listen and Denise at the moment couldn't find the receipt. They interrogated the two separately for over two hours and eventually escorted them from the park. As they were being led out of the park, eureka, Denise found the receipt. She took it to a park employee to verify it, but Disney didn't care or drop the charges.

At the time, Disney would fine shoplifters in addition to contacting police. In the first few years of the 1990s, Disney would collect fines of up to $500 from shoplifting suspects after detaining them. In fact, Denise received a $275 fine from Disney in the mail. If she paid it she could avoid being prosecuted. This fine was one of the ways she found out that Disney didn't drop her charges. Denise paid the fine, and Disney still didn't relent. The two parties went to trial in June 1996. Denise was found not guilty, which set the stage for her to sue Disney for damages. This case also went to trial and Disney lost there as well. A judge awarded Denise $65,000; $30,000 in punitive damages, $35,000 in compensatory damages and the security guard was also ordered to pay her $750.

At first glance, this last story could have probably made its way into "Lights, Camera, Accident!" and maybe even "Mickey Mania." But for some folks, it is all about the money, and that leads us to Randle and his experience at Disneyland.

In April of 1994, Randle was a passenger aboard Disneyland's SkyWay gondola ride. The attraction took guests on an aerial trek between Fantasyland and Tomorrowland. The attraction had a pretty impressive safety record; there were no major accidents or incidents. Randle's trip changed that when he fell over twenty feet out of the gondola and landed in a tree near the Alice in Wonderland attraction.

Randle was rushed to the hospital with back and neck pain. At the time of his release from the hospital, Disneyland said that he had only suffered minor injuries and couldn't imagine how this accident happened. They stated that the ride had a two-step locking process. Both lock and handle had to be opened from the outside in order for the door to open. The attraction was checked that morning before the park opened.

Disney was befuddled as to what happened, even OSHA came to the park to check things out and couldn't determine the cause. Conversely, Randle's attorney (he sued for $25,000, claiming he fell out of the ride) said, "He wasn't doing anything improper and he certainly wasn't trying to get out of the ride. Randle had no warning of the events and just by the grace of God was he able to survive the mishap." This statement was basically a big fat, see you in court!

In the days leading up to the court date, something out of the ordinary happened. No, Disney didn't settle, instead Randle dropped his case. He wrote a letter to the court and to Disney apologizing for his fall from the ride. He did it purposely for a payday. In his letter, he called his lawsuit ill advised, his actions regretful, and was sorry for the negative publicity Disney received.

On that note, next up are the cases where Disney is the hunter and not the hunted. If Randle thought his case brought some negative publicity to Disney, wait until you read about the first story in Pirates of the Courtroom.

6
CHAPTER

Pirates of the Court Room

In 2010, a jury found sixty-year-old John guilty of misdemeanor battery after he was arrested for groping Minnie Mouse at Walt Disney World. He was sentenced to two days in jail and fifty hours of community service.

In April of 1989, three day care centers in Hallandale, Florida (located in southern Florida, much closer to Miami than Orlando) did something they thought was pretty benign. They painted the exterior of their buildings with five-foot murals. The murals depicted everyone's favorite mouse, duck, and dog; Mickey, Minnie, Donald and Goofy. When city officials noticed the outdoor artwork, they did a little investigation.

The centers didn't have a license for their murals. Code enforcement stepped in and notified the owners that they needed a sign variance for their properties. They were also informed that the murals may not take up more than twenty square feet of wall space. Municipal trouble wasn't the only issue sparked by the art. Disney heard of the situation and sent someone down to verify the claims of their copyrighted characters being used without permission. Sure enough, there they were, in all their illegal glory.

Disney reached out to the centers and ordered them to remove their copyright-protected icons. The centers were hovering in the dangerous territory of Disney copyright infringement. After the story made national news, a two-month campaign was waged by a group of toddlers, folks from around the country, and the city of Hallandale, pleading with Disney to allow the murals to stay up.

Disney's response was and will always be a big, fat no! As their legal representatives dug their heels into the sand, they reminded everyone that the day-care centers were breaking copyright laws. Lawbreaking aside, the public may think that Disney had supported or sponsored these centers by allowing the characters to reside on their buildings. Disney does approve of and allows schools all over the country to use their characters inside classrooms and on bulletin boards, but an outside wall may imply they are in business at the location. The murals were ordered off within thirty days.

Disney, through a spokesperson said, "We must protect our copyrights even though we are sympathetic to the children's affection for the characters. If we were to allow them to use the characters, then we would have to allow everyone else to do so. If we don't protect our trademarks and copyrights, we could lose them and be out of business."

Despite the vast majority of the public thinking Disney was being overprotective and a bit of a jerk, the point was taken and the logical argument understood. Not to worry though, a few other legendary copyright-protected characters went on to adorn the day-care centers' walls. Universal Studios was getting ready to start their crosstown rivalry with Mickey in Orlando by opening their own theme park in 1990. In an effort to win over some kids and gain some free PR, Universal's artists came in and eradicated Disney. They painted Woody Woodpecker, Fred Flintstone, George Jetson and other characters owned by Universal and Hanna-Barbera.

The crisis was averted, and all parties were happy, yet some people were still annoyed by Disney's reaction and the turn of events. Mickey debuted in public in 1928, and after all of these years, how are these characters still protected, or better yet, why?

Over the decades, and prominently with their first full-length animated feature back in 1937, the company utilizes stories that are a part of the public domain. Despite all this success from the public domain, Disney themselves aren't necessarily a fan of it; at least in the sense of it being a two-way street. They love to use the centuries-old stories and music from it, but don't want their works to become a part of it.

So what is all this talk about the public domain? Well, it's exactly as it sounds. They are works not protected by copyright. Permission from the creator is not needed to use the work. Be it music, art, literature or, of course, cartoons. No permission needed also means no license, fee, or royalty paid.

The first American Copyright Act was implemented in 1790. It granted the copyright owner fourteen years of protection, which could be renewed for another fourteen years. In 1831, the Act was revised to extend copyright ownership to twenty-eight years with another renewal of fourteen years.

Another amendment to the Act happened in 1909. The initial copyright was still twenty-eight years but the renewal could extend past fourteen years and go to twenty-eight years. The Copyright Act was again amended in 1976. Its framework is for the most part, what stands today. In an effort not to sound like an intellectual property textbook, I'll try and keep it simple. The revision from 1976 extended the copyright term to fifty years after the copyright owner's death. For works created before 1978 that hadn't yet entered the public domain, they were granted another seventy-five years of copyright protection.

When 1998 rolled around, the Copyright Act was amended again. Had it not been, the early 2000's would have seen an even bigger influx of Mickey Mouse products on the market; if that were even possible. The reason for this surge in Mickey would have been due to Disney's most prized possessions entering the public domain. Disney pushed hard for this not to happen. They lobbied for a copyright extension, as they obviously wanted to keep those early works of Mickey (and his profitability) out of the public domain. President Bill Clinton signed the Copyright Term Extension Act, also known as the Mickey Mouse Act, or Sonny Bono Act, into law.

The law did a few things. First, it extended the ownership of copyrights. Instead of the term standing at fifty years after the copyright owner's death, it was extended to seventy years after their death. The extension for corporate works, anonymous works, or works for hire, became ninety-five years from the date of publication or 120 years from the date of creation, whichever expires first.

Next, it basically froze things from hitting the public domain until 2019. Works created and copyrighted in 1923 or after that were still protected as of 1998 will not lose their copyright. Plain and simple, nothing new would enter into the public domain. Most importantly for Disney, the roughly $8 billion a year they generated in 1998 with anything connected to Mickey's name stays under lock and key. It will certainly be interesting to see what happens in 2019.

Disney fought hard in the 1990s to get the Copyright Term Extension Act passed. They formed a lobbying committee and made political donations where they thought it would be most advantageous. With their copyrights still intact, Disney continues to patrol the world looking for those infringing upon their characters in an effort to make a quick buck off one of the most recognizable faces in the world.

Let's be honest, unless you're an expert on intellectual property or work at the United States Patent and Trademark Office, the subject of Disney copyright and trademark infringement can be a bit dry. With Disney being so recognizable and a savvy merchandiser of thousands of products, they encounter an enormous amount of bootleg, fraud, and infringement cases; these are the more interesting ones.

Most of these cases begin when a Disney piracy inspector notices bootlegged items. In the mid-1980s Disney even had investigators that went on-site to retailers and performed piracy "sweeps." In 1986, they sued nearly one hundred retailers in California during one sweep alone. The company also routinely receives submissions from stockholders, consumers that bought bogus products and even anonymous tips. There is an antipiracy tip line and e-mail address on their corporate website, should you be so inclined.

As you can imagine, with a company that licenses and merchandises everything from piñatas to pencils, there are more infringement cases than you can imagine. From 1985 to 1989 alone, they sued 1,700 people for copyright infringements pertaining to just Mickey, and this was in the days before people started to get ubercreative with their computers and the Internet. As Michael Eisner once said, "When it comes to intellectual property, you can't be too litigious."

With that being said, let's dive right into bootleg Mickey. One of the more notable cases to test Disney's patience started in 1971. Dan O'Neill was a successful cartoonist; he had a national newspaper audience and, at the time, was the youngest syndicated cartoonist in history, at age twenty-one during the early 1960s.

Dan was obviously a very talented cartoonist and witty writer to achieve such success at an early age. His comic strip, *Odd Bodkins*, had a loyal following for years. The papers that carried his strip gave him only a few parameters. Keep it benign; no politics, religion or sex. Dan initially stuck to the schematic, but as society and culture changed, Dan couldn't help but insert some of his own cultural commentary into the strip.

Slowly, *Odd Bodkins* became political. This led to a loss of newspapers willing to feature it. By 1970, the San Francisco Chronicle, the very paper that gave him his start, also cut ties with Dan. The strip took aim at many things synonymous with America and American culture. Many of the targets were what the public considered icons of greatness; former presidents, movie stars and the country's favorite mouse.

Apparently, Dan became jaded with society. A society he thought had become too watered down, phony, and artificial. Not everything is always a happily-ever-after story, and Dan thought this country became this way due in part to Walt Disney and Mickey Mouse. With his work out of the mainstream, he decided to zero in on the catastrophic cultural catalyst, Mickey. Dan went "underground" with a group of friends and animators. He decided to make his voice heard. He was going to take the mouse out the best way he knew how: publish a comic titled "Air Pirates" featuring a bootleg Mickey Mouse.

Mickey, known for doing the right thing, was portrayed doing the wrong things. He was drinking, smoking, getting high, and having sex. It would be Mickey and friends as you've never seen them before. The names and identities were not changed, and keep in mind these artists were very creative, not only with the story lines, but also with their artwork. They were all professional artists, so the works looked as if it came from the Disney studio; we're talking a damn near exact Mickey.

In 1971, Dan and crew had around twenty thousand comics printed. They wanted everyone, especially Disney, to see their works. They staged some creative ways to get their comics out to the masses. They hired "winos" to dress up as police and sell the comics on street corners. They even dropped comic books onto a town from a blimp. This creativity still didn't get Disney's attention the way Dan wanted it. He was itching for a fight with a corporate behemoth. Well, if Disney won't come to you, it's time to go to Disney. A friend's father was an executive with Disney. Dan had his friend sneak copies of "Air Pirates" into a board meeting and leave them out for all executives to see. Dan got his wish. Disney sued him for copyright infringement, and a legal fight ensued—one that lasted nearly nine years.

The case could have been open and shut. Dan clearly copied the copyrighted works flawlessly; he even admitted it to court. But this case wasn't going away, and neither was Dan. In 1972, Disney won an injunction against the Air Pirates, barring them from publishing any more comics with Disney characters. In 1975, Disney won $200,000 in damages and a restraining order against Dan, who continued to draw and taunt Mickey and Disney. This eventually lead to a stint in jail after violating court orders and continuing to sell naughty Mickey cartoons; hey, they still needed to pay their legal fees.

Finally, after years of back and forth and a refusal by the Supreme Court to hear the case, an agreement was reached. Dan would stop, and Disney would drop the contempt charge and judgments against him. For Dan, this whole debacle wasn't entirely about his social commentary and Disney's influence over culture. There was more to his motive, and he dubbed it the "Mouse Liberation Front."

Dan argued that his comics were covered under freedom of speech with the First Amendment and under the laws of fair use. A judge ruled that the First Amendment right to expression only applied to the fair use of such material, and "a parody may not consist of a 'substantial' taking or 'outright copying' of a copyrighted work." While the Supreme Court refused to hear the case, Justice Anthony Kennedy, in passing, commented that the Air Pirates were "profiteers who did no more than place the characters from a familiar work in novel or eccentric poses."

The lawsuits ended around 1980 in regards to the Air Pirates. But years later, Dan would sue Disney, claiming they stole one of his copyrighted characters. He claimed Roger Rabbit was based off his drug-dealing rabbit, Roger, from his comic *The Tortoise and the Hare*. The case was eventually dropped.

Going from one high-profile copyright case to another, although this one didn't last nearly as long. This story pitted Mickey against Oscar. In March of 1989, Disney sued the Academy Awards for their illegal use of Snow White in a ten-minute song-and-dance routine during the award ceremony. Days after the award show, Disney filed suit against the Academy of Motion Picture Arts and Sciences for copyright infringement and unfair competition. This suit was settled with a public apology from the Academy.

In the next case, our Disney heroine transforms from Snow White to Ho White. An Australian beer company, the Foundry, took a page out of Dan O'Neill's book and placed Snow White in a compromising position. The fruit-flavored beer purveyor created an advertising beer campaign that put Snow White in bed with her seven little friends. The advertisement featured Ms. White in bed topless with only a blanket covering her. She had a glazed look on her face and was blowing smoke rings. The cartoon had her looking rather ragged, as if she just went seven rounds. The advertisement didn't last very long. It debuted in October of 2009 and made its way around the globe pretty quickly. Shortly after it was picked up by countless news organizations, the company took their ad down. As they put it, they had "brief contact with Disney"—'nuff said there.

The next case takes us over to China, where Disney has a strong presence. Disney has battled trademark and copyright issues in China for a very long time—like so many other American companies. Back in the late 1980s and early 1990s, when Michael Eisner signed a deal with the Chinese government allowing for Disney cartoons to be shown on government television, Disney asked for the government's help in curbing knock-off and bootleg merchandise. Their struggle still continues today, with thousands of counterfeit products being produced in China and making their way into this country.

In 2007, Disney sued a Chinese travel agency over their name. Disney had the Chinese high court order a travel agency named "D Land" change their name, as it could give the impression that the company was a part of the Walt Disney Company. Another case outside of the country had Disney's copyright team circling around a mall in West Edmonton, Canada.

Disney sued the West Edmonton Mall and their amusement park Fantasyland in 1992 over the use of the world Fantasyland. According to Disney's lawyers, Fantasyland didn't exist until Disney invented the word when they opened Disneyland in 1955. They also own the copyright to the word. Disney contended that allowing the West Edmonton Mall to use the

Fantasyland name is like allowing somebody to sell fake Rolex watches as if they were real. The mall's attorneys claimed the distance between Edmonton, Canada, and Anaheim was too great for a person to be confused and think they were going to a Disney property. In addition, the mall had been using the name since 1983, when their park opened. Disney won their case and Fantasyland became Galaxyland in 1995.

A popular story in the history and lore in creating Walt Disney World was Walt's use of "dummy" corporations to purchase his desired land in central Florida. AyeFour Properties, Latin-American Development, and Tomahawk Properties were some of the corporate names utilized to secure the tracts of land at reasonable prices. Walt felt if the landowners knew he was purchasing the land, the prices would skyrocket. He was correct; when word got out that he was making land purchases, neighboring plots of land increased in price substantially.

A group of businessmen took the opposite approach with their Florida real estate and land group in 1970. The year before Walt Disney World opened in 1971, Disney was already defending their name in the sunshine state. Samuel Rose along with Max and Irwin Krauss had the great idea of naming their real-estate business that sold large tracts of land in Florida, Disney Area Acreage Inc. (Disney Land Real Estate must have sounded too generic).

The trio was hauled into court on trademark infringement with claims that their enterprise solely took on the Disney name to "derive benefit from Disney's reputation and goodwill." Using the Disney name would likely cause confusion for prospective purchasers of land, allowing them to think the company is somehow associated with the mouse. Needless to say, the court ordered Disney Area Acreage Inc. dissolved and sent the men back to the corporate drawing board to pick out a new name.

Disney and their intellectual property attorneys continue to bounce around a few entrepreneurs. In 2010 and 2011 Disney sued Bouncing 4 Fun and San Jose Party Rentals of California for selling and renting "bounce houses" or "moon bounces." The bounces were either illegally Disney-themed or featured their copyrighted characters. In both cases Disney sued for upward of $500,000. They were successful in both cases.

Across the country in Lake County, Florida, practically on the mouse's doorstep, Disney sued a family business for $1 million in July of 2008. The family was running a small family entertainment party business. They rented moon bounces and provided live entertainment for the kiddies. The live entertainment was in the way of performers dressing up as Winnie the Pooh, Eeyore, and Tigger. Disney sued them for exploiting the copyright and trademark likenesses in these costumes that were unauthorized reproductions.

The small company claimed they didn't know they were doing anything illegal and bought the costumes on eBay for $500 from a company in Peru. Disney ordered them to stop their entertainment and forfeit their costumes to the company. In their legal documents filed in court addressing Disney's suit, the guilty party noted they were a very small company run by a family currently on public assistance and trying to make ends meet for their children.

This is a situation Disney encounters frequently with the pervasiveness of the Internet. Small vendors, wannabe entrepreneurs, and creative folks aren't safe from Disney either. If you have a keen eye for arts and crafts and Disney, be careful putting your unlicensed creative works up on eBay or Etsy. Disney is known to scour those websites and have auctions and listings removed with an accompanying "cease and desist" letter.

Enough is enough, right? You get the picture. Disney is highly protective of their characters and name. They are the biggest and most lucrative name in family entertainment and a cornerstone of many things in our society today.

No one can escape Disney's copyright grasps; from underground cartoons to mom-and-pop businesses, no one is immune. Well, almost no one. There have been a few diabolical miscreants where even Disney's legal eagles didn't want to get involved, and the mouse had to turn the other ear.

Disney is no stranger to pursuing litigation against companies abroad. In 2007, Disney faced something pretty troubling and devious internationally, the likes of which even they never experienced before. Hamas, the Palestinian Islamic organization, went on Al-Aqsa television to preach Islamic domination and hatred to Israel and the United States.

Ironically, they chose the face and symbol of America known around the world as their voice to spew their messages. A television show geared toward children featured a person dressed in costume as Mickey Mouse. The character was named Farfour and, in a high-pitched Mickey-esque voice, conveyed his anti-American and anti-Zionist views.

Disney certainly took note but chose not to address the situation and bring further recognition to it. As Robert Iger said, "We didn't mobilize our forces and seek to either have the clip taken down or to make any broad public statement about it. I just didn't think it would have any effect. I think it should have been obvious how the company felt about the subject. We were appalled by the use of our character to disseminate that kind of message. I think any time a group seeks to exploit children in that matter, it's despicable. We simply made the decision that we would not either create or prolong a public discourse on the subject by making a loud public statement."

Another state-run television station was guilty of highjacking Mickey, this time with a far less devious message. In the summer of 2012, North Korea held a concert for their almighty leader, Kim Jong Un. The concert was broadcast on television and featured a rather upbeat theme for this snarky government.

The ensemble cast of Mickey, Minnie, Winnie the Pooh, and Tigger paraded around, sang, and danced while an enormous screen behind them played clips from *Beauty and the Beast* and *Snow White*.

Clearly, there was nothing Disney could do about this situation. Our government won't approach this rogue country, as there are no diplomatic relations. That didn't stop the US State Department from voicing its displeasure in the media. They publicly scolded the country and urged them to respect intellectual property rights.

I guess if a government doesn't provide food and care for an enormous amount of their country, they aren't going to care about offending Mickey. This is another interesting example of a group that hates America but loves our mouse. By default, one can surmise that these folks must secretly love our culture, as our powerful mouse is the true cultural king.

CHAPTER 7

It's an Accessible World After All

In March 1997, David went to the restroom at 11:00 a.m. near the entrance of the Magic Kingdom at Walt Disney World. Seconds after he entered, a man came up behind him and put one hand around his mouth; his other hand brandished a stiletto knife. David was robbed of his cash and wallet. Everything happened so fast, and he never got a chance to see the robber's face.

A lengthy Associated Press newspaper article published in June 1984 detailed Walt Disney World's efforts to help ensure a comfortable stay for handicapped and disabled guests. The article encouraged folks needing assistance to write to Disney for their "Disabled Guests Guide Book" in preparation for a trip to see Mickey. The guide was also available to guests already on Disney property. This article was interesting, as it would be six years until federal law required places such as Walt Disney World to make accommodations for handicapped guests.

The guidebook had information about renting wheelchairs, which attractions are wheelchair-accessible, accommodations for sight- and hearing-impaired visitors and parade viewing areas for wheelchair guests. A to Z, it was all there back in the 1980s. Today, much of the same is still offered by Disney. It is conveyed via their bevy of websites and countless other sites on the Internet, from some good folks who share their own experiences and "know-how" in an effort to conquer Disney despite some limitations.

The Disney parks are able to accommodate guests with a variety of disabilities. For those with visual impairments, braille maps, and an audio description device are available to explain many of the attractions and visual elements of the park.

Those who are hearing impaired have their choice of reflective captioning, sign language interpreters, video captioning, or assisted listening devices. All guests, regardless of their disability, be it hearing, visual, or wheelchair bound, are offered modified guest rooms to make their stay comfortable and safe; which wasn't always the case.

As the disability climate evolved for the better over the decades, primarily with the American Disability Act of 1990 (ADA) and an additional amendment in 2008 and modifications in 2010, these laws ensured equal treatment for disabled folks. The laws are an effort to make life as livable as possible for the disabled and thwart any discrimination attempts in a public or commercial setting.

According to some, discrimination wasn't entirely eliminated at Disney. Looking back over the years, many guests complained and sued. The claims were/are that Disney didn't do enough to accommodate some of the folks who frequent their parks.

There was a lawsuit in 1998 complaining about the handicap parking spots at Disney's Animal Kingdom being noncompliant to ADA specifications; along with claims about ill-equipped bathrooms and various ramps around the park without hand rails.

Several lawsuits throughout the early part of the 2000s indicated not enough hotel rooms, facilities and even attractions throughout their Florida resorts and parks were handicap accessible, which denied certain folks the ability to enjoy the full Disney experience. Most lawsuits weren't seeking money but instead seeking corrections to the problems.

We know from our day-to-day lives outside of all things Disney, not everything is one size fits all, so to speak. Disney being a purveyor and provider of countless things to an even greater number of people, at times had trouble keeping up with appropriate accommodations for certain folks. Nearly fifty-seven million people, or 20 percent of the population according to the most recent census, have a disability. At times disabled folks have felt discriminated against or excluded at Disney's parks. The situations needed to be rectified by Disney, and usually were. From time to time, the company needed a little push from a lawsuit or the government.

Despite these "pushes," their plans weren't always incorporated smoothly into their theme parks or without initial resistance. Disney has accommodated and made many attractions accessible for those in a wheelchair. On the resort side of the business, Disney redesigned many pools to be zero entry, along with incorporating chair lifts to assist in getting guests into the pool, but the changes didn't always reflect their attitude and other theme park operators' willingness to make these changes.

In early 2000, articles by the Associated Press outlined proposed changes to the theme park industry for 2001 and 2002. Members of the industry, Disney included, initially called them unfriendly to operators. The changes were deemed restrictive, expensive and even dangerous. Yet, despite the push back from operators, most of these changes were signed into law and are in operation daily at theme parks today. But during this time there were certainly some bumps along the way.

In March of 1997, Disneyland quietly tried to end their twenty-year-old charitable program, Happy Hearts. The program allowed children with disabilities to enjoy Disneyland at a reduced ticket price. The program ran twice a year for six days, usually in February and November. It was always wildly successful as tens of thousands of handicapped children from all over southern California descended upon the park. Once word of the program's demise hit the public, Disney and the Los Angeles Times were inundated with complaints and outrage over their decision. Happy Hearts was starting to sound coldhearted by Disney. A few days of backlash and bad publicity and Disney reinstated the program. Today, Disneyland runs a similar program under a different name, the Community Involvement Program.

In the opening paragraphs of this chapter, Disney's efforts to accommodate handicapped or disabled guests were touched upon. Some applauded their efforts while others lambasted them. They said Disney was not being proactive and was still in violation of the laws, particularly for the visually and hearing impaired.

In September of 2010, three visually impaired women filed a class-action lawsuit against Disney. The women, each long time lovers and visitors to the Disney parks, claimed Disney's websites, parks, and hotels were in violation of the ADA.

The ADA requires companies to respect the needs of visually impaired folks, thus they need to accommodate them with the use of a screen reader (a software program that interprets what is displayed on a computer screen and then is heard audibly with text-to-speech programs or sent to a braille output device). The complaint filed against Disney indicated that many of their websites were full of audio and video trailers, which overpower the audio of the screen readers and can't be turned off by people who can't operate a mouse. The websites also featured the computer program Flash, which the visually impaired can't interpret with their own software programs.

Once inside the Disney parks, the lawsuit claimed that Disney didn't provide menus, maps or schedules in formats for the visually impaired. In addition, Disney wasn't accommodating for those requiring service dogs, nor did they offer discounted admission to support companions the visually impaired need to function on a daily basis. The complaint also contended that Disney denied it owed any social obligation to persons as a group. They made decisions regarding accommodations for their disabled guests on an individual, as-needed basis and not as a company-wide policy.

By 2011, a federal judge certified the class-action status for the four subclasses of the case and allowed for the lawsuit to proceed. The certified complaints brought Disney to the negotiating table. After a bit of give and take, the settlement was reached in January 2013 and was approved by the court. The agreement for the four subclasses, website, communication, service animal, and infrastructure, brought much of the desired justice the suit initially requested.

Some of the more notable settlement terms were: Disney cast members must read menus to visually impaired people if asked. A telephone hotline for impaired guests to receive menu information, park hours, parade schedules and show information would be established. Large fixed-braille maps for both Walt Disney World and Disneyland, and mobile braille maps would be developed for handheld devices that operate via GPS. This would allow guests to meander through the park and navigate to attractions with the device. Disney would provide designated service animal relief areas, along with a temporary kennel to house service animals when they can't join their owner on an attraction. Disney costumed characters must interact with disabled guests without acknowledging the obvious presence of their service animal. Disney must also provide parade preferred viewing areas for visually impaired guests. Lastly, Disney must give one hundred one-day passes each to two charities that support the visually impaired. Disney was given one year to implement these, and other agreed upon, changes from the settlement.

Hearing-impaired guests seeking better accommodations at Disney also received some help from the government but without the need for a class-action lawsuit. In the mid-1990s, the US Department of Justice received a series of complaints from hearing-impaired guests claiming that they were "denied effective communication as required by the ADA" during their visit to Disney. The government agency and Disney collaborated over a period of two years, to create and implement a system within their parks to aid in improving visits for the hearing impaired.

The announcement came in early 1997 and outlined a framework of comprehensive auxiliary aides throughout both Disneyland and Walt Disney World. With advanced notice, parks on both coasts would begin offering sign language interpreters at no cost to the guest. The interpreters were made available for parades, staged performances, and other entertainment featured throughout the parks. Advanced audio-visual aids and closed-captioning systems were also implemented into over one hundred attractions.

Disney attractions that utilize a theatre as their medium to entertain received a system called rear-window captioning. The rear-window system projects captions on a screen in the back of the theatre's wall in mirror image, at the hearing-impaired person's seat, anywhere in the theatre; a small plexiglass panel is placed in front of the guest and catches the reflection of the text that was projected behind them on the theatre wall. The person is now able to read the closed captioning from his or her seat via the specialized panel.

In 2001, a revolutionary personal transportation device took the country by storm. Most people have seen them by now. The two-wheeled, self-balancing, battery-powered Segway that allows people to virtually glide by quietly at up to twelve miles an hour and travel nearly twenty-five miles per charge of the battery. When it debuted, proponents touted it as a vehicle that will change the way we live, and the way we get around day in and day out. Never mind the several thousand dollar price tag, think about how much money will be saved when you ditch your four-wheeled, gas-guzzling car and hop aboard the two-wheeled mystery machine.

Soon cities all over the country and world were offering Segway tours. Disney, always looking to maintain their pop-culture relevancy, climbed aboard the Segway bandwagon with tours at EPCOT (along with a chance for guests to take a spin on one at Innoventions) and Disney's California Adventure.

There was even a story in The Wall Street Journal in 2008, when gas prices were soaring, that profiled a fifty-four-year-old Disneyland employee who commuted twelve miles to work on his Segway. The novel transportation was being utilized not only personally but also commercially with law enforcement and businesses (Disney is one of the largest purchasers of Segways in the country but they are used "back stage"). Even the disabled were starting to deploy them as a means to get around instead of wheelchairs and scooters.

As time progressed, all was not great in the land of the Segway. Many cities and municipalities banned folks from traversing down sidewalks on them. Emergency rooms started to see Segway-related injuries. Broken bones, brain damage, and bumps and bruises were some of the lawsuits filed against Segway dealers and the manufacturer. The same news outlets that flooded the public with news stories about the Segway's ingenuity were featuring stories about the various accidents involving the upwardly mobile. There were riders getting arrested for DWI; one proud owner managed to do this three times. People running over toddlers, others being hit by passing cars, and unfortunately, even death after riding a Segway off a cliff; remember this one for later.

As discussed earlier in the book, Disney has had issues from time to time with guests speeding in their power chairs. Remember Katrina back in 1995, who had her annual pass to Disneyland suspended because she was cited for speeding too many times. With large crowds of people, along with a smattering of wheelchairs and power chairs, Disney thought it would be best to ban the Segway from their parks. Seems fair enough right? Having a large stride can sometimes hinder one from meandering through the crowds at any of the parks, let alone the idea of wheeling about upright on a vehicle that can hit twelve miles per hour.

Well, not everyone was on board with Disney's ban. In fact, there was a growing contingency of disabled folks that used Segways instead of wheelchairs or scooters. Three of them in fact wanted to visit Walt Disney World aboard their vehicle and were denied access; subsequently, the trio filed a lawsuit against the park, citing discrimination under the American with Disabilities Act. The November of 2007 suit claimed that four thousand to seven thousand disabled people rely on their Segway as a primary means of transportation. The Segway offers more mobility and dignity than a wheelchair. One of the plaintiffs suffered from multiple sclerosis, another lost his foot in an accident, and the third suffered from Lou Gehrig's disease.

A similar situation also played out across the country at Disneyland. In May of 2006, Tina, who suffers from muscular dystrophy, inquired to Disneyland if she could visit the park on her Segway to celebrate her birthday with her daughter, as she had never been there. Disneyland informed Tina they would not be able to honor her request for safety reasons. In August of 2007, Tina filed suit against Disney alleging violations of the federal ADA and California law; she also filed similar suits against Sav-On Drug Store, the California Department of Motor Vehicles, and Santa Monica Ford.

This court case, like so many others Disney finds itself involved in, trickled through the overburdened California legal system. Disney's lawyers were steadfast in their argument during the seven years of court proceedings at the state and federal level.

They declared the Segway an unstable two-wheeled device that could accelerate quickly in forward and reverse. These movements could injure not only the rider but also the pedestrians in the vicinity—most notably in close quarters, where someone might inadvertently bump into the Segway, enabling it to lunge forward or backward. Tina and her legal defense continually pressed the issue of her never having an accident and citing the Americans with Disabilities Act and the California Disabled Persons Act. By law, Disney was required to reasonably accommodate her.

Disney's response to that claim was that her Segway was not a reasonable accommodation whereas a wheelchair or scooter was, which she was more than welcome to use. The two sides went back and forth, Disney would prevail and Tina's team would appeal. At one point in 2012, a federal court of appeals sided with Tina. They indicated Tina's use of Segway could be necessary even if she could use a wheelchair or scooter. This victory was short-lived when Disney appealed. While the above statement may be true, it didn't mean Disney must allow for Segways to be used at the park in her situation, Disney's legal defense persisted.

They noted that Segways are in essence always moving; a very small or minute motion will propel the vehicle. Additionally, Disney would have no way to quantify or control the situation or experience and skill level of the rider. Disney used the example of Jimi Heselden, the owner of the company that produced the Segway. He was killed when he lost control of one and went careening over a cliff and died. With this example and a few other tidbits of expert testimony, ultimately, Tina lost her case in July 2013. The courts reaffirmed previous decisions; Disney's ban on Segways doesn't break the Americans with Disabilities Act.

The outcome was similar for the Segway case filed by the three gentlemen in Florida, in regards to Walt Disney World. In this situation, The Supreme Court in April of 2013 put the brakes on forcing Disney to allow the two-wheel mobile at WDW. Instead, Disney came to a settlement; the company agreed to develop a four-wheeled electric stand-up vehicle in lieu of allowing Segways into their parks. Their vehicle debuted at Walt Disney World in May of 2013.

The same month, a Disney-designed stand-up four-wheel vehicle rolled into Walt Disney World, another Disney handicapped story soared into the media. Wednesday Martin, a social anthropologist, was conducting research for an upcoming book. Wednesday heard rumblings about a small faction of unscrupulous and wealthy Manhattan mothers that scammed their way to the head of the line at Walt Disney World.

The mothers would hire a disabled "tour guide" to circumvent the lines at the park. For a *mere* $130 an hour or the bargain price of $1,040 for an eight-hour day, this "disabled" person would enable the family to get the preferential treatment reserved for those actually needing special assistance. Those truly in need of assistance, be it physically or cognitively, were issued a guest assistance card by Disney. The card got the bearer and six accompanying guests an expedited wait time, if any. This was the card the mothers were playing.

When the news story broke in May 2013 and swept through the country like wild fire, a corrupt cottage industry was revealed. The "loophole" that existed to benefit those in need was shamelessly being exploited. As one of the mothers was quoted, "This is how the 1% does Disney. My daughter waited one minute to get on "It's a Small World"—the other kids had to wait two and a half hours. You can't go to Disney without a tour concierge." An interesting quote and use of the words "tour concierge."

The scenario this Manhattan mother described was really nothing new. The situation where someone profited from it other than Disney most certainly was. As cast members and even Disney will tell you, the deception or legal line cutting has been going on for years; it just never had the media buzz as it does today.

The *Wall Street Journal* ran an article in March of 1998 title, "Backdoor Disney: How to Beat the Lines—You Can Be Treated Like a VIP Even If You Aren't One." By and large, the story talked about how to avoid waiting in the never-ending queues for the Disney parks. It mostly centered on paying a fee to Disney and getting a Disney VIP tour guide. The guide can sprinkle some pixie dust and give you a different experience at the parks than most guests ever experience. Aside from the VIP tour guide, the article made mention of another form of special treatment to those who visit the park. Folks who work for companies that do business with Disney—most notably the companies that are corporate sponsors to attractions at the Magic Kingdom and EPCOT—get perks.

At the time of the article, FedEx was the sponsor of Space Mountain. Any FedEx employee could inform a cast member working the attraction that they worked for FedEx, they could then enjoy the corporate sponsorship benefits. They were able to cut the line and head in to the corporate lounge located at the attraction. The same was true at the time for AT&T at Space Ship Earth, among other attractions.

Interesting information about some fringe benefits, but there were actually two other compelling blurbs from the story. The first was Disney's test market in 1994 of their "Exclusive Passport Tour." This program allowed everyone in your party to get to the head of the line by shelling out $1,200 in 1994. This actually made the Manhattan Mom scandal a good deal!

The other storyline in this article was what they coined the "old wheelchair trick." The *Wall Street Journal* recounted the trip of Ira, a forty-eight-year-old attorney from guess where? New York!

Ira explained how he learned from a friend that he could get to the head of the line if someone in his party was in a wheelchair. So on his trip to Walt Disney World for his parents' fiftieth anniversary, he decided to put his eighty-one-year-old father into a Disney-rented wheelchair. To quote Ira, "There was no way I was going to wait," without a trace of guilt. For five dollars a day in the wheelchair rental fee, he knew the whole family could cut in line."

Obviously, Ira wasn't alone; people have been playing the wheelchair card for years and Disney knew it. For years, folks would stroll over to guest services and tell the smiling faces that they had a physical problem that wouldn't allow them to stand for long periods of time, or some other health/medical problem. Disney would hand over a special assistance card and folks would bypass the lengthy wait.

At Disneyland alone, the management knew their program was too lenient. There were days at the park where 20 percent of their visitors possessed the go-to-the-front-of-the-line card. In March 2004, Disneyland implemented changes to the program. They adopted a new solution to accommodate guests with disabilities. As a Disneyland spokesperson said, "tailored solutions to individual needs." The changes were, to ask more questions and see if they could find a better fit for the person and their issues, without freely handing over a pass.

The program introduced in 2004 at Disneyland was modeled after Walt Disney World's guest assistance card program; we now see how that worked out. Which brings us right back to the misbehaving Manhattan mothers. The exposure of their scheme resulted in changes to the guest assistance card program at both Disneyland and Walt Disney World. Maybe the change was long overdue or maybe the change only complicated an already difficult situation for both Disney and specific guests, only time will tell.

The new program, known as the Disability Access Service Card (DAS), was implemented in October of 2013. The DAS is still intended for guests who are unable to wait in a queue. Instead of bypassing the lines, Disney now issues the guest a ticket with a time to come back for immediate entry to the ride. The designated time is based on the current wait times for the attraction. Disney has dubbed this a "virtual wait." The guest is then free to visit another attraction, eat, wander around the park, and so forth.

Disney acknowledges that different situations require different accommodations, and they will try to work on an individual basis, although they are limited legally in what questions they may ask of guests. Disney acknowledges the whole situation is difficult and is sensitive to their guests' needs.

In creating and modifying this program, they consulted with a number of organizations about the best way to rectify the situation; unfortunately, many disabled guests and their families felt that the DAS was a terrible mistake. It was basically another form of the FastPass. Many complained that there was still obviously a wait time; while it wasn't in a queue, it still left families with too much time on their hands with children or those with special needs who have difficulty waiting. Most admitted that they couldn't spend the full day at the park with the physical or mental challenges their loved one faced, and the DAS made for a longer day, with less accomplished.

As noted, Disney consulted with health organizations on the program changes, most notably with the organization Autism Speaks. Ironically, the biggest complaints about the DAS were from families with children on the autism spectrum. In April of 2014, mothers of sixteen children with autism filed a lawsuit against Disney theme parks. They claimed that their children had difficulty waiting for things due to their cognitive issues. It was unreasonable and unrealistic for Disney to expect certain children to sit idle for an extended length of time in this environment. Thus the new program violated the ADA and didn't allow for individualized exceptions. The program's framework was too narrow, especially for those living with autism.

The lawsuit also alleged that there wasn't a widespread problem of abuse of the prior system Disney had in place. If any abuse did exist, persons with cognitive impairments did not commit it. There was no reason to make children and young adults with developmental disabilities collateral damage by withdrawing necessary accommodations. This lawsuit is still pending, and only time will tell how this all plays out.

CHAPTER 8

Morality in the Movies

In 1995, Disney released the controversial film *Powder*, directed by Victor Salva. The film's controversy stemmed from Victor, who was a registered sex offender. Victor was charged with having oral sex with a twelve-year-old boy in 1988. He was sentenced to three years in state prison.

Walt Disney's first foray into exposing the public to his creativity happened in movie theatres during the 1920s. As we know, what is socially acceptable today is vastly different from what was socially acceptable yesterday.

As the years progressed, certain socially acceptable acts were featured in or were a part of the periphery of many Disney classics. Two of these acts were drinking and smoking. Certainly, people drink and smoke today, but socially, things are a bit different as compared with Walt's days.

As our country has evolved, right or wrong, in most public places, being a smoker is in line with being a social pariah. Many cities have legally banned smoking in their restaurants, outdoor spaces, and municipal buildings. Even Disney has curbed the habit throughout most of their parks, dedicating fewer and fewer sections each year to those wishing to light up.

Today, tobacco companies explicitly detail the health risks and warnings on their products and have been shamed into creating nationwide television campaigns detailing the hazards of smoking, primarily to children and teens. Oh, and don't forget—cigarettes haven't been permitted to advertise on television or radio since 1971.

As for alcohol in this country, it is still a staple in our society. Whether it is a vehicle to unwind and relax after a day at work or a social component of nightlife, booze is here to stay, but it isn't without its dangers. In addition to the health and social effects of alcohol abuse, there are the repercussions of drinking and driving, something that has existed since the first wheeled transportation pulled up to a public house.

As alcohol pertains to Disney, spirits were something that by and large were banned at Disneyland and the Magic Kingdom at Walt Disney World for quite some time. EPCOT sells alcohol throughout the World Showcase, and so does Disney's California Adventure. In 2013, alcohol sales were finally permitted at the Magic Kingdom in Walt Disney World.

Obviously, not only Disney but also our society holds different views of both habits today as compared with the 1930s through the 1960s, when many of Disney's full-length animated classics were released. Today, it is unlikely that you would tune into the Disney channel or Disney Junior and see any reference to smoking or drinking. Nor would you see Buzz Lightyear sparking up a cig and then slugging down a beer in a movie.

However, back in the day when Walt was at the helm of animated features, there were instances of smoking and drinking in his animated classics. In 2004, a few social scientists set out to chronicle these instances. *Let Your Conscience Be Your Guide: Smoking and Drinking in Disney's Animated Classics* was a research study that documented the references or portrayals of alcohol and tobacco in the full-length Disney features from 1937 up to 2000.

The study found that over the decades, tobacco use decreased, while alcohol consumption increased. The researchers studied twenty-four G-rated Disney films and found 381 incidents of the two forms of substance abuse. To look at a few of the highlights; *Snow White* had zero tobacco and one very brief exposure to alcohol (a brief view of a beer keg in a scene). *Pinocchio* had seventeen exposures of tobacco and sixteen of alcohol. *Dumbo* had five tobacco exposures and twenty-four of alcohol. *Alice in Wonderland* had sixteen tobacco (or what is purported to be tobacco) exposures and zero alcohol. *Sleeping Beauty* had zero tobacco exposures and fifteen alcohol. *101 Dalmations* had twenty-one tobacco exposures and nine alcohol. Lastly, *Beauty and the Beast* is the big winner here, with zero tobacco and 116 alcohol. It seems as though the alcohol and cigarette portrayals seen in the films by and large parallel our social acceptance of both subjects in America today.

Okay, we've covered alcohol and tobacco as they pertain to Disney's films; how about sex? Disney, for the most part, tries to keep things wholesome. Obviously, there are no explicit or overtly sexual references in their family-centric films. How about subliminally or just under the surface? If you look at the right time, in the right movie and at the right angle, you may have some success.

Deny, Deny, Deny is usually the name of the game when someone is caught with their pants down; sorry for the pun there. This is exactly what Disney did in the mid to late 1990s when rumblings surfaced of some lewd things in their beloved movies. After the denial was over, Disney relied on the always safe "no comment" when questioned about their supposed naughty behavior. No comment works especially well when litigation ensues, which is exactly how this story went.

In December of 1995, Disney was sued for inappropriate subliminal or hidden images and references in several of their films. Janet Gilmer of Fayetteville, Arkansas, filed suit against the Walt Disney Corporation and their subsidiary Buena Vista Home Video for marketing movies with hidden sexual content offensive to children. This lawsuit was intended to become a class-action lawsuit for the entire country. So what was all this about, and how did this happen?

Well, back in September of 1995, the Associated Press picked up a story from a newspaper in Newport News, Virginia, the *Daily Press*. The *Daily Press* reported on a story from a biweekly newsletter published by the American Life League (ALL), the largest Catholic grassroots pro-life group in the country.

ALL was warning parents about a scandalous scene in *The Lion King*. Allegedly, ALL claimed there is a scene where Simba kicks up a cloud of dust, as the clouds float off the screen, the word "SEX" can be seen, only if you pause the video at the appropriate time and are paying careful attention.

When the AP reporter reached out to ALL, he was informed that *The Lion King* wasn't the only movie to feature lewdness. The group went on to explain that a Christian entertainment review magazine, *Movie Guide*, in March of 1995 ran a story titled "Aladdin Exposed." The story detailed a scene where Princess Jasmine, a tiger, and Aladdin are on a balcony and Aladdin mutters the words "all good teenagers take off your clothes."

The objectionable things didn't stop with those two movies. They get a bit more graphic in *The Little Mermaid*. In this movie, the group claimed that a bishop performing a wedding ceremony was aroused and displayed an erection. Religious boners aside, there were also stories of a salacious movie poster and VHS box cover; both featured an erect penis on one of the spires of a castle featured in the background of the scene.

When reporters followed up with Disney about these claims, they were adamant that they were false. In the case of *The Lion King,* Disney spokesperson, Rick Rhoades said, "The American Life League is imagining things in all three movies. They (Disney) are not going to recall VHS tapes of the movies. Seeing anything in *The Lion King* other than a good wholesome family film is purely perception. There is nothing there. It's just ridiculous to think that we'd put that in a movie."

As for *Aladdin,* Rhoades said the line was actually, "Scat, good tiger, take off and go"—which was something that actually may be accurate. The original publisher of the story, *Movie Guide,* sent the film to a professional sound studio and had them decipher the line, syllable by syllable. What they found was that the line was hard to understand. The words didn't sound like what Disney claimed, and it didn't sound like what they published in their story; thus, a retraction was printed in July 1995.

As for the "excited" bishop in *The Little Mermaid,* this time, the animator for the scene, Tom Sito, sounded off in denial, "If I wanted to put satanic messages in a movie, you would see it. That is silly."

Okay, fair enough, but we are talking about sex and lewdness in cartoons aimed at children. We aren't talking about Satanic messages like people claimed to hear in music by playing the record backward; something called back masking and everyone from the Beatles to Led Zepplin are purported to have done it. The satanic urban legends involving back masking was brought about by fundamentalist Christian groups including preacher, Gary Greenwald, and Minister Jacob Aranza, who wrote an entire book about the subject in 1982 called *Backward Masking Unmasked*. Both claimed evil, satanic messages were recorded backward in rock music.

The preacher and the minister claimed that the messages from Satan worked on the unconscious or subconscious level, and were meant to corrupt and brainwash teenagers. Basically, what Tom Sito was referencing in his quote. Well, today we know hidden satanic messages in popular songs and Disney's covert sexual innuendo more than likely aren't working on a subliminal level.

In reality, something may or may not be there but chances are it really doesn't matter. In 1985, researchers Vokey and Read looked into the whole subliminal message notion. The two concluded in their article *Between the Devil and the Media* in the journal of the *American Psychologist*, that messages or potential messages are "a function more of active construction on the part of the perceiver than of the existence of the messages themselves."

So what does this mean? Well, Disney was partially correct when they said people might be imagining things. If you want to see something or be influenced by something that may or may not be there, then perhaps it is possible. Whatever your views may be this reasoning doesn't stop people from suing or make the topic go away. The subliminal situation has now evolved past Disney's denial stage in the controversy, and progressed to the "no-comment" stage, which is when lawyers step in. So back to those lawsuits filed against the mouse…

A judge in Arkansas agreed with Ms. Gilmer's contentions that Disney did indeed have some morally unfit and offensive images. The judge would allow for a trial to proceed. This could have been devastating for Disney, not just in the media but the fact that it would be a class-action suit that would spread throughout the country. In September of 1997, Disney settled out of court. Gilmer's case went away without any further legal action. No numerical figures were released in regards to the settlement, other than a person close to her attorney stating a "small" settlement was received.

In the end, there is no such thing as bad publicity. Clearly this scandal didn't really damage Disney's reputation. Don't sex and scandals sell? Here we are decades later and people are still discussing it. The subject is still very much a relevant topic. A Google search today reveals numerous websites and articles on the subject, many of which have been posted within the past few months. A conspiracy theorist may say Disney inserted these things on purpose to generate "buzz" about the movies. These news stories became free noteworthy publicity that will live on as long as each movie survives. Another theory is: who knows and who cares! Disney denied it and moved on, at least temporarily.

In January of 1999, Disney announced a recall of the home video version of *The Rescuers*. This time, Disney's reaction was quite the opposite of what transpired with *The Lion King*, *Aladdin* and *The Little Mermaid*. Disney offered a recall and exchange of 3.4 million copies of the video due to a photograph of a topless woman that appears in two frames of the film.

At the start of the film, characters Bianca and Bernard are in front of a building. In these frames, the building's window has an image of a topless woman. The frames are on the screen for less than one second but if paused at the appropriate time, a topless woman can be seen. Disney acknowledged the issue and stated that they knew about the image. They claimed it was inserted in a postproduction process when the film was originally released to theaters in 1977. Disney initiated the recall to keep their promise to families that trust and rely on the Disney brand to provide the finest in family entertainment; however, when it comes to recalls of their entertainment that may not be as family centric, that's a different story.

In 1988, Disney released the film *Who Framed Roger Rabbit*. The movie breathed new life into Disney's theatrical releases, was well received and was very profitable. The film won multiple Academy Awards by tapping into Disney's roots of incorporating live action with animated characters. One of these animated characters was a little vixen by the name of Jessica Rabbit. She was like no other Disney animated character in the company's history.

Less than a year before the situations played out in the media with *The Lion King*, *Aladdin*, and *The Little Mermaid*, in March of 1994 *Variety*, the entertainment trade paper, ran a story about scenes where the animated Jessica Rabbit was sans underwear.

In a scene where Jessica is riding along in a taxi, the cab crashes into a light post. The panty-less wonder goes flying through the air with her skirt up and reveals to all, her lack of undergarments. Again, this is only possible for those looking frame by frame and through the power of DVD or in those days, laser disc. The laser disc allowed for scene by scene and even frame by frame viewing, which allowed for this discovery; seriously, who has the time to make these "discoveries."

At the time, Disney dismissed the subject claiming the movie wasn't for children anyway and they would not delete the scenes from future releases. Interestingly, Disney built a popular attraction at Disneyland called Roger Rabbit's Car Toon Spin, as we read about in Lights, Camera, Accident!

Jessica Rabbit's panty-less shot is probably more socially acceptable today than it was in 1988 or 1994. Consider how many celebrities, politicians or public figures, let alone average people, "accidentally" tweet or release some sort of compromising photo of themselves via social media, text or the Internet. Jessica's brief flash is no big deal now, right?

What could be a bigger deal is how Disney created her body image. Despite the film not being directly marketed to children, it is still animated and could be misconstrued and alluring for them. Back in 1988, when Jessica debuted in the movie, there was little talk, if any, about Disney's princesses and their body images impacting young girls. This was primarily because there were only three princesses around: Snow White, Cinderella, and Aurora.

The Disney princess boom didn't start for years after Jessica Rabbit. The princess franchise came together officially as a cohesive brand unto itself in the year 2000. Had the topic of Disney female characters and body image been a hot topic in the late '80s like it is today, Jessica Rabbit would have been at the epicenter of the debate. Today, over twenty years removed from her debut, Jessica is still making headlines. Her full lips and curvaceous features haven't been able to escape the clutches of those who deconstruct Disney. Disney critics argue that the women featured in Disney animated films portray unrealistic body images and types for females. Each princess is a picture beyond aesthetic perfection. This may lead girls to have problems with their self-image and possibly lay the foundation for body dysmorphia, and Jessica Rabbit isn't helping the situation.

Jessica's measurements, if she were real, were estimated at: bust size: 38, waist: 17, hips: 34, and a shoe size of 1, on the basis of her standing six feet tall and weighing 109 pounds. There hasn't been an official estimate on the size of her lips, but in 2012, a young woman from St. Petersburg, Russia wanted to emulate Jessica Rabbit so much, she had over one hundred silicone injections into her lips to look like the Disney vixen.

Jessica's aesthetics, as well as the princesses in the franchise; Snow White, Cinderella, Aurora, Ariel, Belle, Jasmine, Pocahontas, Mulan, Tiana, Rapunzel, Merida, and now *Frozen's* Elsa and Anna may give the impression that all women should be a certain size and possess certain features physically in order to be happy or socially accepted, most notably: tiny waists and an ample bosom.

These portrayals may put unnecessary and unhealthy pressures on young girls to conform to their princess idols, setting the stage for body-image problems as they grow up. Critics beg the question, how can little girls relate to all of this? People come in all shapes, sizes and races and Disney doesn't do a great job of portraying them accordingly.

The criticism is loud and widespread and moves beyond waist and breast size. The critics of the Disney franchise examine every angle, even down to the mega blockbuster hit, *Frozen*. One recent gripe is that Anna's eyeball is much larger than her wrist. The Disney princess criticism doesn't stop with body image; it extends further into gender stereotypes and female roles in the films.

Now, some of this must be put into context with a few of the early films, just like drinking and smoking; the times were different. *Snow White and the Seven Dwarfs*, *Cinderella*, and *Sleeping Beauty* were not yet a Disney princess franchise. These movies were released with almost ten years between each other and in a much different society. The culture of the day in 1937, 1950, and 1959, the years they were released, was drastically different from today.

In those days (and with much less media attention and scrutiny) what was presented, certainly was largely fantasy but not totally radical in a social context. Women were primarily in the home and running the house. Unfortunately, they weren't on a level playing field with men in a large part of society. It didn't mean all women were damsels in distress from the 1930s through the end of the 1950s, nor did it mean their only value was in their looks.

Women don't have to wait for a man to come and rescue them. They aren't too naive or unable to fend for themselves, which is how many Disney films portrayed female characters. Typically, female Disney characters were working in the home, an evil tyrant, or a subservient, insecure beauty. These are hardly things most parents want their daughter to grow up to be.

Herein lie the gripes of parents around the country in regards to the Disney princess franchise. All of this furthers the debate of Disney's role in moral and social responsibility with their entertainment. Is Disney doing children a disservice with all of their storytelling, or is it merely *just* entertainment? Did Walt really know how impactful he would be with the early movies that featured princesses and the aftereffect decades later?

The answer is probably no to both questions. Millions upon millions of little girls watched these movies and grew up to be physicians, lawyers, politicians and, oh yeah, plenty of real life princesses today, like the ones throughout Europe who grew up to be educated independent women.

When Walt set out on his theme park endeavor, he wanted it to be a place both children and parents could enjoy together, something that would appeal and hold the interest of two vastly different audiences. As history reveals, he accomplished it. Perhaps his animated features started out the same way, but didn't evolve with society. They are frozen glimpses in time, a fantasyland of yesterday to escape to and take at face value.

We know women don't need to be rescued by a prince, nor do they need someone to fight their battles in between cleaning their home, but it is still pretty cool to dream and fantasize about being a princess, living the grandiose life of royalty. This is exactly what Disney went for in 2013, without the neediness.

Disney made note of the critics and national media attention in regards to their princess franchise. After five years in development, they created a new princess for the preschool demographic, Sofia the First. Sofia's story follows the nearly identical storyline as many of the other princesses. She was under the care of her unmarried mother; mom meets a king, and then marries him. Sofia now has a stepparent and stepsiblings and a whole new way of life. There is one huge glaring difference though; Sofia doesn't need a prince to save her day.

Disney wholeheartedly faced and acknowledged their princess controversy. Nancy Kanter, senior vice president of original programming and general manager of Disney Junior World Wide, stated:

"We knew we didn't want it to be a young woman looking for a man. Everyone is aware of the princess luggage. We're undoing all that damage."

Disney is starting early with a proactive campaign geared toward the two to five-year-old set, and it seems to be working at least rating wise. Sofia was 2013's most watched cable series for the age group, and of course has spurned plenty of merchandise for the little ones to yearn for; which by the way, is probably the one true thing that is universal to all things Disney: merchandise.

Princess or no princess, when it is all said and done, it obviously comes down to parental preference. Deep down, most of the Disney stories aren't true Disney stories but centuries-old fables the company adapted to their liking. They are usually "coming of age" tales that put the lead character in some sort of difficult situation. This situation needs a villain or some sort of trouble in order for the turmoil, trials and tribulations to happen and a Disney happy ending or lesson to be learned. As Walt was once quoted in 1933: "To be honest about the matter, when our gang goes into a huddle and comes out with a new Mickey Mouse story, we will not have worried one bit as to whether the picture will make the children better men and women, or whether it will conform to the enlightened theories of child psychology."

Subliminal messages, child psychology and princesses aside, the Disney movies are here to stay, and a very small percentage of families cherish them and are very thankful for the emotional doors they've opened.

Owen Suskind was your run-of-the-mill toddler; walking, talking, eating, and playful. Around the age of three, many of these attributes started to disappear, and his communication started to retreat. Owen was diagnosed with regressive autism, a disorder that effects one third of the nearly 1 in 88 children diagnosed with autism. Regressive autism is different from the type of autism some children may be born with. In regressive cases, the children are typical tykes until around the age of eighteen to thirty-six months. At this point, the children start to lose their ability to communicate and their social attributes, which is exactly what happened to Owen.

No longer able to engage his family in conversation and socially connect with his parents on the levels he did previously was devastating for the Suskind family. There was, however, an unconventional and unexpected form of communication lurking in the Suskind household. Despite the onset of regressive autism, one thing didn't leave Owen: his love for Disney movies. Much like millions of other toddlers around the world, Owen loved to watch his favorite Disney characters. He loved these characters and movies so much that he would watch them over and over again.

Owen started to recite lines and songs from his favorite films. There was more to this though. Owen wasn't just repeating what he watched; he was starting to use Disney as a way to communicate through the characters and stories he watched over and over. The little boy who couldn't speak and connect emotionally was now starting to exhibit behavior that was unusual for his disorder; he was adopting the Disney movies into his own form of communication. Disney was helping to unleash that once prominent personality and vibrant emotions. Utilizing Disney as his medium for communication, he was now able to relate and reconnect with his parents, giving them a portal into his feelings.

Remarkably, all of this was discovered one afternoon with Owen's father, Ron (a Pulitzer prize–winning journalist, who should probably expect some more accolades after detailing Owen's story in the book *Life, Animated*) during a chance, life-altering observation. Ron noticed Owens "Disney speak" and tried to join in. He quickly grabbed the puppet of Iago, the parrot from *Aladdin*, and reached out to Owen verbally as the bird. He posed the question, "So, Owen, how ya doin'?" Owen responded, "I am not happy. I don't have friends. I can't understand what people say." For the first time in nearly five years, Ron was connecting with his son in a conversation. Disney movies were resonating with Owen and actually helped a little boy with autism communicate with his family.

As the years went on and Owen got older, the Suskinds embraced Owen's "Disney therapy." The characters, plot lines and stories presented in the countless Disney movies became the vehicle for the family to connect and bond with Owen. For Owen, it allowed him to process and understand the world around him, the best he could under the guise of Disney. But Owen is not alone with his affinity for Disney, as a person living with autism. Disney movies have a special place for many on the autistic spectrum.

Today, Owen is in his early twenties and attends a special school where he is the founder and president of the Disney Club. The club boasts over thirty-five members, who all revel in Disney. The group also uses Disney as a vehicle for members to express themselves, and communicate with the world around them that previously had locked them out.

Many of Owen's peers, who also didn't speak prior to their "Disney therapy," are now speaking and relating to Disney characters. One afternoon, Ron went to visit Owen at school. He sat in on a Disney Club meeting and engaged a young autistic man in a conversation. The man was able to communicate without Disney, but seldom conveyed any emotion or depth. Utilizing Disney movies, he gave Ron a sliver into his mind.

When asked which Disney character he related to or felt a bond with, he replied, "My character is in Pinocchio…because I feel like a wooden boy who is always dreaming about what a real boy feels, and who is born with wooden eyes. I am just learning to see."

These are pretty amazing and moving stories that stretch beyond Owen and his peers in school. More and more across the country, parents with autistic children are living and sharing their Disney experiences with their autistic children.

Former National Football League running back, Curt Warner of the Seattle Seahawks, has twin sons, with what Warner calls "medium autism." Curt says they know everything about Disney movies including each writer and director. Oftentimes they feel as though they are living one of their favorite films by addressing people and family members by Disney character names. Another story, about a young boy, Collin, is similar to Owen's. Collin started to communicate again with his parents via Pixar movies, specifically *Up* and *Ratatouille*—again, pretty phenomenal and touching stories.

Whether it's detrimental or immoral to expose children to this entertainment is up for debate. There certainly are more troubling things out in the world that children are exposed to than a Disney storyline or some subliminal messages. Princesses and their portrayals may be bad, so too may be playing with Barbie dolls with her body type. Watching the legendary non-Disney movies *Annie* or *The Wizard of Oz* with their difficult family situations could also spell doom and gloom.

Today, the media is everywhere and so is Disney. In a day and age when many parents utilize their TV as a quasi babysitter and plant their children in front of the television, they allow a variety of things to stream into their child's mind. Violence, drugs, and sex are imprinting them on a daily basis, and that's just from watching the local six o'clock news.

In the years post-Walt, Disney isn't entirely responsible for chiseling away at the innocence of young children, exposing them to broken families, smoking, drinking, sex, and potential body-image issues (that's what the Internet is for!), but they do have a large role in the education and upbringing of millions of children around the world, good or bad.

Certainly, no company or person is without flaws. When a career such as Walt's reaches the stratosphere as his did, and thus similarly for the company that shares his name, the magnifying glass through which people gaze upon them is that much more powerful.

Many of the situations and life lessons that play out on the big screen from Disney also play out each day in the real world of Disney. Despite the fairy tales and fantasylands, even the sanctity of Disneyland and Walt Disney World with all its jubilation and carefree atmosphere are the setting for many terrible situations. It's regrettable in any circumstance when horrible things happen to unsuspecting and innocent people. Sadly, even the Happiest Place on Earth feels the sting of reality when unfortunate events encroach upon everyone's fantasy world.

As it all relates to Disney, they are unique and special in a lot of ways, but not in the sense of tragic events; however, Disney is very safe on just about every level, and I'm not saying this as a Disney apologist or enthusiast. The numbers don't lie.

Despite the moments of craziness, tragedy and litigation, Disney is diligent, proactive and reactive 99 percent of the time; their business plan and reputation depends upon it. But as the saying goes, shit happens; sometimes Disney is culpable, other times they are not. But one thing is for sure; they are very protective of their multibillion-dollar mouse and try in earnest to keep him out of trouble.

Selected Bibliography By Chapter.

Mickey Mania:

"2-year Sentence for Cancer Scam; Woman Faked Illness." 2-year Sentence for Cancer Scam; Woman Faked Illness. N.p., n.d. Web. 22 May 2014.

"2 Arrested in Armored Truck Heist." Orlando Sentinel 1 May 2008: n. pag. Print.

"Alabama Woman Gets 20 Years For Cancer Fraud Scheme." Associated Press 4 Apr. 2013: n. pag. Print.

Anderson, Dennis. "Mouseketeer Faces Trial On Fraud Charges." Associated Press 30 Nov. 1998: n. pag. Print.

"Boardwalk Inn Hostage Settles With Disney." Orlando Sentinel 15 July 2000: n. pag. Print.

"Cancer Fraud Got Man Disneyland Vacation, Say Utah Police." CBS News 19 Nov. 2012: n. pag. Print.

"Cancer Scam Nets 20 Years For Elmore County Mother." Cancer Scam Nets 20 Years For Elmore County Mother. N.p., n.d. Web. 22 May 2014.

"Captured At Disney." Orlando Sentinel 28 Oct. 2012: n. pag. Print.

Carollo, Kim. "Are Cancer Fraudsters Desperate or Psychopathic." ABC News 12 Aug. 2010: n. pag. Print.

Caulfield, Phillip. "Italian Doctor Kicks 3 Year Old Son In Face At Walt Disney World." New York Daily News 2 July 2012: n. pag. Print.

Chamberlain, Gethin. "Disney Factory Faces Probe into Sweatshop Suicide Claims." The Observer. Guardian News and Media, 28 Aug. 2011. May2014.<http://www.theguardian.com/law/2011/aug/27/disney-factory-sweatshop-suicide-claims>.

"Chemo Buddies Head to Disney World Together." - KSLA News 12 Shreveport, Louisiana News Weather & Sports. N.p., n.d. Web. 22 May 2014. <http://www.ksla.com/story/24169666/chemo-buddies-head-to-disney-world-together>.

Chmielewski, Dawn. "Man Indicted On Securities Fraud In Disney Marvel Acquisition." Los Angeles Times 8 Oct. 2013: n. pag. Print.

Clark, Lesley. "New Disney Hires Now All Undergo Criminal Checks." Orlando Sentinel 16 Oct. 1998: n. pag. Print.

Clary, Susan. "Trial Starts In Hostage Incident At Disney." Orlando Sentinel 17 Jan. 2002: n. pag. Print.

Clary, Susan. "Jury Delivers Split Verdict For Disney Hostage Taker." Orlando Sentinel 19 Jan. 2002: n. pag. Print.

"Code of Conduct for Manufacturers." The Walt Disney Company. 22 May 2014. <http://thewaltdisneycompany.com/citizenship/respectful-workplaces/ethical-sourcing/ils/code-conduct-manufacturers>.

"Colo. Mom Charged with Abuse for Telling Her 6-year-old He Was Terminally Ill ." NY Daily News. N.p., n.d. Web. 22 May 2014.

Conservatorship of the Estate of MICHELLE A. LUND. WILLIAM S. LUND Et Al., Petitioners and Appellants, v. MICHELLE A. LUND, Objector and Respondent. COURT OF APPEAL OF CALIFORNIA, FOURTH APPELLATE DISTRICT, DIVISION THREE. 10 Dec. 2013. Print.

"Construction Begins on State-of-the-Art Laundry Facility at Walt Disney World Resort." Walt Disney World News. N.p., n.d. Web. 22 May 2014. <http://wdwnews.com/releases/2014/03/25/construction-begins-on-state-of-the-art-laundry-facility-at-walt-disney-world-resort/>.

Curtis, Henry. "Disney Accused of Profiling Black Teens." Orlando Sentinel 27 June 2007: n. pag. Print.

Curtis, Henry. "Teens Face Crackdown At Downtown Disney." Orlando Sentinel 22 June 2007: n. pag. Print.

Decker, Twila. "Jasmine's New Parents: Aunt And Uncle." Orlando Sentinel 7 Nov. 1998: n. pag. Print.

"Disney Breaks Ground on Cutting-Edge Laundry." TRSA. N.p., n.d. Web. 22 May 2014. <http://www.trsa.org/news/disney-breaks-ground-cutting-edge-laundry>.

"Disneyland Zoo Sued Over Dog Attack Involving Girl." Daily News OF Los Angeles 25 Sept. 2008: n. pag. Print.

"Disney & McDonald's Linked to $0.06/Hour Sweatshop in Vietnam." Disney & McDonald's Linked to $0.06/Hour Sweatshop in Vietnam. N.p., 2 May 1997. Web. 22 May 2014. <http://www.hartford-hwp.com/archives/54/103.html>.

"Disney Sweatshops Alleged." CNN Money, 18 Aug. 2005. Web.

"Disney Obsession?: Alexander Pera, Ill. Restaurant Manager, Allegedly Stole Customer Credit Info to Pay for Frequent Disney Vacations." CBSNews. CBS Interactive, 9 July 2013. Web. 22 May 2014.

"Disney Speedster Cops Ban." Herald Sun 25 Aug. 1995: n. pag. Print.

"Disney Secretary Admits To Insider Trading Scheme - Law360." Disney Secretary Admits To Insider Trading Scheme - Law360. N.p., n.d. Web. 22 May 2014.

"Disney Secretary Avoids Jail Time For Trading Scheme - Law360." Disney Secretary Avoids Jail Time For Trading Scheme - Law360. N.p., n.d. Web. 22 May 2014.

Dorman, Nick. "Crew Snorting 'cocaine' on Disney Cruise - Pictures." Mirror. N.p., 18 Aug. 2012. Web. 22 May 2014.

"Emma La Garde: Son of Sickest Mum in Britain Tells How She Convinced Him He Was Dying of Cancer." Mirror. N.p., n.d. Web. 22 May 2014.

"Emma La Garde Apologises to Son She Tricked into Believing He Was Dying from Cancer." Mirror. Daily Mirror, Apr. 2013. Web. 22 May 2014.<http://www.mirror.co.uk/news/uk-news/emma-la-garde-apologises-son-2142670>.

"Emma La Garde: Mum Shaved Son's Head and Eyebrows in Fake Cancer Benefit Scam." Mirror. N.p., 14 Nov. 2012. Web. 22 May 2014. <http://www.mirror.co.uk/news/uk-news/emma-la-garde-mum-shaved-1433746>.

"Ex-Disney Employee Accused of Stealing $122K in Fraudulent..." WFTV Channel 9 Orlando, Daytona Beach, Melbourne, Central Florida. N.p., n.d. Web. 22 May 2014.

"Ex-Disney Clerk Charged With Stealing Park Passes." Orlando Sentinel 18 Sept. 1996: n. pag. Print.

"Faking Cancer for Donations and Sympathy." Msnbc.com. N.p., n.d. Web. 22 May 2014.

Fenton, Reuven. "Staten Island Couple Allegedly Stole Sick Elderly Patients Identities To Fund Disney World Trip." New York Post 17 July 2013: n. pag. Print.

"Former Hilliard Investment Adviser Pleads Guilty in Ponzi Scheme." The Columbus Dispatch. N.p., n.d. Web. 22 May 2014. <http://www.dispatch.com/content/stories/business/2013/05/30/investment-adviser-pleads-guilty.html>.

"Former Hilliard Man Sentenced to 5 Years in Ponzi Scheme." The Columbus Dispatch. N.p., 7 Mar. 2014. Web. 22 May 2014. <http://www.dispatch.com/content/stories/business/2014/03/06/kelly-sentenced-in-ponzi-scheme.html>.

"The Friendliest Interrogator Of World War II Was A German - KnowledgeNuts." KnowledgeNuts. N.p., n.d. Web. 22 May 2014. <http://knowledgenuts.com/2014/01/31/the-friendliest-interrogator-of-world-war-ii-was-a-nazi/>.

Gandhi, Prakash. "Robbers Take Thousands In Disney Tunnel." Orlando Sentinel 3 Jan. 1986: n. pag. Print.

Gardner, Joshua. "Not So Magic Kingdom: Twin Grandchildren of Walt Disney Battle It Out Over Disputed $400 Million Inheritance." Mail Online. Associated Newspapers, 25 Nov. 2013. Web. 22 May 2014.

"Girl with Cancer Gets Disney Princess Parade." HLNtv.com. N.p., 22 May 2014. <http://www.hlntv.com/article/2014/02/20/claire-lankford-princess-parade-terminal-cancer>.

Grier, Peter. "The Walt Disney Company Pulls out of Bangladesh: Will That Make Workers Safer?" The Christian Science Monitor. The Christian Science Monitor, 03 May 2013. Web. 21 May 2014. <http://www.csmonitor.com/USA/2013/0503/The-Walt-Disney-Company-pulls-out-of-Bangladesh-Will-that-make-workers-safer>

Gutierrez, Pedro. "Ex-Hostage: I Was Afraid for My Life." Orlando Sentinel 1 July 2000: n. pag. Print.

Gutierrez, Pedro. "New Charge Hits Hostage Taker." Orlando Sentinel 4 Aug. 2000: n. pag. Print.

Gutierrez, Pedro. "Marital Strife Led To Disney Hostage Crisis." Orlando Sentinel 16 July 2000: n. pag. Print.

Gutierrez, Pedro. "Police Find Jasmine's Mom." Orlando Sentinel. N.p., 6 Feb. 1998. Web. 23 May 2014.

Gutierrez, Pedro. "Cops: Disney Worker Took Boy." Orlando Sentinel 14 Apr. 1999: n. pag. Print.

Harris, Kenneth. "Baby Born At Disney Doing Fine." Orlando Sentinel 19 Nov. 1997: n. pag. Print.

"He Spends $700,000 on 'Work Trips'" He Spends $700,000 on 'work Trips'<http://news.asiaone.com/News/The%2BNew%2BPaper/Story/A1Story20090403-133130.html>.

"In the Valley, Heirs Embroiled in Disney Feud." In the Valley, Heirs Embroiled in Disney Feud. Web. 22 May 2014. <http://www.azcentral.com/arizonarepublic/news/articles/2010/10/08/20101008phoenix-area-family-disney-trust-fund-fight.html>

"Italian Tourist Accused of Kicking Son in Face at Epcot." Italian Tourist Accused of Kicking Son in Face at Epcot. N.p., n.d. Web. 22 May 2014. <http://mynews13.com/content/news/cfnews13/news/article.html/content/news/articles/cfn/2012/7/1/italian_tourist_accu.html>.

Johnson, Pamela. "Hostage Taker At Disney Surrenders To Police." Orlando Sentinel 30 June 2000: n. pag. Print.

Johnson, Pamela. "Hostages Held At Disney." Orlando Sentinel 30 June 2000: n. pag. Print.

Kennedy, Brendan. "Woman Faked Cancer To Raise Money." The Star—Canada 6 Aug. 2010: n. pag. Print.

"Khir's RM1.7m Disney Trips | TheSundaily." Khir's RM1.7m Disney Trips | TheSundaily. N.p., 2 Apr. 2009. Web. 22 May 2014. <http://www.thesundaily.my/node/157274>.

Krantz, Matt. "Former Walt Disney Aide Arrested In Fraud." USA Today 28 May 2010: n. pag. Print.

Leithauser, Tom. "Police Seek 3 In Disney Robbery." Orlando Sentinel 10 July 1996: n. pag. Print.

Leithauser, Tom. "Suspect Knew Disney Details, Officials Say." Orlando Sentinel 31 July 1996: n. pag. Print.

"Little Girl with Terminal Cancer Gets a Hometown Princess Parade." PEOPLE.com. N.p., 21 Feb. 2014. Web. 22 May 2014. <http://www.people.com/people/article/0%2C%2C20789424%2C00.html>.

Lopez, Steve. "Disneyland Workers Answer To Electric Whip." Los Angeles Times 19 Apr. 2011: n. pag. Print.

"Man Admits Stealing Cash Registers From Disney World." St. Augustine Record 3 May 2006: n. pag. Print.

"Man Sentenced To 6 Years In Disney World Robbery." Orlando Sentinel 6 Dec. 1996: n. pag. Print.

Martin, Adam. "Couple Arrested In Most Romantic Fraud Case Ever." New York Magazine 18 July 2013: n. pag. Print.

McShane, Larry. "Lovebirds Stole Staten Island Doctor's Office To Fund Disney World Engagement." New York Daily News 17 July 2013: n. pag. Print.

"Mom Accused In Cancer Scam Indicted On Theft Charges." Chicago Tribune 3 Dec. 2003: n. pag. Print.

Moran, Lee. "Drunken Joyride Around Disney Doesn't Have Fairy Tale Ending." New York Daily News 29 May 2013: n. pag. Print

"Mother of Baby Left In Toilet Traced To Philippines DNA Nails Baby Jasmine's Mom." Spokesman-Review 6 Feb. 1998: n. pag. Print.

Murdock, Sebastian. "Sandy Nguyen Allegedly Fakes Son's Cancer, Takes Donations To Disneyland." The Huffington Post. TheHuffingtonPost.com, 16 Mar. 2014. Web. 22 May 2014.

"Newborn Pulled From Theme Park Toilet Doing Fine." Associated Press 10 Nov. 1997: n. pag. Print.

News, CBC. "Cancer Faker Kirilow Spared Jail." CBCnews. CBC/Radio Canada, 07 Apr. 2011. Web. 22 May 2014

"No Happily Ever After for Disney Heirs - Morris, Hall and Kinghorn, P.L.L.C." Morris Hall and Kinghorn PLLC. N.p., n.d. Web. 22 May 2014. <http://morristrust.com/articles/no-happily-ever-after-for-disney-heirs/>.

Oliver, Myrna. "Hanns Scharff: Creator of L.A., State Capital Mosaics." Los Angeles Times 12 Sept. 1992: n. pag. Print.

Owens, Sherri. "1 Year Later Jasmine Has New Life." Orlando Sentinel 8 Nov. 1998: n. pag. Print.

"Ponzi Schemer Went Underground at Disney World." Ponzi Clawbacks. Web. <http://www.ponziclawbacks.com/2013/06/04/ponzi-schemer-went-underground-at-disney-world/>.

Powers, Scott. "Disney Reverses 4 Teens Lifetime Ban." Orlando Sentinel 29 June 2007: n. pag. Print.

"Robber Sought In Holdup of 2 Workers." Orlando Sentinel 12 July 1996: n. pag. Print.

Rockrohr, Phillip. "Police: IDs Stolen to Pay for Disney Obsession - Chicago Sun-Times." Police: IDs Stolen to Pay for Disney Obsession - Chicago Sun-Times. Sun Times, 8 July 2013. Web. 22 May 2014.

Rocha, Veronica. "Disneyland Scamster Arrested Again In Glendale." Los Angeles Times 11 June 2013: n. pag. Print.

Schabner, Dean. "Alleged Cancer Hoaxster Ashley Kirilow's Father Ashamed." ABC News 8 Aug. 2010: n. pag. Print.

Secret, Mosi. "Prosecutors Say Five Ran A Credit Card Fraud Ring." The New York Times 17 July 2013: n. pag. Print.

"Scharff and Scharff." Scharff and Scharff. N.p., n.d. Web. 22 May 2014. <http://www.scharffandscharff.com/>.

Sheehan, Daniel. "Disney Tattoo Guy Saying Farewell." Morning Call 6 Jan. 2012: n. pag. Print

Sheehan, Daniel. "Officials: Disney Tattoo Guy Attacked, Imprisoned Woman." Orlando Sentinel 8 July 2011: n. pag. Print.

Silverman, Billy. "Bonnie Hoxie, Disney Exec's Assistant, Charged In Trade Scheme." The Huffington Post. TheHuffingtonPost.com, 26 May 2010. Web. 22 May 2014.

Sprouse, Martin. Sabotage in the American Workplace: Anecdotes of Dissatisfaction, Mischief, and Revenge. San Francisco: Pressure Drop, 1992. Print.

Stebner, Beth. "Mother Returning from Disney Cruise with Husband and Two Children JAILED over 22-year-old Warrant after She Stole Pack of Cigarettes in 1991." Mail Online. Associated Newspapers, 23 Jan. 2013. Web. 22 May 2014.

Stratton, Jim. "Disney Tries Again To Toughen Ticket Fraud Law." Orlando Sentinel 7 Mar. 2014: n. pag. Print.

Stutzman, Rene. "Disney Scam: Homeless Man Lived In Hotels For Years On Stolen Credit Cards." Orlando Sentinel 25 Oct. 2012: n. pag. Print.

Thompson, Paul. "Disney Hotel Housekeeper Suspected of Stealing Guests' Money Is Caught in Sting Operation ." Mail Online. Associated Newspapers, 22 Aug. 2013. Web. 22 May 2014.

Tracy, Erin. "Ceres Couple Arrested In Disneyland Ticket Scam." Modesto Bee 19 Feb. 2014: n. pag. Print.

"Utah Couple Secretly Weds on Pirates of the Caribbean Ride | KSL.com." Utah Couple Secretly Weds on Pirates of the Caribbean Ride | KSL.com. N.p., 18 Oct. 2013. Web. 22 May 2014.

Verrier, Richard. "Hostage Plans to Sue Disney Over Incident." Orlando Sentinel 12 July 2000: n. pag. Print.

"Walt Disney—Sweatshop Retailer of the Year." Walt Disney—Sweatshop Retailer of the Year. N.p., 18 June 2001. Web. 22 May 2014. <http://www.organicconsumers.org/corp/disneysweat.cfm>.

"Wells Fargo Worker Jailed, May Have Stolen $20,500." Orlando Sentinel 24 Mar. 1993: n. pag. Print.

Weiner, Jeff. "Former Disney Employee Accused of Falsifying $120,000 In Liability Claims." Orlando Sentinel 11 Oct. 2012: n. pag. Print.

"Wheelchair Speeder Loses Disneyland Pass." Spokesman-Review 25 Aug. 1995: n. pag. Print.

"While Checking For Terrorists on Disney Cruise, Police Arrest Woman For Stealing Pack of Cigarettes in 1991." Riptide 2.0. N.p., n.d. Web.<http://blogs.miaminewtimes.com/riptide/2013/01/while_checking_for_terrorists.php>.

Woodyard, Chris. "Disney Faces $400,00 Fine For Illegal Workers." Los Angeles Times 7 May 1993: n. pag. Print.

"Woman Admits Guilt in Fake Cancer Story." Associated Press 15 May 2004: n. pag. Print.

Woodruff, Mandi. "Police Say These Guys Outsmarted Disney World To Score 4 Years Of Free Vacations." Business Insider. Business Insider, Inc, 31 May 2012. Web. 22 May 2014.

"The WWII Interrogator Who Used Kindness Over Violence." BBC News. BBC, 15 Oct. 2012. Web. 21 May 2014. <http://www.bbc.co.uk/history/0/19923902>

Lights, Camera, Accident!
"2 Improve in Disney Air Crash That Killed Parents, Sister." Pittsburgh Press 24 Nov. 1984: n. pag. Print.

"8 Hurt In Disney Ferry Crash." Orlando Sentinel 29 Dec. 2002: n. pag. Print.

"$15M Tower of Terror Lawsuit Against Disney Dropped." $15M Tower of Terror Lawsuit Against Disney Dropped. Arrington Law Firm Blog, 27 Dec. 2012. Web. <arringtonlawfirm.com/blog>.

2002 The Walt Disney Company Report of Safety.

2009 The Walt Disney Company Report on Safety.

"3 Bodies Found in Disney Pond." CBSNEWS.Com 22 June 1999: n. pag. Print.

"3 Killed in Plane Crash at Disney World Lot." The New York Times 22 Nov. 1984: n. pag. Print

"Accident At Disney Kills One." Ocala Star Banner 16 Feb. 1999: n. pag. Print.

"Anaheim: Court Upholds Finding in Favor of Disneyland." Los Angeles Times 27 May 1987: n. pag. Print.

Anne Noel v. Disney Parks and Resorts. United States District Court of Massachusetts. 31 Mar. 2011. Print.

"Appellate Court Overturns Disney Accident Jury Award." Ocala Star Banner 2 July 1994: n. pag. Print.

Associated Press. "Disney Ride Death Investigated." Boca Raton News 4 Jan. 1984: n. pag.

Associated Press. Family Sues Disney Over Boy's Traffic Death 7 July 1995: n. pag. Print.

Associated Press. Report: Error Caused Disney Death 31 Dec. 1998: n. pag. Print.

Associated Press. "Police School Disney On Accidents." 11 Jan. 1999: n. pag. Print.

Associated Press. "Disney Ride Death Investigated." Boca Raton News 4 Jan. 1984: n. pag. Print.

"Authorities ID Water Park Guest Who Died." Orlando Sentinel 17 Mar. 2007: n. pag. Print.

Berkman, Leslie. "Youth Killed By Disneyland Ride." Los Angeles Times 8 June 1980: n. pag. Print.

Blumfield, Michael. "Accidents Worry Disney's Indiana Jones Stunt Workers." Orlando Sentinel 17 Dec. 1989: n. pag. Print.

Blumfield, Michael. "Disney Performer Hurt During Show." Orlando Sentinel 13 Dec. 1989: n. pag. Print.

Blumfield, Michael. "U.S. Fines Disney For Stunt Risks." Orlando Sentinel 1 Mar. 1990: n. pag. Print.

"Body of One of Missing Vacationers Is Identified." St. Petersburg Times 25 June 1999: n. pag. Print.

"Boy Critically Hurt on Ride At Disneyland." Los Angeles Times 17 May 1964: B. Print.

"Boy Killed in Fall At Disneyland." Los Angeles Times 23 Aug. 1967: n. pag. Print.

"Boy Pulled From Disney Resort Pool Dies." CNN.com 14 Mar. 2013: n. pag. Print.

Boyd, Christopher. "Disney World Death on Everest Roller Coaster Blamed On Tourist's Heart Condition." Orlando Sentinel 20 Dec. 2007: n. pag. Print.

"Brain Bleeding Killed Disney Space Rider." St. Petersburg TImes 15 Apr. 2006: n. pag. Print.

Cetin N, Blackall D.Naegleria fowleri meningoencephalitis. Blood 2012 Apr 19;119(16):3658.

Clary, Mike. "Animal Deaths Cast Pall Over Disney Theme Park." Los Angeles Times 13 Apr. 1998: n. pag. Print.

Colarossi, Anthony. "Lawsuit Against Disney In Fatal Monorail Crash Apparently Settled." Orlando Sentinel 26 Mar. 2011: n. pag. Print.

"Commonly Used Statistics." Commonly Used Statistics. OSHA, n.d. Web. 20 May 2014. <https://www.osha.gov/oshstats/commonstats.html>.

"Compensation Needed in Disney Case: Juror." Ocala Star Banner 10 Mar. 1985: n. pag. Print

Curtis, Henry. "Disney's Animal Kingdom Worker Dies of Injuries." Orlando Sentinel 14 Mar. 2011: n. pag. Print

DeBarros, Anthony. "Death After Disney Ride Sparks Call for Federal Review." USA Today 14 June 2005: n. pag. Print.

"Disneyland Reopens Show That Killed Girl." Los Angeles Times 11 July 1974: C3. Print.

"Disneyland Guest Hurt; Police Begin Inquiry." Los Angeles Times 22 Jan. 1999: n. pag. Print.

"Disneyland Prank Under Monorail Kills Youth." Los Angeles Times 18 June 1966: 1. Print.

"Disney Keeps Its Visitors' Hearts in Mind With AED Interactive Page." Disney Keeps Its Visitors' Hearts in Mind With AED Interactive Page. AED.com, 29 Aug. 2013. Web. <Aed.com/blog/Disney>.

"Disney Sued By Coma Girl." The Daily Mirror 13 Feb. 2009: n. pag. Print.

"Disney Opening STOL Airport." Lakeland Ledger 22 Oct. 1974: n. pag. Print.

"Disney Fined $6,300 for Pluto Worker's Death." USA Today 11 Aug. 2004: n. pag. Print.

"Disney's Mystery Rider Remains In Medical Center." Los Angeles Times 19 June 1991: n. pag. Print.

"Disney Worker Injured on Ride Platform." Orlando Sentinel 29 Nov. 2007: n. pag. Print.

"Disney Worker Dies After Fall From Platform." Orlando Sentinel 30 Nov. 2007: n. pag. Print.

"Disney World Had Rigorous Safety Inspections Even before Accident." Rigorous Safety. N.p., n.d. Web. 22 May 2014. <http://www.birket.com/articles/103-reading-room/articles/131-rigoroussafety>.

"Disneyland Cited for 36 Violations of Worker Safety Rules by OSHA." Los Angeles Times. Los Angeles Times, 15 Apr. 1988. Web. 22 May 2014. <http://articles.latimes.com/1988-04-15/local/me-1429_1_serious-safety-violations>.

Dizon, Lily. "Disneyland's Mystery Rider Had Been Enjoying Birthday." Los Angeles Times 20 June 1991: n. pag. Print.

Estate of Moses Bamiwamye v. Disney Parks and Resorts. 9th Judicial Court, Orange County, Florida. 11 Jan. 2007. Print.

"Father Urges Inquest in Fatal Disneyland Ride." Los Angeles Times 22 May 1964: 28. Print.

Ferris, Gerrie. "Buyers Warned of Contaminated Juice." The Atlanta Journal and Constitution 17 Aug. 1995: n. pag. Print.

Flores, Ike. "Say Salmonella In Orange Juice Sickens 63 People at Disney." Associated Press 16 Aug. 1995: n. pag. Print

Fryer, Dean. "Cal/OSHA Cites Disneyland for December Accident." Cal/OSHA Cites Disneyland for December Accident. California OSHA, 25 Mar. 1999. Web. 22 May 2014 http://www.dir.ca.gov/dirnews/1999/IR99-02.html>.

Gandhi, Prakash. "Construction Worker Dies, 3 Hurt At Disney Water Park." Orlando Sentinel 26 Apr. 1988: n. pag. Print

Garcia, Jason. "Disney World Stunt Worker's Death Not Caused by Safety Violations, OSHA Says." Palm Beach Post 17 Feb. 2010: n. pag. Print.

Garcia, Jason. "Disney Cited For Safety Violations Following Death of Mechanic on Animal Kingdom Rollercoaster." Orlando Sentinel 16 Sept. 2011:

Garcia, Jason. "Disney Coaster to Remain Closed Through Summer as Fatal Accident Probe Continues." Orlando Sentinel 7 June 2011: n. pag.

Garcia, Jason. "Disney's Move Just May Save Your Life." Orlando Sentinel 10 Jan. 2009: n. pag. Print.

Garcia, Jason. "Investigators: Lack of Safety Protocols at Disney Contributed to 2009 Monorail Accident." Orlando Sentinel 31 Oct. 2011: n. pag. Print.

Garcia, Jason. "Boy Killed in Disney Bus Accident in Fort Wilderness." Orlando Sentinel 2 Apr. 2010: n. pag. Print.

Garcia, Jason. "Disney World Limits Use of Onboard Bus Computers." Orlando Sentinel 20 July 2010: n. pag. Print.

Garcia, Jason. "Disney World Bus Accidents: GPS Units on Buses Were Distracting, Critics Say." Orlando Sentinel 16 Apr. 2010: n. pag. Print.

Garcia, Jason. "Disney World to Lock Hotel Swimming Pools Overnight." Orlando Sentinel 26 Sept. 2013: n. pag. Print.

Gottlieb, Jeff. "Disneyland Closes Space Mountain After Accident Hurts 9." Los Angeles Times 2 Aug. 2000: n. pag. Print.

Gutierrez, Pedro. "Psychics Join Search For Men." Orlando Sentinel 23 Nov. 1998: n. pag.

Gutierrez, Pedro. "Witnesses Told Disney About Sick Man." Orlando Sentinel 8 Nov. 2000: n. pag. Print.

Harwood, Anthony. "Man Killed By Derailed Disney Rollercoaster." The Daily Mirror 6 Sept. 2003: n. pag. Print.

"He Tried To Join His Friends." Los Angeles Times 19 June 1966: n. pag. Print.

Hernandez, Salvador. "Boy Badly Hurt in 2000 Roger Rabbit Accident Dies." Orange County Register 26 Jan. 2009: n. pag. Print.

Hill-Holtzman, Nancy. "Davis Signs Theme Park Inspection Bill." Los Angeles Times 5 Oct. 1999: n. pag. Print.

"Indiana Jones Show Taking A Break At Disney-MGM." Orlando Sentinel 13 Jan. 2000: n. pag. Print.

"Injury Statistics." Amusement Ride Safety. IAAPA, n.d. Web. 22 May 2014. <http://www.iaapa.org/safety-and-advocacy/safety/amusement-ride-safety/injury-statistics#sthash.gU6tpPES.dpuf>.

Injuries, All. "Injury Facts." The Odds of Dying (n.d.): n. pag. The National Safety Council. Web. <www.nsc.org>

"Inquest Ruled Out In Fatal Disneyland Fall." Los Angeles Times 27 May 1964: A1. Print.

"Investigation of Monorail Collision Begins." Palm Beach Post 26 June 1985: n. pag. Print.

Jacobson, Susan. "Massachusetts Man Dies After Walking In Front of Disney Bus At Port Orleans." Orlando Sentinel 27 Dec. 2010

Jacobson, Susan. "Disney Employee Killed, 2 Hurt When Disney Bus Rear-Ends Car Near EPCOT." Orlando Sentinel 17 Aug. 2013: n. pag. Print.

Jung, Carolyn. "Parents, Disney Settle Suit $250,000 to Be Paid in Boy's Drowning." Sun Sentinel 15 June 1988: n. pag. Print.

"Jury Can Hear of Changes to Disney Ride After Death." Orange County Register 12 Dec. 2006: n. pag. Print.

Kassab, Beth. "A Closer Look Behind the Magic." Orlando Sentinel 4 Mar. 2007: n. pag. Print.

Kassab, Beth. "Tamer Spaceship Ride Makes Debut At EPCOT." Orlando Sentinel 20 May 2006: n. pag. Print.

Kennedy, Kelli. "Disney to Offer Tamer Mission Space Ride." Associated Press n.d.: n. pag. Print.

King, Larry. "Disney World Sued for Boy's 2005 Death." Philadelphia Inquirer 15 June 2006: n. pag. Print.

"Lack of Fuel Cited In EPCOT Crash." Sarasota Herald Tribune 29 Nov. 1984: n. pag. Print.

Lancaster, Cory. "65 Year Old Custodian Killed While Cleaning Disney Ride." Sun Sentinel 16 Feb. 1999: n. pag. Print.

Lancaster, Cory. "Disney Forced To Change Safari Ride." Orlando Sentinel 4 Apr. 1998: n. pag. Print.

Lane, Mark. "Mother May Sue Disney World Over Son's Drowning." Daytona Beach Morning Journal 23 Dec. 1982: n. pag. Print.

"Lightning Kills Giraffe At Disney Park." Orlando Sentinel 24 July 2003: n. pag. Print.

Liston, Barbara. "Mourning Death At the Magic Kingdom." TIME 21 Aug. 2009: n. pag. Web.

Luna, Claire. "Family, Disney Settle Suit Over Ride Death." Los Angeles Times 3 Dec. 2005:. pag. Print.

"Man Killed at Disneyland Bled to Death, Autopsy Says." Los Angeles Times 10 Sept. 2003: n. pag. Print.

Mariano, Willoughby. "Disney Performer Dies During Rehearsal." Orlando Sentinel 18 Aug. 2009: n. pag. Print.

Mariano, Willoughby. "Teen Went On Ride Too Many Times." Orlando Sentinel 14 July 2005: n. pag. Print

Mariano, Willoughby. "Teen Critical After Terror Ride." Orlando Sentinel 13 July 2005: n. pag. Print.

Marietta Goode v. Walt Disney World. Florida Fifth District Court. 14 Jan. 1987. Print.

Martin, Hugo. "Amusement Park Rides: Thrills and Ills." Los Angeles Times 3 Jan. 2014: n. pag. Print.

"Mission Space Ride Faces No Delays." Orlando Sentinel 13 May 2002: n. pag. Print.

Mussenden, Sean. "Disney Worker Killed In Parade." Orlando Sentinel 12 Feb. 2004: n. pag. Print.

Mussenden, Sean. "Mission Space Ride Has Sent 6 To Hospital." Orlando Sentinel 6 May 2004: n. pag. Print.

Newkirk, Ingrid. "Animals Are Worst Part of Disney's Animal Kingdom." Orlando Sentinel 8 May 1998: n. pag. Print.

Oliver, Mike. "Words Fail As Teens Mourned." Orlando Sentinel 15 July 1990: n. pag. Print.

Owens, Darryl. "Sarasota Teen Critically Injured In Fall From Ride At Disney." Orlando Sentinel 20 Oct. 1991: n. pag. Print.

Pack, Todd. "Theme Parks Say Rides Are Safe." The Orlando Sentinel 13 Sept. 2003: n. pag. Print.

Palm, Anika. "Woman Injured In Boat Crash At Disney." Orlando Sentinel 27 Apr. 2010: n. pag. Print.

Pankowski, Mark. "Victim's Kin Sue Disney Over Fatal Boat Collision." Orlando Sentinel 25 Feb. 1990: n. pag. Print.

"Passengers Escape From Burning Car on Disney Train." Palm Beach Post 28 June 1985: n. pag. Print.

Pfeifer, Stuart. "Disneyland Rider Dies in Roller Coaster Accident." Los Angeles Times 6 Sept. 2006: n. pag. Print.

Pisa, Nick. "Jailed Sex Criminals Make Lion King Lamps for Disney." Daily Mirror 8 Sept. 1998: n. pag. Print.

"Plane Crash Victims In Serious Condition." Ocala Star Banner 23 Nov. 1984: n. pag. Print.

Postal, Leslie. "Animal Kingdom Worker Suffers Head Injury." Orlando Sentinel 13 Mar. 2011: n. pag. Print.

Powers, Scott. "Disney's Animal Kingdom Ride Gets Added Safety Features." Orlando Sentinel 5 Mar. 2008:

Powers, Scott. "OSHA Hits Disney With Violations, Fine for Animal Kingdom Accident." Orlando Sentinel 24 May 2008:

Powers, Scott. "Boy, 12, Dies After Disney Coaster Ride." Orlando Sentinel 30 June 2006: n. pag. Print.

Powers, Scott. "Autopsy Shows Heart Defect." Orlando Sentinel 1 July 2006: n. pag. Print.

Powers, Scott. "Thrills, Chills On Mission Space." Orlando Sentinel 25 June 2006: n. pag. Print.

Powers, Scott. "Everest Ride In Disney." Orlando Sentinel 19 Dec. 2007: n. pag. Print.

"Principal Drowns At Disney World." The Washington Afro American 21 Aug. 1979: n. pag. Print.

Reckard, E. Scott. "Disneyland, Family Settle Suit Over 1998 Death." Los Angeles Times 5 Oct. 2000: n. pag. Print.

Reckard, E. Scott. "Disneyland Casualty Back on Job." Los Angeles Times 16 Mar. 2000: n. pag. Print.

Ritchie, Lauren. "Friends Car Ride Ends In Death." Orlando Sentinel 11 July 1990: n. pag. Print.

Roy, Roger. "Couple Sue Disney Over Monorail Fire." Orlando Sentinel 14 Nov. 1987: n. pag. Print.

"Safety and Security." The Walt Disney Company. N.p., n.d. Web. 22 May 2014. <http://thewaltdisneycompany.com/about-disney/security>.

Saffian, Sarah. "The Hidden Danger of Amusement Parks: After Her Son Was Tragically Injured on a Roller Coaster, Kathy Fackler Decided to Do Something to Make Theme Parks Safer for Everyone By Sarah SaffianRedbook, May, 2000." Sarah Saffian. N.p., n.d. Web. 22 May 2014. <http://www.saffian.com/danger.htm>.

Sampson, Jenna. "Disney's Policy Change Highlights Drowning Prevention Efforts." Aquatics International 21 Oct. 2013: n. pag. Print.

Samsock, Karen. "Boating Accident Kills Woman Visiting Disney." Orlando Sentinel 10 Oct. 1989: n. pag. Print.

Savino, Lenny. "Recovery of Body Helped Mom Heal." Orlando Sentinel 29 Aug. 1999: n. Pag

Scheen, David. "Shawnee, Executive Start STOL Service to Orlando." Sarasota Herald Tribune 24 Oct. 1971: n. pag. Print.

Schneider, Mike. "Large Theme Parks in Florida Escape State's Safety Laws." Online Athens. N.p., n.d. Web. 22 May 2014. <http://onlineathens.com/stories/061805/new_20050618021.shtml>.

Strodder, Chris. The Disneyland Encyclopedia: The Unofficial, Unauthorized, and Unprecedented History of Every Land, Attraction, Restaurant, Shop and Major Event in the Original Magic Kingdom. Santa Monica, CA: Santa Monica, 2012. Print.

Stutzman, Rene. "Family Sues Disney Over Auto Death." Orlando Sentinel 19 Sept. 1995: n. pag. Print

"Teenager Drowns On Outing At Disneyland." Los Angeles Times 5 June 1983: n. pag. Print.

"Teen Hurt At Disney World Returns Home." Sarasota Herald Tribune 2 Nov. 1991: n. pag. Print.

Terrie Marie Roscoe v. Walt Disney World. 9th Judicial Court In Orange County, Florida. 5 Oct. 2012. Print.

Thomas, Josh. "State Ride Inspections Exempt Busch Gardens and Disney." - WFLA News Channel 8. N.p., Feb. 2014. Web. 22 May 2014. <http://www.wfla.com/story/24728820/state-ride-inpsections-exempt-busch-gardens-and-disney>.

Thompson, Paul. "British Teenager Sues Disney After Tower of Terror Ride Left Her Brain Damaged." The Daily Mail 12 Feb. 2009: n. pag. Print.

Trager, Louis. "Monorail Fire Began in Wheel, State Says." Orlando Sentinel 28 June 1985: n. pag. Print.

Tripoli, Steve. "Disneyland Ride Victim Loses Lawsuit." Los Angeles Times 8 Mar. 1985: n. pag. Print.

Truesdell, Al. "Disney Loses Appeal of $1.5 Million in Drowning." Orlando Sentinel 5 Dec. 1986: n. pag. Print.

Verrier, Richard. "Magic Kingdom Ride Fatality Has Investigators Perplexed." Orlando Sentinel 7 Nov. 2000:

Verrier, Richard. "Disney Ride Had Record of Trouble." Orlando Sentinel 24 Nov. 2000: n. pag. Print.

Wade, Betsy. "Mosquito Alert At Walt Disney World." The New York Times 7 Sept. 1997: n. pag. Print

"Walt Disney World Fined in Skyway Way Worker's Death." St. Petersburg Times 30 Apr. 1999: n. pag. Print.

"Walt Disney World Fun Facts." The Walt Disney Company (n.d.): n. http://corporate.disney.go.com/media/news/Fact_WDW_Fun_Facts_08_06.pdf>.

"Walt Disney World Resort Prepares for Sudden Cardiac Arrest." Walt Disney World Resort Prepares for Sudden Cardiac Arrest. N.p., 15 Aug. 2013. Web. <www.sca-aware.org/sca-news/waltdisneyworld.html>.

Weber, Tracy. "Disneyland Death: The Cost." Los Angeles Times 13 Dec. 1999: n. pag. Print.

"Workers Hurt At Water Park." Orlando Sentinel 3 Nov. 2000: n. pag. Print.

"Yesterland.com: River Country Closed by Brain-Eating Amoeba? (Part 1 of 2)." Yesterland.com: River Country Closed by Brain-Eating Amoeba? (Part 1 of 2). <http://www.yesterland.com/rivercountry.html>.

"Youth Dies After Swimming At Disney." The Lakeland Ledger 28 Aug. 1980: n. pag. Print.

Yoshino, Kimi. "Brandon Zucker Dies at 13." Los Angeles Times 27 Jan. 2009: n. pag. Print.

Yoshino, Kimi. "Dead Women's Kin Sue Disney Over Indiana Jones Ride." Los Angeles Times 26 Sept. 2001: n. pag. Print.

Yoshino, Kimi. "Disney Settles Injury Suit." Los Angeles Times 21 June 2001: n. pag. Print.

Yoshino, Kimi. "Disney Again Faulted in Ride Accident." Los Angeles Times 28 Aug. 2004: n. pag. Print.

Yoshino, Kimi. "Even Fans of Ride Starting to Have Doubts." Los Angeles Times 10 July 2004: n. pag. Print.

Yoshino, Kimi. "Family of Boy Injured on Ride Tells of Painful Bedside Wait." Los Angeles Times 12 Jan. 2001: n. pag. Print

Yoshino, Kimi. "State's Order to Alter Disneyland Ride Opens New Era For Theme Parks." Los Angeles Times 5 Jan. 2001: n. pag. Print.

Yoshino, Kimi. "Thrill Rides' G-Forces Also Being Felt in Court." Los Angeles Times. Los Angeles Times, 27 May 2002. Web. 22 May 2014. <http://articles.latimes.com/2002/may/27/local/me-brain27>.

Yoshino, Kimi. "Witnesses: Disney Workers Wouldn't Let Them Aid Boy." Los Angeles Times 29 Sept. 2000: n. pag. Print.

Peter Pan's Fight:
"3 Shot in Disneyland Fight." Reuters 13 Jan. 1975: n. pag. Print

"80 At Disneyland Irritated After Pepper Spray Dispute." 16 Mar. 1993: n. pag. Print.

"Anaheim: Conviction Overturned In Disneyland Murder." Los Angeles Times 3 May 1989: n. pag. Print.

Blankstein, Andrew. "Disneyland Employee Held In Toon Town Dry Ice Bomb Explosion." Los Angeles Times 29 May 2013: n. pag. Print.

"Barricaded Man in Celebration Found Dead." Osceola County Sherriff's Office. Osceola.org, 3 Dec. 2010. Web.

Bartkewicz, Anthony. "Murder In Disney Town: Two Years After Celebration, Fla's First Homocide, Shocking Revelations About Victims Past." New York Daily News 11 Sept. 2012: n. pag. Print.

Bernal, Maria. "Man Arrested After Beating Up Three Disney Employees in Epcot." Nbcmiami.com. N.p, 15 Oct. 2013. Web.

Boylan, Peter. "Disney Hotel Kicks Out Hawaii Families after Brawl." Honolulu Advertiser 12 Dec. 2007: n. pag. Print.

Breen, David. "Felony Charge Might Be Filed After Fight at Disney Youth Soccer Tournament." 21 July 2013: n. pag. Print.

Carlton, Jim. "Girl Wounded At Disneyland Improves." Los Angeles Times 13 Feb. 1990: n. pag. Print.

"Caught On Tape: Belligerent Man Repeatedly Pepper Sprayed During Wild Fight At Disneyland - CBS Los Angeles." CBS Los Angeles. N.p., 19 Feb. 2012. Web. 23 May 2014.

Copeland, Jeff. "Bobby Brown Pays off Accuser." Eonline.com. N.p., 7 Nov. 1996. Web.

Curtis, Henry. "David Murillo, First Person Convicted of Murder In Celebration, Sentenced To Life In Prison." Orlando Sentinel 26 Apr. 2013: n. pag. Print.

Curtis, Henry. "Attorney: Celebration Murder Defendant Grabbed Axe Out Of Fear." Orlando Sentinel 23 Jan. 2013: n. pag. Print.

Curtis, Henry. "Jury In Celebration Slaying Find Man Guilty of Second Degree Murder." Orlando Sentinel 25 Jan. 2013: n. pag. Print.

Curtis, Henry. "Celebration Murder Defendant: I Knew I Was Going to Hurt Him." Orlando Sentinel 24 Jan. 2013: n. pag. Print.

Curtis, Henry. "Murder Plot Tied to Guard at Disney." Orlando Sentinel 30 Dec. 2004: n. pag. Print.

Curtis, Henry. "Finger Pointing Continues after Fight Marred Disney Cup Youth Soccer Championship Fight." Orlando Sentinel 22 July 2013: n. pag. Print.

"Deputy Tasers Teen in Disney Brawl." Associated Press 22 May 2007: n. pag. Print.

"Disney Knifing." Orlando Sentinel 13 Jan. 1995: n. pag. Print.

"Disneyland Hires Ambulance Service after Controversy." Associated Press 20 Apr. 1981: n. pag. Print.

"Disney Security Guard Arrested in Murder for Hire Plot." Associated Press 30 Dec. 2004: n. pag. Print.

"Disneyland Must Pay $600,000 In Park Murder." New York Times 24 July 1986: n. pag. Print.

Eckinger, Helen. "Jurors in Disney World Tea Cup Battle Hear Conflicting Accounts." Orlando Sentinel 10 Apr. 2008: n. pag. Print.

Eckinger, Helen. "Defendant in Disney Tea Cup Case Sentenced to 90 Days." Orlando Sentinel 24 Apr. 2008: n. pag. Print.

Eckinger, Helen. "Trial Over Battle at Disney's Mad Tea Party Ride Ends with Guilty Verdict." Orlando Sentinel 12 Apr. 2008: n. pag. Print.

Eckinger, Helen. "Disney's Tea Cups Trial Paused for Possible New Witnesses." Orlando Sentinel 11 Apr. 2008: n. pag. Print.

Eckinger, Helen. "Attack at Disney Tea Cup Ride Near Orlando Has Damaged Victim, Witnesses Testify." Orlando Sentinel 9 Apr. 2008: n. pag. Print.

"Extortion Threats Fail against Disney Parks." Associated Press 19 Dec. 1974: n. pag. Print.

"Family of Teenager Stabbed At Disneyland Files $60 Million Lawsuit." The New York Times 13 Apr. 1981: n. pag. Print.

"Five Arrested at Disney World." UPI 22 May 2007: n. pag. Print.

"Girl Wounded At Disneyland Is Doing Well." Los Angeles Times 13 Feb. 1990: n. pag. Print.

"Grandmother Arrested for Carrying Weapons at Walt Disney World." Azcentral.com. N.p., 10 Dec. 2007. Web.

"Hara Charged with Disney Bomb Attempt." Associated Press 28 June 1972: n. pag. Print.

"Hara Indicted for Disney Bombs." Associated Press 28 June 1972: n. pag. Print.

Hernandez, Arelis. "Sailor, Marine Describe Alleged Attack by Navy Ensign at Disney." Orlando Sentinel 16 Oct. 2013: n. pag. Print.

Hicks, Jerry. "Disneyland Incident: Ex-Guard Acquitted of Filing False Report." Los Angeles Times 12 Apr. 1985: n. pag. Print.

Holewa, Lisa. "Police: Teens With No Criminal Record Go On Crime Spree." Associated Press 10 May 1996: n. pag. Print.

Howley, Kathleen. "Pixie Dust Loses Magic As Foreclosures Slam Utopian Disney Town." Bloomberg.com 14 Dec. 2010: n. pag. Print.

Hunt, April. "2 Moms Duke It out at Disney in Real Tempest at the Tea Cups." Orlando Sentinel 19 July 2007: n. pag. Print.

"Judge Drops Charges in Disney Bomb Plot." Associated Press 30 Jan. 1973: n. pag. Print.

Krikorian, Greg. "Disney Chooses Security Overseer." Los Angeles times 18 July 2004: n. pag. Print.

LaGanga, Maria. "Teenager Killed In Brawl At Disney Lot." Los Angeles Times 8 Mar. 1987: n. pag. Print.

Lee, Caroline. "Florida Man Forgets Loaded Gun on Disney World Ride." Upi.com. N.p., 30 May 2013. web.

Leusner, Jim. "Painful Split Preceded EPCOT Death." Orlando Sentinel 14 Sept. 1992: n. pag. Print.

"Man Arrested for Disney World Threat." Associated Press 4 May 1974: n. pag. Print.

"Man Shoots Himself At EPCOT Center." Orlando Sentinel 13 Sept. 1992: n. pag. Print.

"Man Fires At Guards, Takes Hostages At EPCOT Center Before Killing Himself." Associated Press 14 Sept. 1992: n. pag. Print.

"Man Slain at Disneyland." Associated Press 9 Mar. 1981: n. pag. Print.

"Man Stabbed At Disney." Orlando Sentinel 15 Aug. 1994: n. pag. Print.

"Man with Grenade Arrested Near Entrance to Disney World." Associated Press 20 Oct. 1982: n. pag. Print.

Martinez, Michael. "Disneyland Employee Pleads Not Guilty In Dry Ice Bomb Explosions." CNN.com. N.p., 30 May 2013. Web.

Molloy, Joanna. "Bobby Brown Arrested in Assault at Disney World." New York Daily News 27 Apr. 1995: n. pag. Print.

Moye, David. "Christian Barnes, Ex-Disneyland Worker, Sentenced For Dry-ice Bombs." The Huffington Post. TheHuffingtonPost.com, 04 Nov. 2013. Web. 23 May 2014.

"Murder Suspect Arrested at Disney." Associated Press 13 Aug. 1995: n. pag. Print.

"Naval Academy Graduate Allegedly Attacks 3 Walt Disney World Employees." Foxnews.com. N.p., 14 Oct. 2013. Web.

"Osceola Deputies Capture 2 Out of State Fugitives." Orlando Sentinel 11 Aug. 1995: n. pag. Print.

Pacheco, Walter. "Standoff Ends in Disney Town of Celebration, Gunman Dead." Orlando Sentinel 3 Dec. 2010: n. pag. Print.

Pacheo, Walter. "German Tourist Arrested in Disney Bomb Plot." Orlando Sentinel 30 Nov. 2009: n. pag. Print.

"Police: Employee's Ex-Boyfriend Takes Hostages, Kills Self At EPCOT." Associated Press 13 Sept. 1992: n. pag. Print.

Pristin, Terry. "Manhunt Ends in Disney World." The New York times 11 Aug. 1995: n. pag. Print.

Quinn, Christopher. "Singer Used Fake Name to Extend Stay at Disney." Orlando Sentinel 29 Apr. 1995: n. pag. Print.

Reckard, Scott. "Judge Dismisses Ex-Mouseketeer's Suit." Los Angeles Times 23 Aug. 1997: n. pag. Print.

Salamone, Debbie. "Bobby Brown In The Clear As Beating Case Wraps Up." Orlando Sentinel 8 Jan. 1997: n. pag. Print.

Spano, John. "Doctor Testifies in Disneyland Stabbing Death." Los Angeles Times 17 July 1986: n. pag. Print.

Spano, John. "Testimony in Wrongful Death Suit Over Disneyland Stabbing." Los Angeles Times 15 July 1986: n. pag. Print.

Spano, John. "Ex-Disney Guard Loses Suit Challenging Firing." Los Angeles Times 3 May 1988: n. pag. Print.

"Suspect Arrested in Disney Extortion." Associated Press 22 Dec. 1974: n. pag. Print.

"Teenager Killed, Another Wounded In Shooting In Disneyland Parking Lot." Los Angeles Times 8 Mar. 1987: n. pag. Print.

"Teenager Slain at Disneyland, Couple Booked." Associated Press 10 Mar. 1981: n. pag. Print.

Whaley, Floyd. "Judge Reinstates Guard's Suit Against Disneyland." Los Angeles Times 20 July 1988: n. pag. Print.

Whitcomb, Dan. "Disneyland Employee Arrested In Suspected Dry Ice Explosion." Reuters.com. N.p., 29 May 2013. Web.

Deviant Disney:
"9 Investigates Crackdown on Sex Offenders Inside Disney World." WFTV Channel 9 Orlando, Daytona Beach, Melbourne, Central Florida. N.p., 25 Apr. 2013. Web. 23 May 2014.

"Alleged Disney Pool Groper a Youth Minister in Victor." - RochesterHomepage.net. N.p., 8 July 2009. Web. 23 May 2014.

Anton, Mike. "Disney Worker Charged with Sexually Assaulting Girl." Latimes.com. N.p., 24 June 2013. Web.

Bennetto, Jason. "Disney Face Puppet Man Sex Law Suit." Independent UK 3 June 1999: n. pag. Print.

Breen, David. "Washington Man Gets 2 Year Sentence for Molestation at Typhoon Lagoon." Orlando Sentinel 28 Oct. 2011: n. pag. Print.

"Brits to Sue Disney World Over Sex Attack." Daily Mail 12 Jan. 1999: n. pag. Print

Catalanello, Rebecca. "Man Accused of Abusing Pinellas Girl at Disney." St. Petersburg times 8 Sept. 2009: n. pag. Print.

Clark, Lesley. "New Disney Hires Now All Undergo Criminal Checks." Orlando Sentinel 16 Oct. 1998: n. pag. Print.

Colarossi, Anthony. "Jury Finds Former Disney Clerk Not Guilty of Rape." Orlando Sentinel 16 Nov. 2011: n. pag. Print.

Curtis, Henry. "Employee Raped at Magic Kingdom." Orlando Sentinel 8 May 1999: n. pag. Print.

Curtis, Henry. "Missing Tourist Tells Cops He Was Held as Sex Slave." Orlando Sentinel 14 Apr. 1999: n. pag. Print.

Curtis, Henry. "Disney Worker Accused of Raping Woman in Caribbean Beach Resort." Orlando Sentinel 24 Feb. 2011: n. pag. Print.

Curtis, Henry. "Scout's Parents Sue Schools." Orlando Sentinel 12 Apr. 1995: n. pag. Print.

Davis, Phil. "Former Disneyland Employee Indicted on Charges of Sexual Assault on Minors." Nj.com. N.p., 19 Dec. 2013. Web.

Deane, Joel. "The Rise and Fall of Patrick Naughton | ZDNet." ZDNet. N.p., 12 Mar. 2000. Web. 23 May 2014.

Desimone, Jim. "Disney's Crime Reporting Questioned." Orlando Sentinel 28 Mar. 1996: n. pag. Print.

Dickerson, Marla. "Disney Riders Show Bare Necessities." Los Angeles times 12 Jan. 1997: n. pag. Print.

"Director of Disney Film about Troubled Teen Is Registered Sex Offender." Associated Press 24 Oct. 1995: n. pag. Print.

"Disney Cruise Line Crew Member Charged with Molesting Girl." Wesh.com. N.p., 10 Apr. 2014. Web. 23 May 2014.

"Disney Worker Was Raped, Claims Negligence in Suit." Orlando Sentinel 26 Nov. 1992: n. pag. Print.

"Disney and Dancers Settle Lawsuit over Peeping Tom." Orlando Sentinel 5 Dec. 1996: n. pag. Print

"Disney Employee Is among 38 Arrested in Polk Child Sex Case." Tampa Tribune 12 June 2012: n. pag. Print.

"Disney Employee Arrested Trying to Meet 14 Year Old Girl for Sex." Wftv.com. N.p., 14 Sept. 2007. Web.

"Disney Security Guard Amassed Child Porn, Enjoyed Children's Innocence." Orlando Sentinel 30 Jan. 2013: n. pag. Print.

"Disney Workers Get Background Check." Associated Press 17 Oct. 1998: n. pag. Print.

"Disney Worker Faces Child Porn Charges." Associated Press 10 Feb. 2007: n. pag. Print.

"Disney Worker Arrested on Child Porn." Nbc-2.com. N.p., 31 Jan. 2013. Web.

Goldberg, Michael. "Trial Set for Lansdale Man Accused of Taking Photos of Boy in Disney World." The Reporter 12 Dec. 2013: n. pag. Print.

"Goofing around Lands Disney Staff in Dog House." Canada.com 15 Oct. 2006: n. pag. Print.

Gutierrez, Pedro. "Disney Cook Held in Rape." Orlando Sentinel 9 July 1998: n. pag. Print.

"Harbor Blvd. Now Part of Prostitutes' National Map." Los Angeles times 12 Feb. 1989: n. pag. Print.

Hua, Thao. "Lawuit Alleges Sexual Assault at Disneyland." Los Angeles times 7 June 1997: n. pag. Print.

Jacobson, Susan. "Disney Electrician Arrested in Indecent Exposure, Lewdness Charges." Orlando Sentinel 25 Feb. 2011: n. pag. Print.

Jacobson, Susan. "Man Acquitted of Disney Rape Says He Never Should Have Been Charged." Orlando Sentinel 17 Nov. 2011: n. pag. Print.

Jacobson, Susan. "Cops: Man Peeped on Women in Disney Bathroom Stall." Orlando Sentinel 11 Nov. 2011: n. pag. Print.

Jacobson, Susan. "Disney Guest Charged with Voyeurism." Orlando Sentinel 17 Aug. 2013: n. pag. Print.

Kassab, Beth. "Disney Steps up Vigilance against Sex Predators." Orlando Sentinel 10 Oct. 2007: n. pag. Print.

Koli, David. "California Woman: I Was Groped on Disney Ride." New York Post 3 Feb. 2010: n. pag. Print.

Lancaster, Cory. "Disney Will Fire Suspect in Rape." Orlando Sentinel 10 July 1998: n. pag. Print.

Leithhauser, Tom. "Rape at Disney Hotel Was a False Report." Orlando Sentinel 7 Oct. 1993: n. pag. Print.

Leusner, Jim. "Rape Victim Sues Disney over 911, Security." Orlando Sentinel 24 June 1993: n. pag. Print.

Lundy, Sarah. "Woman Is Molested at Disney Water Park." Orlando Sentinel 27 Oct. 2009: n. pag. Print.

Macdonald, Peggy. "12 Year Old Girl Allegedly Raped at Disney's Fort Wilderness Resort near Magic Kingdom." Examiner 6 Sept. 2009: n. pag. Print.

"Man Accused of Exposing Himself, Assault." Orlando Sentinel 15 Mar. 2008: n. pag. Print.

"Man Accused of Molesting Boy at Water Park." Upi.com. N.p., 17 July 2009. Web.

Mckinnon, Jim. "Plum Man Guilty of Abusing Adoptee." Pittsburgh Post Gazette 24 Aug. 2005: n. pag. Print.

"Meet Masha, Adopted by a Pedophile." Oprah.com. N.p., n.d. Web. 23 May 2014.

Miller, Greg. "Exec's Defense in Sex Case: The Net Is a Fantasy World." Los Angeles times 6 Dec. 1999: n. pag. Print.

Miller, Greg. "Online Exec Is Accused of Using Net to Solicit Sex." Los Angeles times 18 Sept. 1999: n. pag. Print.

Miller, Greg. "In Sentencing Deal, No Jail Time for Ex-online Exec in Sex Case." Los Angeles times 10 Aug. 2000: n. pag. Print.

Miller, Greg. "Internet Exec's Child Porn Conviction Tossed out." Los Angeles times 22 Jan. 2000: n. pag. Print.

Morris, Bob. "This Rat in Dressing Room Wall Had 2 Legs." Orlando Sentinel 28 Feb. 1992: n. pag. Print.

Pacheco, Walter. "Man Accused of Molesting Girls at Disney's Typhoon Lagoon." Orlando Sentinel 6 July 2009: n. pag. Print.

Pacheco, Walter. "Disney Character Actor Accused." Sun Sentinel 11 Feb. 2007: n. pag. Print.

Palm, Anika. "Trial Begins for Ex-Disney Worker Accused of Rape." Orlando Sentinel 14 Nov. 2011: n. pag. Print.

Parry, Ryan. "Goofy Held for Kid Porn." Daily Mirror 10 Feb. 2007: n. pag. Print.

Pierce, Jessica. "Disney Groping Suspect Is Youth Minister." Mpnnow.com. N.p., 9 July 2009. Web.

Pinsky, Mark. "Priest Suspended in Sex Scandal Went to Work for Disney." Orlando Sentinel 21 June 2002: n. pag. Print

Pipitone, Tony. "Disney Cruise Line Fails to Promptly Report Molestation of 11-year-old Girl in Port." WKMG. N.p., 20 May 2013. Web. 23 May 2014.

"Police: Man Arrested for Peeping in Disney Restroom." Cbsnews.com. N.p., 11 Nov. 2011. Web.

Prieto, Bianca. "Emotional Testimony during Ex-Disney Clerk's Rape Trial." Orlando Sentinel 15 Nov. 2011: n. pag. Print.

Prieto, Bianca. "Sex Offender Accused of Lewd Punching at Disney's Typhoon Lagoon." Orlando Sentinel 12 Aug. 2011: n. pag. Print.

Quinn, Christopher. "Deputies Didn't Know of Rape Right Away." Orlando Sentinel 3 Nov. 1992: n. pag. Print.

Quinn, Christopher. "Woman Arrested in Disney Rape Hoax." Orlando Sentinel 4 Dec. 1993: n. pag. Print.

Reporter, Daily Mail. "Disney World Employee Tried to Rape Single Mother after Luring Her There with Discount Offers'" Mail Online. Associated Newspapers, 25 Feb. 2011. Web. 23 May 2014.

Rojas, Rick. "Man Faces Charges of Sexual Assault on 3 Girls, Including Relatives." Los Angeles times 12 July 2013: n. pag. Print.

Salamone, Debbie. "Woman in Rape Hoax Enters Guilty Plea." Orlando Sentinel 7 May 1994: n. pag. Print.

Schneider, Mike. "Girl in Abuse Photos at Disney Found Safe." Ocala.com. N.p., 14 May 2005. Web.

"Security Guard Raped at Disney's Magic Kingdom." Associated Press 8 May 1999: n. pag. Print.

"Sex Clip Takes the Mickey." Associated Press 13 Oct. 2006: n. pag. Print.

Stennett, Desiree. "Ex-Disney Worker Accused of Watching Child Porn Released from Jail Booted as a Pastor." Orlando Sentinel 16 May 2013: n. pag. Print.

Stroshane, Matt. "Walt Disney World Employees Arrested: Florida Authorities Arrest 22 in Child Sex Sting." Cnn.com. N.p., 12 Oct. 2003. Web.

Sturgeon, Marjorie. "Former Disney Worker, Pastor Arrested for Child Porn Again." Former Disney Worker, Pastor Arrested for Child Porn Again. N.p., 19 Oct. 2013. Web. 23 May 2014

"Surrounded by Sin." Knight Ridder 30 Oct. 1979: n. pag. Print.

"Teenager Gets 15.7 Years for Rape of Disney Tourist." Orlando Sentinel 10 Mar. 2000: n. pag. Print.

Thompson, Paul. "Child Sex Sting at Disney." Daily Mirror 8 Oct. 2007: n. pag. Print.

Tully, Sarah. "Disney Union Distributes Flyers Warning of Pedophiles." Orange County Register 21 Oct. 2010: n. pag. Print.

"Videotape Shows Disney Encounter Was Consensual Sex, Not Gang Rape." Associated Press 3 Mar. 2006: n. pag. Print.

Warren, Lydia. "U.S. Olympian Suzy Favor-Hamilton Who Led Double Life as $600-an-hour Vegas Call Girl Is BANNED from Competing at Disneyland Half Marathon as Sponsors Drop Runner." Mail Online. Associated Newspapers, 22 Dec. 2012. Web. 23 May 2014.

Making A Mint off The Mouse:
"4,000 Employees and Retirees Sue Disney for Health Benefits." Associated Press 17 Mar. 1999: n. pag. Print.

Arellano, Gustavo. "Disneyland Settles White Rabbit Is Racist Lawsuit." Orange County Weekly 30 Dec. 2013: n. pag. Print.

Armitage, Alex. "Disney Wins Bear of 13 Year Lawsuit." Associated Press 30 Mar. 2004: n. pag. Print.

Armstrong, Mark. "Jury: Disney Bullied Dying Exec." Eonline.com. N.p., 21 Apr. 2000. Web.

Bayot, Jennifer. "Judge Rules for Walt Disney Directors in Ovitz Case." New York times 9 Aug. 2005: n. pag. Print.

"Beastly Behavior Real Life Mouse." New York times 19 May 1985: n. pag. Print.

Beck, Julie. "Muslim Woman Sues Disney for Forbidding Head Scarves." Inside Counsel Aug. 2012: n. pag. Print.

Bernstein, Sharon. "The Lady and the Lawsuit." Los Angeles times 19 Feb. 1991: n. pag. Print.

"Boudlal v. Disney." Aclu of Southern California. N.p., 13 Aug. 2012. Web.

Brazil, Jeff. "Pixie Dust Case Takes Not So Magical Turn for Disney." Orlando Sentinel 16 May 1992: n. pag. Print.

Burnis Simon v. Disney. Court of Appeal California Fifth District. 8 Jan. 2004. Print.

Carr, David. "A Hollywood Blogger Feared by Executives." New York times 17 July 2009: n. pag. Print.

Chavez, Erika. "Disneyland Loses Suit over False Accusation." Los Angeles times 25 Apr. 1998: n. pag. Print.

Clark, Andrew. "Disney Wins Winnie the Pooh Copyright Case." Theguardian.com. N.p., 30 Sept. 2009. Web.

Collins, Glenn. "Peggy Lee Is Suing Disney." New York times 17 Nov. 1988: n. pag. Print.

Conyers, David. "Disney Sued by Sleeping Beauty." St. Petersburg times 6 Mar. 1990: n. pag. Print.

"Court Declines to Grant Disney's Wish." Daily Variety 6 July 1992: n. pag. Print.

"Court: New Jersey Has No Jurisdiction for Mickey Mouse Suit." Associated Press 28 June 1989: n. pag. Print.

Davies, Emily. "Black Family Accuses Disneyland's White Rabbit of Racism after It 'Refused to Touch Their Kids'" Mail Online. Associated Newspapers, 07 Feb. 2013. Web. 24 May 2014.

Deborah Thomas v. the Walt Disney Company. United States District Court for the Northern District of California. 14 Feb. 2008. Print.

Decker, Twila. "3 Firefighters Settle Sexual Harassment Suit with Reedy Creek." Orlando Sentinel. N.p., 29 Oct. 1996. Web.

Diorio, Carl. "Mouse Loses Cheese over Sports Complex." Daily Variety 14 Aug. 2000: n. pag. Print.

Dipaola, Jim. "Beauty Suit Put to Bed." Orlando Sentinel 1 June 1990: n. pag. Print.

Dipaola, Jim. "Court Lays Sleeping Beauty Argument to Rest." Orlando Sentinel 12 July 1990: n. pag. Print.

"Disney Sued by Man Who Says *Honey I Shrunk the Kids* Based on His Idea." Associated Press 7 June 1991: n. pag. Print.

"Disney Settles Suit over Sports Complex." Los Angeles times 26 Sept. 2002: n. pag. Print.

"Disney's Image, No More Valedictorians." Thisweek.com. N.p., 19 June 2008. Web.

"Disneyland Settles Lawsuit over Detention." Associated Press 28 Sept. 1992: n. pag. Print.

Ernst, Amanda. "Appeals Court: Epcot Did Not Infringe on Painting." Law360.com. N.p., 23 Jan. 2007. Web.

Faturechi, Robert. "Disneyland Bends on Employee Who Wore Hijab, Muslim Rights Group Says." Los Angeles Times. Los Angeles Times, 28 Sept. 2010. Web. 24 May 2014.

"Finding Nemo Copyright Claim Deemed Fishy." The Hollywood Reporter 14 Feb. 2008: n. pag. Print.

Finkelstein, Alex. "Disney Firefighter Sues, Charges Male Sexual Harassment." Orlando Business Journal 21 July 1997: n. pag. Print.

Finkelstein, Alex. "Male Firefighter Sues Disney for Condoning Sex Abuse." Orlando Business Journal 28 Oct. 1996: n. pag. Print.

Finkelstein, Alex. "Firefighter Douses Sex Bias Suit Against Disney," Orlando Business Journal 20 July 1998: n. pag. Print.

Finkelstein, Alex. "Disney, Reedy Creek Ask Judge to Stay Firefighter Suit." Orlando Business Journal 2 Feb. 1998: n. pag. Print.

Finkelstein, Alex. "Firefighters: No Sexual Harassment at Reedy Creek Station." Orlando Business Journal 6 Apr. 1998: n. pag. Print.

Fiore, Faye. "Magic Kingdom Visit a Nightmare for Idaho Family." Los Angeles times 14 July 1990: n. pag. Print.

Gardner, Eriq. "Disney Sued over Toy Story 3 Evil Stuffed Bear Character." The Hollywood Reporter 11 Feb. 2014: n. pag. Print.

Garcia, Jason. "Publix, Disney Aim to Cut Lawsuit Awards for Accident Victims." Orlando Sentinel 10 July 2013: n. pag. Print.

Granelli, James. "Suit Claims Park Violated Civil Rights." Los Angeles times 30 Apr. 1985: n. pag. Print

Greenbaum, Kurt. "Disney Hit by Awakened Beauty's Suit." Orlando Sentinel 12 May 1989: n. pag. Print.

Greenbaum, Kurt. "Disney Loses Lawsuit Singer Peggy Lee Wins on Video Issue." Orlando Sentinel 6 Apr. 1990: n. pag. Print.

Haring, Bruce. "$200 Million Suit Targets Sister Act." Variety 11 June 1993: n. pag. Print.

Harper, Jennifer. "Sikh Sues Disney over Right to Wear Turban." The Washington times 18 June 2008: n. pag. Print.

Harper, Thomas. "It's a Small World After All." Florida Employment Law Letter 1 Nov. 1996: n. pag. Print.

Henry, Mark. "Children Who Saw Sex Movie Win Damages." Los Angeles times 12 Nov. 1986: n. pag. Print.

Holpuch, Amanda. "Disney Sued for Discrimination by Former Employee over Muslim Hijab." The Guardian.com. N.p., 14 Aug. 2014. Web.

"Imane Boudlal, Who Clashed with Disney over Wearing Hijab on Job Sues with Aclu Assist." Aclu of Southern California. N.p., 13 Aug. 2012. Web.

Irving, Doug. "Disney, Knotts Frequent Targets of Lawsuits." Orange County Register 01 June 2012: n. pag. Print.

Jake Mandeville-Anthony v. the Walt Disney Company. United States District Court for the Central District of California. 28 July 2011. Print.

James, Meg. "Disney Wins Ruling on Winnie the Pooh Rights." Los Angeles times 26 Sept. 2007: n. pag. Print.

James, Meg. "Disney Controls Winnie the Pooh Trademarks, Court Rules." Los Angeles times 21 Dec. 2012: n. pag. Print.

James, Meg. "Roger Rabbit's Creator Sues Walt Disney Co." Los Angeles times 30 May 2001: n. pag. Print.

Jarlson, Gary. "Can't Redheads Have a Little Fun, Too?" Los Angeles times 1 May 1985: n. pag. Print.

Jeffrey Kouf v. Walt Disney Pictures. United States Court of Appeals Ninth Circuit. 17 Feb. 1994. Print.

"Journalist's Case against Disney Upheld by Court of Appeal." Associated Press 29 July 2003: n. pag. Print.

Kafka, Peter. "Eisner-Ovitz Ends in a Win for Disney." Forbes.com. N.p., 9 Aug. 2005. Web.

Kenneally, Tim. "Nun Sues Disney for $1 Billion over Sister Act." Reuters 3 Sept. 2012: n. pag. Print.

Lancaster, Cory. "Deal Falls Apart between Disney and Retirees." Orlando Sentinel 17 June 1998: n. pag. Print.

Landis, David. "*Fantasia* Suit." USA Today 7 May 1992: n. pag. Print.

Mather, Kate. "Woman's Lawsuit Accuses Disneyland of Bias." Los Angeles Times. Los Angeles Times, 14 Aug. 2012. Web. 24 May 2014.

Mather, Kate. "Disney Says Muslim Woman Had Options in Head Scarf Dispute." Los Angeles Times. Los Angeles Times, 13 Aug. 2012. Web. 24 May 2014.

"Mickey Mouse Cleared." Sunday Mail 2 July 1989: n. pag. Print.

Nichols, Peter. "Home Video." New York times 18 Mar. 1993: n. pag. Print.

Nikki Finke v. the Walt Disney Company. State of California Second Appeallate District Division Seven. 28 July 2003. Print.

"No Pussycat in Court, Peggy Lee Nips Disney for $3.8 Million." People 8 Apr. 1991: n. pag. Web.

Norris, Kim. "Disney Sued over Uniform Flap." St. Petersburg times 18 July 1996: n. pag. Print.

Orrin Monroe Corwin v. Walt Disney Company. United States Court of Appeals for the Eleventh Circuit. 2 Nov. 2006. Print.

"Passings: Paul Alter." Los Angeles times 16 June 2011: n. pag. Print.

Pettersson, Edward. "Disney Wins on Last Claims in Winnie the Pooh Copyright Suit." Bloomberg.com. N.p., 29 Sept. 2009. Web.

"Philadelphia Orchestra Disney Settle Score." Associated Press 23 Oct. 1994: n. pag. Print.

"Philadelphia Orchestra Sues Disney over *Fantasia*." Associated Press 12 Oct. 1994: n. pag. Print.

Powers, Scott. "Sikh Musician Sues Disney over Job." Orlando Sentinel 17 June 2008: n. pag. Print.

Randles, Jonathon. "Supreme Court Puts Brakes on *Cars* Copyright Appeal." Law360.com. N.p., 29 Apr. 2013. Web.

Reckard, Scott. "Disney Agrees to Settle Retirement Benefits Suit." Los Angeles times 21 Aug. 1999: n. pag. Print.

Reporter, Daily Mail. "Second Family Accuses Disneyland of Racism after Donald Duck Refuses to Hug Their Son." Mail Online. Associated Newspapers, 09 Feb. 2013. Web. 24 May 2014.

Rosenzweig, David. "Disney Treatment of Dying Executive Is Focus of Trial." Los Angeles times 5 Apr. 2000: n. pag. Print.

Rosenzweig, David. "Disney Had No Right to Deny Benefits to Executive, Jury Rules." Los Angeles times 22 Apr. 2000: n. pag. Print.

Rowe, Jeff. "Man Who Sued Disney over His Fall from Ride Now Apologizes for Suit." Orange County Register 24 Sept. 1996: n. pag. Print.

Roy, Roger. "Disney Lawyers Take Dim View of Glitter." Orlando Sentinel 23 Feb. 1991: n. pag. Print.

Sallah, Michael. "Lawsuits Are Nothing New for Disney." Toledo Blade 2 July 2000: n. pag. Print.

Scheibel, Steve. "Man Who Fell from Aerial Gondola Sues Disneyland." Los Angeles times 17 Mar. 1995: n. pag. Print.

Schneider, Mike. "Disney Sued over Sports Complex." Associated Press 7 Aug. 2000: n. pag. Print.

Shields, Gerard. "2 Families Sue Disney for Charge of Shoplifting." Orlando Sentinel 4 Apr. 1996: n. pag. Print.

Shields, Gerard. "Little Known Shoplifting Law Flawed, Critics Say." Orlando Sentinel 19 Sept. 1995: n. pag. Print.

"Shoplifting Statistics." Shopliftingpreventon.org. National Shoplifting Prevention Coalition, 2014. Web.

Sistrunk, Jeff. "Disney Sued over Toy Story 3 Character Lotso Bear." Law360.com. N.p., 10 Feb. 2014. Web.

Smith, Steven. "Mickey Mouse Suits." Los Angeles times 28 Sept. 1975: n. pag. Print.

Smith, Ethan. "Walt Disney Surrenders to Navy's Seal Team 6." The Wall Street Journal 26 May 2011: n. pag. Print.

Tully, Sarah. "Woman Defies Disney Dress." Orange County Register 22 Aug. 2010: n. pag. Print.

Toufexis, Anastasia. "Law: No Mickey Mousing Around." Time 11 Mar. 1985: n. pag. Web.

Verrier, Richard. "Verdict against Disney Stands." Orlando Sentinel 15 Nov. 2000: n. pag. Print.

Weber, Tracy. "Disneyland a Fierce Foe in Court." Los Angeles times 31 Jan. 1999: n. pag. Print.

Wilkinson, Mike. "Disney Sued over Design of Epcot." Toledo Blade 20 Nov. 2002: n. pag. Print.

"Woman Sues Disney, Saying Drunk Mickey Mouse Attacked Her Son." Associated Press 24 Sept. 1986: n. pag. Print.

Wong, Tony. "Architect Settles Disney Suit." Toronto Star 26 Sept. 2002: n. pag. Print.

Pirates of The Courtroom:
Bernaski, Kaitlyn. "Saving Mickey Mouse: The Upcoming Fight for Copyright Extension in 2018." Seton Hall Law Student Scholarship Review (2014): n. pag. Web.

"Cartoon Figures Run Afoul of Law." Chicago Tribune 27 Apr. 1989: n. pag. Print.

"City, Disney Tell 3 Preschools to Get Rid of Mickey Mouse Murals." Orlando Sentinel 8 Apr. 1989: n. pag. Print.

Conrad, Eric. "Disney's Dark Side." Sun Sentinel 30 Sept. 1991: n. pag.

Costello, D. "Disney Cheesed Off by Mickey Murals." Daily Mail 2 May 1989: n. pag. Print.

"Disney Drops Suits over Snow White Oscar Skit." Associated Press 8 Apr. 1989: n. pag. Print.

"Disney Explains Reaction to Hamas Use of Mickey Mouse Image." Usa Today 21 May 2007: n. pag. Print.

"Disney Sues." Courier Mail 30 June 1986: n. pag. Print.

"Disney's Penchant for Lawsuits Called Grumpy and Mean Spirited." Video Age International 1 Oct. 1991: n. pag. Print.

"Disney Suing Theatre over Lion King, Mary Poppins Copyright Infringement." Broadwayworld.com. N.p., 26 Sept. 2013. Web.

"Disney Sues Edmonton Mall over Use of Fantasyland Name." Associated Press 2 Nov. 1993: n. pag. Print.

Disney Enterprises v. San Jose Party Rental. United States District Court for the Northern District of California. 10 Mar. 2010. Print.

Disney Enterprises v. Bouncing 4 Fun. United States District Court for the Eastern District of California. 9 Sept. 2011. Print.

Easton, Nina. "Disney Sues Over Use of Snow White at Oscars." 31 Mar. 1989: n. pag. Print.

Gladwell, Malcolm. "For Disney, Shirts Aren't a Mickey Mouse Issue." Washington Post 4 Sept. 1987: n. pag. Print.

"Grandfather Found Guilty of Groping Minnie Mouse on Family Holiday to Disney World." Mail Online. Associated Newspapers, 12 Aug. 2009. Web. 24 May 2014.

Heer, Jeet. "Free Mickey!" Boston Magazine 28 Sept. 2003: n. pag. Print.

"Ho White and the Seven Dwarves Beer Advert Angers Disney." The Daily Telegraph 16 Oct. 2009: n. pag. Print.

Horn, John. "Disney Turns Grumpy over Copyright Infringements." Associated Press 20 May 1991: n. pag. Print.

Hudak, Stephan. "Disney Takes Lake County Business to Federal Court." Orlando Sentinel 10 July 2008: n. pag. Print.

"It's Mouse vs. Mice in Court Disney Accuses Stores of Selling Counterfeits." Orlando Sentinel 25 Dec. 1986: n. pag. Print.

Lee, Timothy. "15 Years Ago, Congress Kept Mickey Mouse Out of the Public Domain. Will They Do It Again?" Washington Post 25 Oct. 2013: n. pag. Print.

Liles-Morris, Shelly. "Mickey's Legal Eagle Cuts No Slack." USA Today 25 Aug. 1989: n. pag. Print.

Long, Lyda. "Disney Denies Bid to Keep Characters 3 Hallandale Day Care Centers Are given 1 Month to Remove Murals." Orlando Sentinel 18 May 1989: n. pag. Print.

"Mall Lost in Fantasyland as Disney Wins Suit." Daily Variety 6 July 1992: n. pag. Print.

Shan, Janet. "Raunchy Beer Ad Entitled Ho White and the Seven Dwarves, Angers Disney." Newstex 16 Oct. 2009: n. pag. Print.

Schmalz, Jeffrey. "Nastiness Is Not a Fantasy in Movie Theme Park War." New York Times 13 Aug. 1989: n. pag. Print.

Tsui, Yvonne. "Travel Agency Must Change D Land Name." South China Morning Post 6 Dec. 2007: n. pag. Print.

"U.S. Scolds North Korea for Unauthorized Disney Show." Cbsnews.com. N.p., 10 July 2012. Web.

Walt Disney World Company v. Disney Area Acreage. United States District Court for the Southern District of California. 21 May 1970. Print.

"X-rated Ho White Beer Ad Reportedly Riles Disney." Foxnews.com. N.p., 17 Oct. 2009. Web.

It's An Accessible World After All:
"Agreement between the United States of America and Walt Disney World Co. under the Americans with Disabilities Act Concerning the Use of Auxiliary Aids at Walt Disney World." Ada.gov. N.p., n.d. Web.

Chapman, Beverly. "Disney's World a Dream Come True for the Disabled." Orlando Sentinel 26 Sept. 1991: n. pag. Print.

"Class Action Lawsuit Against Disney Alleges Inaccessible Websites and Failure to Accommodate Blind Persons." Law360.com. N.p., 18 Feb. 2011. Web.

Cohen, Adam. "Does Disneyland Discriminate Against the Disabled." Time 23 July 2012: n. pag. Web.

"Disabled Trio Sue Disney over Its Ban on Segways." Associated Press 12 Nov. 2007: n. pag. Print.

"Disabled Plaintiffs Ada Claims against Walt Disney World Dismissed." Class Action Law Monitor 31 Oct. 2009: n. pag. Print.

"Disney Autism Ada Lawsuit." Dogali Law Group. N.p., Apr. 2014. Web. <dogalilawgroup.com>.

"Disney Parks Disability Access Service Card Fact Sheet." Disney Parks Blog http://disneyparks.disney.go.com/blog/disney-parks-disability-access-service-card-fact-sheet/>.

"Disney, Epcot Offer Guides for Handicapped." The Evening Independent 8 June 1984: n. pag. Print.

"Disney Helps Hearing Impaired." New York times 1 Mar. 1997: n. pag. Print.

"Disney Sued for Lack of Accommodations." Accomdations Strategies 6.6 (2000): n. pag. Web.

"Disneyland Discontinues Event for Disabled Youths." Orlando Sentinel 23 Mar. 1997: n. pag. Print.

"Disneyland Ends Program for Disabled." United Press International 22 Mar. 1997: n. pag. Print.

"Disneyland Ditches One Size Fits All Approach to Providing Services." Disability Compliance Bulletin 22 Mar. 2004, Vol 27 ed., No 7 sec.: n. pag. Print.

Eden, Richard. "King Questions Why There Are No Disabled Princesses." The Sunday Telegraph 31 Jan. 2010: n. pag. Print.

"Florida, California Parks Disney Agrees to Adapt for the Deaf." The Globe and Mail 22 Jan. 1997: n. pag. Print.

Garcia, Jason. "Citing Abuse, Disney Theme Parks Change Rules for Disabled Visitors." Orlando Sentinel 23 Sept. 2013: n. pag. Print.

Gentile, Gary. "Disneyland's Redesigned Sub Ride Accommodates Disabled Guests." Associated Press 11 June 2007: n. pag. Print.

Gold, Kerry. "Blind Advocates Don't Buy Disney Defense of Mr. Magoo." Vancouver Sun 11 July 1997: n. pag. Print.

"Guest Claims Disney Violates Disabilities Law." Associated Press 11 Nov. 1998: n. pag. Print.

Harris, Kenneth. "Man Robbed at Knife Point in Magic Kingdom." Orlando Sentinel 10 Mar. 1997: n. pag. Print.

Hetter, Katie. "Disney Tightens up Resort Disability Program." Cnn.com. N.p., 25 Sept. 2013. Web.

Himmelberg, Michele. "Disney Theme Parks Want Able Bodied Back in Line; but Special Pass Is Harder for Disabled Too." Orange County Register 5 Feb. 2004: n. pag. Print.

"Hunchback Draws Anger of the Disabled." Associated Press 6 July 1996: n. pag. Print.

Kelly, Joe. "Disney Brings Electric Standing Vehicle to Magic Kingdom." News965.com. N.p., 3 May 2013. Web.

Levs, Josh. "Disney World Vows Action after Report of Wealthy Hiring Disabled to Skip Lines." Cnn.com. N.p., 15 May 2013. Web.

Mcafee, David. "Disney Segway Ban Doesn't Break Ada: California Appeals Court." Law360.com. N.p., 18 July 2013. Web.

Murphy, Pat. "9th Circuit Says Ada May Require Disney to Allow Segways." Lawyers Weekly Usa 20 July 2012: n. pag. Print.

"Nearly 1 in 5 People Have a Disability in the U.S." United States Census. N.p., n.d. Web. <census.gov>.

Keates, Nancy. Backdoor Disney: How to beat the lines --- you can be treated like a VIP even if you aren't one; 'No way I would wait'. Wall Street Journal 27 March 1998

Ofgang, Kenneth. "Disabled Woman Cannot Use Segway at Disneyland." Metropolitan News 19 July 2013: n. pag. Print.

Ogintz, Eileen. "Disney World Excels for Its Disabled Guests." The Bergen Record 8 Apr. 2007: n. pag. Print.

Palmeri, Tara. "Rich Manhattan Moms Hire Handicapped Tour Guides so Kids Can Cut Lines at Disney World." New York Post 14 May 2013: n. pag. Print.

"Parents of Autistic Kids Sue Disney over New Line Waiting Policy." Foxnews.com. N.p., 10 Apr. 2014. Web.

Schneider, Mike. "Amusement Park Industry: Rule to Make Rides Disabled Friendly Too Restrictive." Associated Press 18 Jan. 2000: n. pag. Print.

Schneider, Mike. "Disabled Activists File Discrimination Lawsuit against Disney." Associated Press 4 Aug. 2000: n. pag. Print.

Strachan, Deshayla. "Disney Can Settle Florida Case over Segways." Court House News 4 Sept. 2012: n. pag. Print.

Tina Baughman v. Walt Disney Company. State of California Fourth Appellate District. 18 July 2013. Print.

Tully, Sarah. "Disneyland Can Prohibit Segways, Appeal Court Says." Orange County Register 24 July 2013: n. pag. Print.

"Walt Disney: Blind Persons File Suit over Inaccessible Web Sites." Class Action Reporter 30 Mar. 2011, Vol. 13 ed.: n. pag. Print.

"Walt Disney: Theme Park Settlement on the Verge of Collapse." Class Action Reporter 23 Nov. 2012, Vol. 14 ed.: n. pag. Print.

"Which Disney Princess Are You?--Disabled Disney Princess?" The Independent—u.k. 28 Jan. 2014: n. pag. Print.

Williams, Mari-jane. "Disney Parks Changing Guest Assistance Card Program for Patrons with Disabilities." Washington Post 24 Sept. 2013: n. pag. Print.

Woo, Stu. "Segway Glides as Gasoline Jumps." The Wall Street Journal 16 June 2008: n. pag. Print.

Yoshino, Kimi. "A Sinking Feeling on Small World Ride." Los Angeles times 9 Nov. 2007: n. pag. Print.

Morality In The Movies:
Arthurs, Deborah. "That's One Swell Pout! Woman Desperate to Look like Jessica Rabbit Gets World's Biggest Lips after 100 Injections (and She's Not Stopping There)." Mail Online. Associated Newspapers, 23 Nov. 2011.

Associated Press. "Disney Sued Over Alleged Hidden Messages in Films." Lodi News Sentinel [Lodi, California] 5 Sept. 1996: n. pag. Print.

Associated, Press. "Sex in Disney Cartoons Claim Is Ridiculous." 27 Sept. 1995
Bannon, Lisa. "How a Rumor Spread About Subliminal Sex in Disney's *Aladdin*." The Wall Street Journal 24 Oct. 1995:

Balraj, Belinda. "The Construction of Family in Selected Disney Animated Films." International Journal of Humanities and Social Science 3.11 (2013):

Brooks, Rosa. "Resist the Princess." Los Angeles Times 27 Mar. 2008:

"The Cartoon's Contribution to Children." Overland Monthly and Outwest Magazine Oct. 1933: n. pag. Web.

"Children with Autism and Thomas the Tank Engine." The National Autistic Society website. http://www.autism.org.uk/About-autism/Our-publications/Reports/Our-policy-and-research-reports/Children-with-autism-and-thomas-the-tank-engine.aspx>.

"Dear Pixar, Thank You - RYAN D. SULLIVAN." RYAN D SULLIVAN. <http://www.ryandsullivan.com/dear-pixar-thank-you/>.

Diament, Michelle. "Disney Show Goes Sensory Friendly." Disability Scoop. Diabilityscoop.com, Mar. 2014. Web.

"Disney Show Goes Sensory Friendly." NASET News Alert RSS. N.p., n.d. Web. 07 Apr. 2014. <http://www.naset.org/807.0.html

England, Dawn E. "Gender Role Portrayal and the Disney Princess." Sex Roles 64 (2011): 555-67.

Fleming, Michael. "Jessica Rabbit Revealed." Variety [Los Angeles] 13 Mar. 1994: n. pag.

"Football Great Curt Warner Opens Up about Autism." The Penn Stater Magazine. N.p., n.d. Web. 22 May 2014.

Gabler, Neal. Walt Disney: The Triumph of the American Imagination. New York: Knopf, 2006. Print.

Gerbner, G. (1998). "Cultivation analysis: An overview". Mass Communication and Society, ¾, 175-194.

Goldstein, Seth. "Risks in Disney's Subliminal Suit Settlement." Billboard 13 Sept. 1997: 87.

Harris, James. "Non-Traditional Families May Be Typical American Family; Applying Disney Films to the Discussion." The Houseparent Network (n.d.): n. pag. Web.

Hoerrner, K. L. "Gender Roles in Disney Films: Analyzing Behaviors from Snow White to Simba." Women's Studies in Communications 19 (n.d.): 213-28.

Horn, John. "Christian Group Claims Other Disney Films Have Racy Messages." Associated Press 1 Sept. 1995:

Hubka, David. "Child Maltreatment in Disney Animated Feature Films: 1937-2006." The Social Science Journal 46 (2009): 427-41. Web.

Laderman, Gary. "The Disney Way of Death." Journal of The American Academy of Religion March 2000:

Orenstein, Peggy. Cinderella Ate My Daughter: Dispatches from the Front Lines of the New Girlie-girl Culture. New York, NY: HarperCollins, 2011. Print.

Rosman, Katherine. "Test-Marketing a Modern Princess." The Wall Street Journal 9 Apr. 2013: n. pag. Print.

Ryan, Erin L. "Let Your Conscience Be Your Guide: Smoking and Drinking in Disney's Animated Classics." Mass Communication & Society 7.3 (n.d.): 261-78.

Skouteris, Helen. "Do Young Children Get the Message? The Effects of Repeated Video Viewing on Explicit and Implicit Information." Australian Journal of Educational & Developmental Psychology 7 (2007): 98-107

Smith, Leef. "Disney's Loin King? Group Sees Dirt in the Dust." The Washington Post 1 Sept. 1995

Suskind, Ron. Life, Animated: A Story of Sidekicks, Heroes, and Autism. N.p.: Kingswell, 2014. Print.

Suskind, Ron. "Reaching My Son Through Disney." The New York Times 7 Mar. 2014: n. pag. Print.

Thomas, Bob. Walt Disney: An American Original. New York: Simon and Schuster, 1976. Print.

Vokey, J. R., & Read, J. D. (1985). Subliminal messages: Between the devil and the media. American Psychologist, 40, 1231-1239.

Weintraub, Karen. "Autism Rates Soar, Now Affects 1 in 68 Children." USA Today 27 Mar. 2014: n. pag. Print.

Another great book by Aaron Goldberg

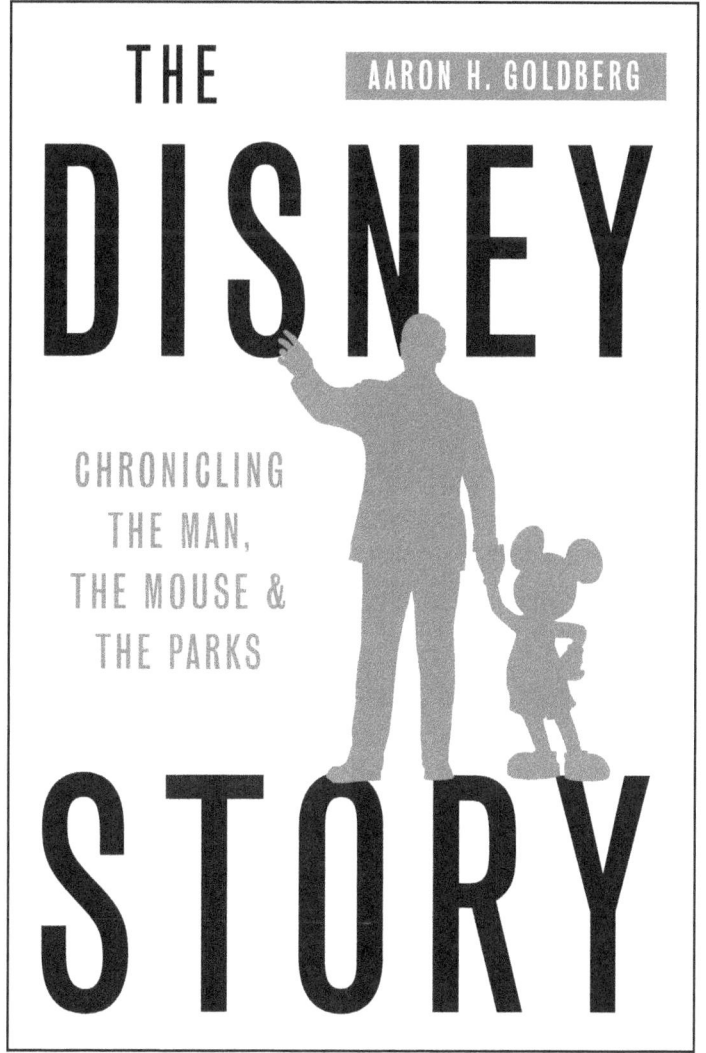

www.ingramcontent.com/pod-product-compliance
Lightning Source LLC
Chambersburg PA
CBHW051942290426
44110CB00015B/2078